EXPERIMENTALIST COMPETITION LAW AND THE REGULATION OF MARKETS

This book charts the emergence of experimentalist governance in the implementation of EU competition law as a response to uncertainty and the limits of hierarchical enforcement, in an increasingly dynamic and heterogeneous economic environment. It contributes to ongoing debates about the current state of EU competition law, and provides an innovative account of emergent enforcement trends and its future direction. It also argues that an experimentalist evolution of competition law and market regulation attenuates concerns about the competitive strictures of EU law on national economic and regulatory institutions.

Through its focus on experimentalist governance, the book provides guidance on completing experimentalist infrastructures for market regulation, as well as on the role of courts in triggering and sustaining experimentalist solutions. As such, it offers a novel perspective on implementing competition law in the EU and beyond.

Volume 27 in the series Hart Studies in Competition Law

Hart Studies in Competition Law

The Interface between Competition and the Internal Market: Market Separation under Article 102 TFEU
Vasiliki Brisimi

Anti-Cartel Enforcement in a Contemporary Age: Leniency Religion
Edited by Caron Beaton-Wells and Christopher Tran

Public Procurement and the EU Competition Rules
Albert Sánchez Graells

The Concept of Abuse in EU Competition Law: Law and Economic Approaches
Pınar Akman

The Competitive Effects of Minority Shareholdings: Legal and Economic Issues
Panagiotis Fotis and Nikolaos Zevgolis

The More Economic Approach to EU Antitrust Law
Anne C Witt

Private Power, Online Information Flows and EU Law
Angela Daly

The Role of Competitors in the Enforcement of State Aid Law
Fernando Pastor-Merchante

The Legality of Bailouts and Buy Nationals: International Trade Law in a Crisis
Kamala Dawar

A Critical Account of Article 106(2) TFEU: Government Failure in Public Service Provision
Jarleth Burke

Dawn Raids Under Challenge
Helene Andersson

A Framework for European Competition Law: Co-ordinated Diversity
Christopher Townley

Evidence Standards in EU Competition Enforcement: The EU Approach
Andriani Kalintiri

The Metaphysics of Market Power: The Zero-sum Competition and Market Manipulation Model
George Raitt

Competition Law's Innovation Factor: The Relevant Market in Dynamic Contexts in the EU and US
Viktoria H.S.E. Robertson

Competition, Effects and Predictability: Rule of Law and the Economic Approach to Competition
Bruce Wardhaugh

Fighting Cross-Border Cartels: The Perspective of the Young and Small Competition Authorities
Pierre Horna

Conceptualising Procedural Fairness in EU Competition Law
Haukur Logi Karlsson

Experimentalist Competition Law and the Regulation of Markets

Yane Svetiev

•HART•
OXFORD • LONDON • NEW YORK • NEW DELHI • SYDNEY

HART PUBLISHING

Bloomsbury Publishing Plc

Kemp House, Chawley Park, Cumnor Hill, Oxford, OX2 9PH, UK

1385 Broadway, New York, NY 10018, USA

HART PUBLISHING, the Hart/Stag logo, BLOOMSBURY and the Diana logo are trademarks of Bloomsbury Publishing Plc

First published in Great Britain 2020

A catalogue record for this book is available from the British Library.

Library of Congress Cataloging-in-Publication data

Names: Svetiev, Yane, author.

Title: Experimentalist competition law and the regulation of markets / Yane Svetiev.

Description: Oxford, UK ; New York, NY : Hart Publishing, an imprint of Bloomsbury Publishing, 2020. | Series: Hart studies in competition law ; volume 27 | Includes bibliographical references and index.

Identifiers: LCCN 2020028628 (print) | LCCN 2020028629 (ebook) | ISBN 9781509910670 (hardback) | ISBN 9781509910656 (ePDF) | ISBN 9781509910663 (Epub)

Subjects: LCSH: Antitrust law—European Union countries. | Competition, Unfair—European Union countries.

Classification: LCC KJE6497 .S84 2020 (print) | LCC KJE6497 (ebook) | DDC 343.2407/21—dc23

LC record available at https://lccn.loc.gov/2020028628

LC ebook record available at https://lccn.loc.gov/2020028629

ISBN: HB: 978-1-50991-067-0
ePDF: 978-1-50991-065-6
ePub: 978-1-50991-066-3

Typeset by Compuscript Ltd, Shannon

PREFACE

This book is the result of a longer-term reflection and study of the evolving role of competition law in the regulation of markets in the EU and beyond. It has benefited from my participation in a number of collective research projects, charting experimentalist governance in the EU and beyond, studying the regulatory role of European private law, as well as the evolution of transnational governance.

At first blush, it would seem that experimentalist governance, even if it provides an attractive framework for regulatory problem-solving, would be of limited applicability in competition law as an *ex post* legal enforcement tool. Two observations changed this initial perception. One was that in complex antitrust cases in dynamic markets, much of the focus was on remedial design, with the remedial protocols and mechanisms implemented resembling experimentalist remedies in public service delivery. The second observation arose out of interviews with enforcement officials from around the world, where it became apparent that whenever they were faced with a competition problem, they rarely sought or obtained definitive guidance from the texts of their domestic competition statutes, preferring instead to consult either prior local precedents or the experiences of their peers in other jurisdictions. But both local enforcement precedents and transnational experiences did not always provide adequate guidance for the case at hand, not least because there was often poor understanding of the actual market effects of those prior local or foreign enforcement efforts.

Focusing more specifically on the EU, much of the emphasis in the early 2000s was on the adoption of the more economic approach in competition law as well as sectoral regulation. While this might have been a project for technocratic closure of competition law, it had the benefit of re-orienting enforcement towards the question of effects. As such, it signals the abandonment of any project to define the 'essence' of anti-competitive conduct. Scholars of the history of antitrust may have regarded both projects (to identify the essence of anti-competitive conduct and to narrow the focus of antitrust on some variant of efficiency) as doomed to failure. On both sides of the Atlantic, in the US and Germany for example, the public policy treatment of interfirm coordination and collaboration, associational forms of production and large firm conduct has changed over time, along with changes in the understanding of public policy problems and priorities. Yet such changes often seem to have followed long periods of path-dependence of stabilised rules and analytical techniques, resulting in either overenforcement or underenforcement. If antitrust enforcement inevitably changes to reflect novel problems and policy priorities, an experimentalist enforcement framework is more nimble and adaptable. It allows – ideally – for course-corrections in real time, rather than after long periods of observing the failures of the old rules and analytical categories. In fact, even as this manuscript is going to print, competition enforcement and market regulation around the world are adjusting to challenges presented by a global pandemic.

This book has greatly benefited from my participation in the European Regulatory Private Law Project, financed by the European Research Council. This project studied the transformation of European private law from a justice-oriented discipline to a discipline that is functional to promoting competition and regulating markets. In the many interviews the project team conducted with market regulatory and competition officials from around the EU, we observed numerous institutional innovations pursued by different actors, which aimed to hybridise different regulatory objectives rather than simply prioritise market competition or 'economisation'. Typically such innovations involve novel forms of review and dynamic adjustment in implemented measures. Sometimes such innovations disclose a fully experimentalist architecture. At other times, experimentalism seems to be within the grasp of regulatory actors, but may be precluded by habits of thought, or an unwillingness to openly acknowledge uncertainty (which may be viewed as a mark of incompetence), or by concerns about judicial review. This is one of the reasons why the book seeks to rationalise new developments through the experimentalist frame, showing both how some observed solutions incorporate all elements of experimentalism as well as how, with minor adjustments or simple re-orientations in the modes of justification, experimentalist governance can be more fully realised.

Finally, I also greatly benefited from my contribution to the project on 'Power Shifts in Transnational Regulation' at the Universities of Geneva and Lucerne, funded by the Swiss National Science Foundation (Schweizerischer Nationalfonds zur Förderung der Wissenschaftlichen Forschung). The work with my colleagues in this project afforded me the opportunity to study transnational cooperation frameworks and their influence on the domestic adoption and enforcement of competition law and market regulation.

Financial support for this book project was also provided by the faculty research funds at Bocconi University (Italy) and the University of Sydney Law School (Australia). In addition, I would like to thank a number of institutions for hosting me as a visiting scholar while I was writing the book, including the Oñati International Institute for the Sociology of Law (Spain), the Humboldt University Faculty of Law (Germany), the Center for the Advanced Study of the Behavioral Sciences at Stanford (US) and the University of Colorado (US).

While many have both directly and indirectly contributed to the work presented in this book, special thanks are due to the participants in the European Regulatory Private Law Project, including Hans Micklitz, Thomas Roethe, Guido Comparato, Marta Cantero-Gamito, Betül Kas and Baarend van Leeuwen, as well as the participants in the Power Shifts project, including Sandra Lavenex, Lei Wang,

Omar Serrano, Ivo Križić and Tim Büthe. I also wish to thank my colleagues with whom I have been grappling with experimentalism for quite some time, including Charles Sabel, Jonathan Zeitlin and Grainne de Búrca. For comments on the entire draft, I wish to thank in particular Giacomo Tagiuri and for research assistance Mitheran Selvendran, Riccardo Haupt, Giulia Schneider and Jemma Sturgis. Maciej Bernatt, Shaun Wilson and Marta Cantero-Gamito also provided comments on parts of the manuscript. I also wish to thank the colleagues at Hart Publishing/ Bloomsbury for their continued support and Jon Lloyd for his careful copyediting.

Mount Victoria,
March 2020

CONTENTS

Introduction

This book aims to provide an account of the recent evolution of competition law enforcement in the European Union (EU) in the face of contemporary challenges, including the growth and increasing diversity of the EU itself, novel competition problems presented by dynamic high-technology markets, as well as incipient scepticism about the benefits of competition in the internal market. The main argument is that the model of experimentalist governance, based on learning from difference and recursive problem-solving, rationalises a number of emergent developments in the orientation of competition law and enforcement techniques at the EU and national levels, which can be observed also beyond the EU. To provide the background to the argument, we will begin with a brief account of the transformation of competition law from a relatively blunt instrument for building the internal market to a tool that must balance a richer set of policy objectives in the regulation of markets. Notwithstanding the growing influence of economic analysis, the role of competitive strictures imposed by EU law has been challenged in both public and scholarly debate, undermining any account of competition law as a tool for pursuing narrow economic efficiency goals either through litigation or technocratic regulation. Instead, reforms in both the law and practice of competition enforcement and market regulation at the EU and national levels have created the scope for the experimentalist elaboration of competition policy as a diagnostic tool to identify problems in the operation of both markets and regulatory regimes, to develop prototype solutions for such problems, and to adjust or scale up such prototypes through peer review and recursive learning.

I. Transformation of EU Competition Law: From Cross-border Transactions to Economic Efficiency?

Promoting competitive markets and the enforcement of competition law have been among the foundational building blocks of the EU's internal market project, which was itself seen as a stepping stone towards closer political integration. Enhancing competition through competition law was one of the tasks of the European Coal and Steel Community and also of the European Economic Community. It reflected an appreciation – or at least a perception – that both protectionism and cartelisation contributed towards totalitarianism and the disastrous wars in the first half of the twentieth century. Moreover, since national market regulation tended to restrain competition, whether through corporatism, state provision or subsidies, the Member States lacked both the broader vision and the regulatory capacity to be entrusted with competition policy.[1] The incorporation of competition disciplines in the treaties demonstrated a recognition that any trade liberalisation pursued by disciplining public restraints to trade could be undone through private arrangements restricting market access.

Notwithstanding its foundational contribution to the European project, at least when viewed from the present perspective, it may be argued that the objectives of promoting competition in the common market were to some extent inchoate. Theories of trade and market structure would have suggested gains from specialisation and trade, dead-weight losses of market power and potential improvements in consumer or total welfare from more competitive market structures. At the same time, the early Commission competition practice, supported by the court jurisprudence, did not appear to have some variant of either deconcentration of markets or efficiency as principal objectives, focusing instead on the goal of promoting greater economic interpenetration of national markets. Such interpenetration would serve the creation of a common market as the basis of economic interdependence, which was to contribute to the broader political objectives of maintaining peace and coping with the threats of the Cold War division on the continent. While this may seem like a limited or even unsophisticated understanding of the role of competition law, the idea of promoting peace and interdependence through commerce had the imprimatur of a line of scholars stretching back to the Enlightenment.[2]

Putting competition law in the service of market integration offered a relatively simple recipe for its implementation. Despite drawing inspiration from the more long-standing US antitrust model, a key focus of the early competition interventions by the European Commission and the Court of Justice of the European Union (CJEU) was the promotion of cross-border transactions and cross-border market entry by weakening private trading restrictions that fragmented national markets. The benefit of such an approach to competition policy is a neat analytic alignment between means and goals through a focus on apparently discriminatory private

[1] There were some exceptions, notably Germany, where before the Second World War, the ordoliberal school already identified competition as an important disciplining force on market actors, as distinct from either state regulation or state-promoted cartelisation. See M Siems and G Schnyder, 'Ordoliberal Lessons for Economic Stability: Different Kinds of Regulation, Not More Regulation' (2014) 27 *Governance* 377.

[2] DP Fidler, 'Competition Law and International Relations' (1992) 41 *International and Comparative Law Quarterly* 563, 571 (arguing that for Kant, 'interdependence slowly forces States to require peace in order to pursue their interests'); *cf* H Brunkhorst, 'European Crisis: The Kantian Mindset of Democracy under Pressure of the Managerial Mindset of Capitalism' in H Brunkhorst, C Gaitanides and G Grözinger (eds), *Europe at a Crossroad: From Currency Union to Political and Economic Governance?* (Baden-Baden, Nomos Verlagsgesellschaft, 2015) 71 (contrasting the revolutionary foundation with the managerial trajectory of European integration).

restraints on competition that fragment national markets.[3] If business practices and conduct in competition law are assessed along the single dimension of their effects on cross-border transactions (as with national regulatory rules in freedom of movement law), it is feasible to devise simple relatively bright-line competition rules to tackle such restrictions.

At the same time, merely promoting cross-border competition may be regarded as a relatively shallow variant of the internal market project[4] if economic interpenetration is pursued for its own sake and without sufficient regard to other market and policy objectives valued at the national or supranational level.[5] The key difficulty with competition rules being focused principally on the internal market objective, without much inquiry into the reasons for business practices and their possible effects, is that they can become both over-inclusive (sacrificing valuable policy goals and business strategies on the altar of interpenetration of economic activity) and under-inclusive (ignoring other anti-competitive effects of market conduct). The existence and costs of such policy trade-offs have become more apparent as competition law instruments have extended into more economically important and socially sensitive sectors, including services, and particularly with the substitution of private for public provision of essential services through market liberalisation.

The need to re-evaluate the application of competition policy in different markets, in the face of shifting market constellations and public policy objectives, has not been unique to the EU. As has been extensively documented, US antitrust enforcement has undergone a number of shifts since the original enactment of the Sherman Act, including periodic re-orientation of the goals, instruments and the aggressiveness of antitrust enforcement. In the first half of the twentieth century, it vacillated between deconcentration and trust-busting (to address consolidation of economic power) and encouraging coordination in times of crisis.[6] In the post-Second World War period, an activist antitrust policy implemented by US courts and agencies – through relatively simple bright-line rules of prohibition on price-setting across firm boundaries, exclusionary conduct, as well as predation – promoted business autonomy, while targeting market concentration.[7] Generalist

[3] See, eg, Case 26/76 *Metro-SB-Groß-Märkte GmbH & Co KG v Commission of the European Communities* [1977] ECR 1875, 1904 (effective rivalry is defined as 'the degree of competition necessary to ensure the observance of the basic requirements and the attainment of the objectives of the Treaty, in particular the creation of a single market achieving conditions similar to those of a domestic market').

[4] *cf* Y Svetiev, 'The EU's Private Law in the Regulated Sectors: Competitive Market Handmaiden or Institutional Platform?' (2016) 22 *European Law Journal* 659.

[5] See G Amato, *Antitrust and the Bounds of Power: The Dilemma of Liberal Democracy in the History of the Market* (Oxford, Hart Publishing, 1997).

[6] WE Kovacic and C Shapiro, 'Antitrust Policy: A Century of Economic and Legal Thinking' (2000) 14 *Journal of Economic Perspectives* 43.

[7] ibid.

courts could elaborate an active competition policy precisely because the rules they fashioned largely ignored the reasons for or likely effects of business conduct on a range of objectives. As such, courts could eschew difficult balancing exercises in antitrust litigation, invoking a presumption that enhancing competition enhances the public interest.[8]

Political and economic developments triggered a further re-evaluation of US antitrust policy by highlighting the economic benefits of firm size and vertical integration at times of a perceived loss of competitiveness of American industry during the 1970s.[9] The so-called economics revolution in US antitrust sought to incorporate economic learning about the reasons for and possible effects of certain market conduct into antitrust doctrines.[10] One effect of the economics revolution was the re-orientation of both the goals – towards efficiency and consumer welfare – and the analytical instruments of antitrust – towards the economic evaluation of business conduct. However, the need to re-absorb the new economic learning into legal doctrines in light of the limited capability of generalist courts to engage in the complex evaluation of evidence on economic effects on a case-by-case basis[11] meant that US antitrust became much more tolerant towards business conduct and increased market concentration.[12]

EU competition law has not been immune to such re-examination. After all, US antitrust has always been an important source of inspiration and learning for EU competition enforcement. The diffusion of practices between the two jurisdictions has been fuelled both by strategic competition concerns and by ever greater intensity of communication between the antitrust epistemic communities on both sides of the Atlantic. Moreover, EU and US enforcers have increasingly grappled with the same conduct and proposed mergers of multinational firms operating in global markets increasing the need for both communication and coordination.[13] Such investigations have even led to divergent decisions, which were sometimes accompanied by criticisms from the US antitrust community that EU competition law was outmoded in its orientation.[14]

In addition to the transnational dialogue, there have also been internal criticisms that a narrow focus of EU competition enforcement without reference

[8] *National Society of Professional Engineers v United States* 435 US 679, 695 (1978); *Federal State Commission v Indiana Federation of Dentists* 476 US 447, 459 (1986).

[9] N Lamoreaux, 'The Problem of Bigness: From Standard Oil to Google' (2019) 33 *Journal of Economic Perspectives* 94.

[10] JE Kwoka, Jr and LJ White (eds), *The Antitrust Revolution* (Boston, Scott, Foresman and Co, 1989).

[11] JE Lopatka and WH Page, 'Economic Authority and the Limits of Expertise in Antitrust Cases' (2004) 90 *Cornell Law Review* 617.

[12] T Wu, *The Curse of Bigness: Antitrust in the New Gilded Age* (New York, Columbia Global Reports, 2018).

[13] C Damro and T Guay, 'Translantic Merger Relations: The Pursuit of Cooperation and Convergence' (2012) 34 *Journal of European Integration* 643.

[14] EM Fox, 'We Protect Competition, You Protect Competitors' (2003) 26 *World Competition* 149.

to effects undermined arrangements – sometimes long-standing ones – that promoted competitive advantage and efficiency in certain industrial sectors of the Member States by allowing firms to collaborate in order to overcome problems in industrial organisation and contracting.[15] Given the more limited role of courts in the elaboration of EU competition law, the EU Commission could contextualise competition policy to different market settings through innovative regulatory tools, such as the block exemptions from the operation of Article 101 that were implemented for specific sectors (in industries such as automobiles[16] or insurance)[17] or transversally (on vertical contracting practices,[18] joint ventures[19] or intellectual property).[20] On the one hand, such tools lead to a fragmentation of competition law, but on the other hand, they allow competition policy to be more sensitive to specific sectoral problems and policy objectives, including not only allocative efficiency, but also quality, innovation, research and development, and essential service provision.

At least since the early 2000s, the EU Commission has also emphasised a shift towards a more economic approach in EU competition enforcement.[21] Such an approach involves a greater focus on the effects of market conduct, particularly on economic efficiency and consumer welfare, and consequently greater openness to economic input in gauging such effects. In an evaluation of EU competition policy on its fiftieth anniversary, Vives noted a substantial transatlantic convergence in antitrust policy, arguing that one of its 'main driving forces … has been the application of economic reasoning grounded in the analysis of industrial organization using game theory and empirical methods as a fundamental toolbox'.[22] Apart from

[15] See, eg, DJ Gerber, *Law and Competition in Twentieth Century Europe: Protecting Prometheus* (Oxford, Oxford University Press, 1998). This had been a long-standing view of interfirm collaboration and associational cooperation in Germany as well as in other countries. See G Herrigel, *Industrial Constructions: The Sources of German Industrial Power* (Cambridge, Cambridge University Press, 2000).

[16] Commission Regulation (EC) 1400/2002 of 31 July 2002 on the application of Article 81(3) of the Treaty to categories of vertical agreements and concerted practices in the motor vehicle sector [2002] OJ L203/30.

[17] Council Regulation (EEC) 1534/91 of 31 May 1991 on the application of Article 85(3) of the Treaty to certain categories of agreements, decisions and concerted practices in the insurance sector [1991] OJ L143/1; Commission Regulation (EC) of 24 March 2010 on the application of Article 101(3) of the Treaty to certain categories of agreements, decisions and concerted practices in the insurance sector [2010] OJ L83/1.

[18] Commission Regulation (EU) 330/2010 of 20 April 2010 on the application of Article 101(3) of the Treaty on the Functioning of the European Union to categories of vertical agreements and concerted practices [2010] OJ L102/1.

[19] Commission Notice of 2 March 1998 on the concept of full-function joint ventures under Council Regulation (EEC) No 4064/89 on the control of concentrations between undertakings [1998] OJ C66/1.

[20] Commission Regulation (EU) 316/2014 of 21 March 2014 on the application of Article 101(3) of the Treaty on the Functioning of the European Union to categories of technology transfer agreements [2014] OJ L93/17.

[21] AC Witt, *The More Economic Approach to EU Antitrust Law* (Oxford, Hart Publishing, 2016).

[22] X Vives, *Competition Policy in the EU: Fifty Years on from the Treaty of Rome* (Oxford, Oxford University Press, 2009) 1.

bolstering its internal capacities for economic analysis by establishing the Chief Economist's Unit within the Directorate General (DG) Competition and including economists as part of the case teams responsible for antitrust investigations, the Commission issued guidelines on the economic approach to analysing various competition violations. The 2009 guidance on its enforcement priorities in application of Article 102[23] is said to represent the high watermark of this evolution.[24] It is worth pausing to note that the more economic approach to competition enforcement was not implemented through novel legal provisions. Further, the EU courts have maintained adherence both to the internal market as an important objective and to the relevance of non-economic objectives in competition decision-making.

II. A New Equilibrium for EU Competition Law: Legalism or Regulation?

The foregoing changes in emphasis for both the objectives and the enforcement approaches of EU competition law have led both scholars and practitioners to question whether EU competition law is converging upon a 'new equilibrium', analogous to the economics revolution in US antitrust.[25] By way of background to the main argument presented in this book – that EU competition law is evolving into an experimentalist tool of market regulation – it may be useful to sketch out two alternative views about the new equilibrium of EU competition law in its more mature phase. Notably, these views are to some extent incompatible with each other, which may provide further support for the argument that experimentalist governance provides a more useful synthesis of recent developments in EU competition policy and market regulation more broadly.

One view, which emphasises both the procedural and substantive convergence of EU competition law on the US antitrust model, suggests that EU competition law is a paradigmatic example of a distinct form of juridification of EU internal market law or 'Eurolegalism'.[26] According to this view, the enforcement of EU competition law is just another instance of regulation through litigation. Its

[23] European Commission, Communication from the Commission – Guidance on the Commission's Enforcement Priorities in Applying Article 82 of the EC Treaty to Abusive Exclusionary Conduct by Dominant Undertakings, OJ C45, 24 February 2009. See P Akman, 'The European Commission's Guidance on Article 102 TFEU: From Inferno to Paradiso?' (2010) 73 *Modern Law Review* 605 (pointing out that the guidance followed a four-year review and criticism of the lack of economic sophistication of the Commission's approach).

[24] W Sauter, *Coherence in EU Competition Law* (Oxford, Oxford University Press, 2016) 45.

[25] D Gerard and I Lianos, 'Introduction' in D Gerard and I Lianos (eds) *Reconciling Efficiency and Equity: A Global Challenge for Competition Policy* (Cambridge, Cambridge University Press, 2019). *cf* EM Fox, 'Modernization of Antitrust: A New Equilibrium' (1981) 66 *Cornell Law Revue* 1140.

[26] RD Kelemen, *Eurolegalism: The Transformation of Law and Regulation in the European Union* (Cambridge, MA, Harvard University Press, 2011) 194.

juridification was enhanced by the trifecta of cases[27] of the CJEU recognising that a private right of action for compensation of private harm from competition violations subsists in the Treaty articles to ensure their effective implementation. In fact, repeated attempts by the Commission to stimulate private antitrust litigation at a national level has even culminated in a harmonisation directive.[28] Recognising the deregulationist impact of economics-based US antitrust rules, some authors argued that apart from the substance of antitrust regulation, 'its mode has been attuned with the *laissez-faire* variety of capitalism' so that the 'changes in policy goals and enforcement practices' may be understood as part of a 'substantial shift from the Rhenish to the Anglo-Saxon variety of capitalism'.[29]

An alternative view of the new equilibrium is that EU competition law is converging on a new mode of regulation. This account emphasises the substantial empowerment of regulatory actors, such as the Commission and national competition authorities (NCAs), inherent in the shift towards an effects-based competition law relying on complex economic assessments of market conduct. Rather than being limited to an *ex post* characterisation of conduct based on rules or precedents, regulatory enforcement is forward-looking and based on technocratic expertise, which in turn benefits from a substantial margin of deference by EU courts to complex factual and economic assessments.[30] Apart from a shift in the analytical toolkit, the economic approach to competition law has led to a proliferation of regulatory mechanisms, such as administrative guidance,[31] market studies[32] and competitive impact assessments,[33] as well as more complex remedies requiring ongoing oversight and monitoring.[34] Further, the liberalisation and privatisation of key service sectors has diffused competition law analytical tools and remedies into sectoral regulation.[35] The combined effect of such developments

[27] Case C-453/99 *Courage Ltd v Bernard Crehan* and *Bernard Crehan v Courage Ltd and Others* [2001] ECR 1; Joined Cases C-295/04–C-298/04 *Vincenzo Manfredi and Others v Lloyd Adriatico Assicurazioni SpA and Others* [2006] ECR I-6619; Case C-557/12 *Kone AG and Others v ÖBB-Infrastruktur AG* [2014] 5 CMLR 5.

[28] Council Directive 2014/104/EU of 26 November 2014 on certain rules governing actions for damages under national law for infringements of the competition law provisions of the Member States and of the European Union [2014] OJ L349/1.

[29] A Wigger and A Nölke, 'Enhanced Roles of Private Actors in EU Business Regulation and the Erosion of Rhenish Capitalism: The Case of Antitrust Enforcement' (2007) 45 *Journal of Common Market Studies* 487, 505.

[30] I Forrester, 'Panel Discussion' in C Ehlermann and M Marquis (eds), *European Competition Law Annual, Antitrust Settlements under EC Competition Law* (Oxford, Hart Publishing, 2010) 610.

[31] O Stefan, *Soft Law in Court: Competition Law, State Aid, and the Court of Justice of the European Union* (London, Kluwer Law International, 2012).

[32] See the European Commission's Sector Inquiries: https://ec.europa.eu/competition/antitrust/sector_inquiries.html.

[33] DG Communication, 'Better Regulation: Why and How', https://ec.europa.eu/info/law/law-making-process/planning-and-proposing-law/better-regulation-why-and-how_en.

[34] Y Svetiev, 'Settling or Learning: Commitment Decisions as a Competition Enforcement Paradigm' (2014) 33 *Yearbook of European Law* 466.

[35] PL Parcu, 'The Surprising Convergence of Antitrust and Regulation in Europe' (2011) Working Paper, EUI RSCAS, 2011/35, Florence School of Regulation, https://cadmus.eui.eu/handle/1814/17934.

suggests that competition law is evolving into a variant of regulation as opposed to a form of *ex post* legal enforcement.[36]

The regulatory model of competition law could be further reinforced by the networking of competition authorities at the EU and national levels so as to stimulate the adoption of similar analytical approaches and enforcement practices – with economics as a common language[37] – making them technocratic trustees of economic efficiency.[38] Given the more limited role of the courts in the elaboration of EU competition law compared to the US, competition regulators would be at liberty to use more sophisticated empirical and theoretical economic tools to shape the competition policy agenda. In other words, the Commission and NCAs could aim to implement an economic effects-based competition policy not by incorporating economic analysis into legal-doctrinal rules, but through regulatory means.

III. The Status of Competition in the EU Internal Market: Competitive Markets and Public Interest Objectives

In understanding the plausibility of the foregoing two accounts of EU competition law's new equilibrium, it is worth recognising that the function of competition and the objectives of competition policy in the EU internal market have come under considerable scrutiny in contemporary scholarly and public discussion. Such scrutiny has ranged from the macro-level role of competition within the EU treaties to the micro-level interaction of EU competition policy with other policies at EU and national levels. An overarching concern expressed in various settings relates to whether the competitive strictures underlying EU competition law (including antitrust, merger control and state aid), but also freedom of movement law and sectoral regulation, may impede the achievement of a range of public policy goals, including the goal of the social market economy.[39]

[36] See, eg, J Drexl and F Di Porto (eds), *Competition Law as Regulation* (Cheltenham, Edward Elgar, 2015); N Dunne, *Competition Law and Economic Regulation* (Cambridge, Cambridge University Press, 2015); PI Colomo, 'On the Application of Competition Law as Regulation: Elements for a Theory' (2010) 29 *Yearbook of European Law* 261.

[37] DJ Gerber, 'Two Forms of Modernization in European Competition Law' (2007) 31 *Fordham International Law Journal* 1235.

[38] G Majone, 'State, Market, and Regulatory Competition in the EU: Lessons from the Integrating World Economy' in A Moravcsik (ed), *Centralization or Fragmentation? Europe Facing the Challenges of Deepening, Diversity and Democracy* (New York, Council of Foreign Relations, 1998) 117 (professionals are 'oriented by goals, standards of conduct, cognitive beliefs, and career opportunities that derive from their professional community' allowing a 'cooperative partnership of national and supranational regulators').

[39] FW Scharpf, 'The Asymmetry of European Integration, or Why the EU Cannot Be a "Social Market Economy"' (2010) 8 *Socio-Economic Review* 211.

A more visible moment of re-examination of the status of competition law in EU integration involved the apparent demotion of the role of competition in the Treaty of Lisbon following the rejection of the Constitutional Treaty project. The Constitutional Treaty had defined competition and competition policy as, in themselves, objectives of the EU.[40] Following the abandonment of the Constitutional Treaty project, at the insistence of the then-French President Nicolas Sarkozy, the reference to competition as an ultimate objective of EU integration was removed from the Treaty of Lisbon. Within the resulting framework, competition retained the status of an instrument for building the EU internal market, rather than being an object in and of itself.

Quite apart from such symbolic demotion,[41] provisions have been introduced into the EU treaties that arguably strengthen permissible derogations from the competitive strictures of EU law writ large so as to pursue broader public policy objectives. One example is provided by the strengthening of the concept of 'services of general economic interest' (SGEI) by the introduction of (now) Article 14 of the Treaty on the Functioning of the European Union (TFEU) and its inclusion in Article 36 of the Charter of Fundamental Rights. Apart from providing a legislative competence for SGEIs at the EU level, the Lisbon Treaty also introduced a Protocol on SGEIs re-affirming the 'essential role' and 'wide discretion of national, regional and local authorities' in the provision of SGEIs 'as closely as possible to the needs of the users', the 'diversity between various [SGEIs]' and the 'needs and preferences of users' resulting from 'different geographical, social or cultural situations'. The Protocol further affirms that the EU Treaties 'do not affect in any way' Member States' competence to provide 'noneconomic services of general interest'.[42]

In addition, in the aftermath of the EU enlargement, scholars who once lauded the deliberation-enhancing effects of EU integration, including with respect to the quality and inclusiveness of national policy-making and regulation,[43] have suggested a fundamental incompatibility between the competitive principles of EU law and a broad range of non-economic policies at the national level. In particular, the competition-enhancing effects of EU law and a single-minded pursuit of cross-border competition have been said to undermine national regulation that

[40] Article I-3 of the Treaty Establishing a Constitution for Europe mentioned among the EU's objectives 'an internal market where competition is free and undistorted' (Treaty Establishing a Constitution for Europe [2004] OJ C310/1, art I-3.2). Such mention of competition is not present in art 3 of the Treaty on European Union.

[41] E Loozen, 'Strict Competition Enforcement and Welfare: A Constitutional Perspective Based on Article 101 TFEU and Sustainability' (2019) 56 *Common Market Law Review* 1265, 1273 (arguing that the demotion had no legal consequences).

[42] Sauter has argued that these amendments may 'add little of substance' in part due to the Member States' inability to 'conceptualise within the EU legal framework what it is they want from SGEIs'. W Sauter, 'SGEI and Universal Service in EU Law', TILEC Discussion Paper No. 17 (2008) 9.

[43] C Joerges and J Neyer, 'From Intergovernmental Bargaining to Deliberative Political Processes' (1997) 3 *European Law Journal* 273.

embodies solidaristic or social policy objectives.[44] While such criticisms have focused on freedom of movement law, they are extended *a fortiori* to competition law, where the status of other policy objectives in decision-making is at best uncertain and often discouraged for the sake of coherence.[45] In the aftermath of the financial and sovereign debt crises, EU-level strictures imposing fiscal austerity in the affected Member States together with the promotion of competitive markets were seen as mutually reinforcing parts of a neoliberal policy package.[46] Somek has explicitly made the argument that the strictures of competition, freedom of movement and fiscal austerity reflect the link between the ordoliberal pedigree of EU legal integration and neoliberal economic policy, suggesting that:

> Arriving at constructive solutions demands rethinking radically, the ordoliberal straightjacket [*sic*] that … the European legal order [has] created for states. It may well be necessary to abandon the strictures that European competition law presents for states. States are necessary, not only to provide public services, but to offer employment for those who do not want to live competitive lives.[47]

The foregoing discussion suggests reasons for caution about any claim that EU competition law could converge upon either a legal or a regulatory tool to promote a narrow goal of economic efficiency. In fact, more nuanced understanding of the benefits and shortcomings of competition in delivering public policy objectives in markets can be observed in both legislative and judicial pronouncements at the EU level, including in the regulated sectors, such as energy, telecommunications and finance. In such sectors, EU interventions steered Member States to liberalise previously regulated markets and open them up to competitive entry (including cross-border entry) as a way of promoting the internal market, while increasing competitive rivalry and improving the cost and quality of service delivery.[48] One stated aim of EU interventions in such markets was 'progressively to reduce *ex-ante* sector specific rules as competition in the markets develops' so that ultimately they would 'be governed by competition law only'.[49] Examining the compatibility of national energy price regulation with the EU energy liberalisation package,

[44] C Joerges and F Rödl, 'Informal Politics, Formalised Law and the "Social Deficit" of European Integration: Reflections after the Judgments of the ECJ in *Viking* and *Laval*' (2009) 15 *European Law Journal* 1.

[45] Sauter (n 24) 71.

[46] H Brunkhorst, 'A Curtain of Gloom is Descending on the Continent: Capitalism, Democracy and Europe' (2017) 23 *European Law Journal* 335.

[47] A Somek, 'Europe: Political, Not Cosmopolitan' (2014) 20 *European Law Journal* 142.

[48] H Schweitzer, 'Services of General Economic Interest: European Law's Impact on the Role of Markets and of Member States' in M Cremona (ed), *Market Integration and Public Services in the European Union* (Oxford, Oxford University Press, 2011) 60.

[49] Recital 5 of Directive 2009/140/EC of the European Parliament and of the Council of 25 November 2009 amending Directives 2002/21/EC on a common regulatory framework for electronic communications networks and services, 2002/19/EC on access to, and interconnection of electronic communications, networks and associated facilities, and 2002/20/EC on the authorisation of electronic communications networks and services [2009] OJ L337/37.

Advocate General Ruiz-Jarabo Colomer observed that: 'Since the Single European Act, when competition was installed as the new deity on the altar of political ideas, public service has become an obstacle to be overcome in the name of a liberalisation on which all hopes were pinned.'[50]

However, precisely because in the regulated services sectors, multiple public policy objectives are engaged, it is in such markets that we can observe a more fine-grained re-examination of the effects of competition on the public interest at both the EU and national levels. For example, the 2007 Roaming Regulation[51] was motivated by explicit recognition of the limits of competition and the analytical tools of competition law in both completing the internal market and delivering favourable market outcomes. Such limits included the difficulty in identifying undertakings with significant market power in international roaming markets and the fact that telecommunications operators had no incentive to pass on lower wholesale charges through to retail prices, given the nature of competitive rivalry and consumer behaviour in roaming markets.[52] As such, not least to promote communication in the internal market, the legislation relied on a strong form regulation of retail prices, in an intervention that was limited in time (through a sunset clause) to allow for a re-evaluation of the measure in an evolving market with complex competitive dynamics.[53]

Following similar reasoning, the CJEU has also held that Member States can maintain price regulations in the energy sector, even if such limits on the freedom to set prices constitute 'an obstacle to the realization of an operational internal market'. As the Court has recognised, Member States can pursue public service obligations for different policy reasons, including protecting consumers from excessive price rises, if there is either insufficient rivalry in the market or if rivalry is not delivering desired market outcomes. However, such national regulation must be clearly defined, transparent, non-discriminatory and verifiable, and must guarantee equality of access for undertakings. Proportionality requires that Member States differentiate between different classes of customers benefiting from price regulation and make regulatory instruments subject to a sunset clause to allow for the re-evaluation of the adopted measures.[54]

Finally, the aftermath of the financial crisis revealed weaknesses in the Member States' regulatory frameworks for ensuring financial stability. However,

[50] Opinion of Advocate General D. Ruiz-Jarabo Colomer of 20 October 2009 in Case C-265/08 *Federutility v Autorità per l'Energia Elettrica e il Gas* [2009] ECLI: EU:C:2009:640, para 2.

[51] Regulation (EC) No 717/2007 of the European Parliament and of the Council of 27 June 2007 on roaming on public mobile telephone networks within the Community amending Directive 2002/21/EC [2007] OJ L176/37.

[52] ibid Recital 6. See Svetiev, 'The EU's Private Law' (2016).

[53] Case C-58/08 *Vodafone and Others v Secretary of State for Business, Enterprise and Regulatory Reform* [2010] ECLI:EU:C:2010:321.

[54] *Federutility* (n 50) [6], [33]; see also Case C-36/14 *European Commission v Republic of Poland* ECLI: EU:C:2015:570.

the crisis also revealed consequences of promoting market competition, including through competition enforcement, in financial services for the policy goal of financial stability. Given the specific features of financial services, increasing competitive pressures on financial institutions may not always deliver desired market outcomes. For example, increasing competitive pressure on financial institutions by forcing them to compete more intensely for customers may lead to the lowering of quality of services and mis-selling of products to inappropriate target customers.[55] Competition also incentivises financial innovation, resulting in greater product complexity, so that the ordinary competitive disciplines on market actors through disclosure to enhance customer autonomy and choice become less effective.[56] Herd behaviour among financial institutions, whereby they mimic each others' product development and marketing strategies, exacerbates the foregoing problems. As Aglietta and Scialom have argued, 'reflexivity of individual actions and the reactions of others' as a way of managing uncertainty and limited knowledge in financial markets mean that individual transactions come to have systemic consequences.[57]

The foregoing arguments suggest that increasing rivalry and competitive pressure in finance – including through competition law and sectoral regulation that aids free movement – can undermine financial stability unless it is combined with mechanisms to ensure customers can properly evaluate and conserve their interests in financial transactions. Furthermore, if competition enforcement aims to promote cross-border entry and service provision – such as by treating cross-border mergers favourably – this encourages the creation of large financial institutions that become threats to systemic stability at Member State and EU levels.[58] Given their size and systemic importance, the market conduct of such financial institutions, including failures in their product design and contracting, can have significant cross-border effects, destabilising the financial system and requiring bailouts. As such, post-crisis responses required coordination of competition policy, financial supervision and investor protection.[59]

The above discussion illustrates a few key points. First, the introduction of competitive rivalry in some markets does not always produce the intended benefits, even in terms of consumer welfare through lower prices or improved

[55] HJ Allen, 'The Pathologies of Banking Business as Usual' (2015) 17 *University Journal of Business Law* 861.

[56] ibid.

[57] M Aglietta and L Scialom, 'For a Renewal of Financial Regulation' in E Brousseau and J-M Glachant (eds), *The Manufacturing of Markets* (Cambridge, Cambridge University Press, 2014) 333–35.

[58] E Carletti, P Hartmann and S Ongena, 'Cross-border Banking and Competition Policy' (2006) 4 *Research Bulletin, European Central Bank* 7; ME Stucke, 'Lessons from the Financial Crisis' (2010) 77 *Antitrust Law Journal* 313.

[59] DMB Gerard, 'Managing the Financial Crisis in Europe: Why Competition Law is Part of the Solution, Not of the Problem' (2008) 12 *Global Competition Review* 1; HW Micklitz, 'The Transformation of Private Law through Competition' (2016) 22 *European Law Journal* 627, 638 (arguing that competition was 'suspended' in responding to the crisis).

quality. Such outcomes may depend both on the bases of competitive rivalry and other structural features of the market and transactions, including the ability of consumers to effectively exercise choice. Moreover, competition enforcement – whether to promote the internal market or enhance consumer welfare – may have unintended consequences for other public policy objectives, including non-market objectives. As such, observed poor performance of a particular market may require a response from competition law, sectoral regulation or consumer law. Such observations suggest caution about the viability of any equilibrium in which EU competition law can become a self-sufficient legal or technocratic tool for the promotion of either the shallow version of the internal market or a narrow goal of economic efficiency. Moreover, contrary to any idea of a relentless pursuit of an abstract model of competitive markets, the examples above disclose interventions at both the EU and national levels that can be tailored to respond to specific problems in market operation, subject to experimentalist disciplines of justification, review and periodic re-evaluation.

IV. Competition Law and Experimentalist Governance

This book aims to provide an alternative account of the evolution of the orientation and instruments of EU competition law as an instance of experimentalist governance. Scholars[60] have shown that experimentalist architectures of policy-making and regulation can be observed across a variety of regulatory fields in the internal market that were traditionally seen to embody distinct policy modes.[61] Moreover, the literature also demonstrates that through various channels of diffusion – and often through the EU's involvement – experimentalist governance architectures can be detected in different global regulatory regimes.[62]

The remainder of the Introduction will set out the key features of an experimentalist governance architecture and the main background conditions that can lead to its emergence, formalisation and use. It will also be argued that these background conditions are salient in the implementation of competition law as a market regulatory tool more generally. Given the broader salience of these scope conditions, while this book mainly draws upon instruments and examples from the EU as a forum in which the emergence of experimentalist mechanisms may be most evident, the argument presented is also applicable outside of the EU.

[60] CF Sabel and J Zeitlin, 'Learning from Difference: The New Architecture of Experimentalist Governance in the EU' (2008) 14 *European Law Journal* 271, 280 and the contributions in CF Sabel and J Zeitlin (eds), *Experimentalist Governance in the European Union: Towards a New Architecture* (Oxford, Oxford University Press, 2010).

[61] *cf* H Wallace et al (eds) *Policy-Making in the European Union* (Oxford, Oxford University Press, 2015).

[62] J Zeitlin (ed), *Extending Experimentalist Governance? The European Union and Transnational Regulation* (Oxford, Oxford University Press, 2015).

The literature suggests that an experimentalist regulatory architecture is likely to emerge in the face of two background factors, or 'scope conditions', namely: (i) strategic uncertainty about the selection of regulatory means through which to pursue identified policy objectives; and (ii) polyarchy,[63] whereby a single actor is unable to impose their own preferred solutions on all other participating actors.[64] These background conditions for regulation may be expected to lead to inaction or minimalist solutions with a deregulationist tendency.[65] But assuming that all participating actors can agree that there is a problem which requires a solution and that they can perceive benefits from continued mutual engagement (whether in continuing mutually beneficial trade or even in engaging in mutual policy learning), one alternative approach involves: (i) agreeing to a set of common (or framework) objectives to be pursued; and (ii) granting autonomy to each individual lower-level actor[66] to tailor the local means through which to pursue those objectives.[67] While this is not always made explicit in the experimentalism literature, in fashioning local solutions to pursue shared objectives, lower-level actors can take into account specific contextual factors relevant to the local environment (which make 'one-size-fits-all' regulatory templates inappropriate), they can draw upon existing policy knowledge (including about previous local policy solutions) and they should also be able to incorporate local policy preferences.[68]

As described above, an experimentalist regulatory architecture suggests a move away from binding and legally enforceable harmonised rules, given the identified need for autonomy to tailor locally appropriate solutions. As such, experimentalism may be regarded as a species of 'new governance' that relies on flexible mechanisms, such as soft law and informal learning and exchange.[69] However, what marks out experimentalist governance is the incorporation of a set of formal obligations that discipline the discretion of participating actors through joint learning rather than verification of compliance. These formal mechanisms include: (i) an obligation

[63] Sabel and Zeitlin, 'Learning from Difference' (2008).

[64] ibid.

[65] The idea of market fundamentalism, after all, may be understood as a preference for (or faith in) market solutions, even in the face of poor market outcomes, given difficulties in devising effective public regulation. See F Block and MR Somers, *The Power of Market Fundamentalism* (Cambridge, MA, Harvard University Press, 2014).

[66] As we will observe in successive chapters, local actors are conceived broadly in the experimentalism literature to include national authorities in the EU or transnational context, as well as firms or trading associations through which regulatory solutions are implemented in regulatory capitalism. See Sabel and Zeitlin (n 60); J Braithwaite, *Regulatory Capitalism: How it Works, Ideas for Making it Work Better* (Cheltenham, Edward Elgar, 2008).

[67] ibid.

[68] As we will underscore throughout the book, the ability to hybridise common with local policy objectives may be seen as one hallmark of experimentalist as opposed to technocratic transnational governance. See Svetiev (n 4).

[69] In the EU context, one frequently cited example of soft or informal governance is the Open Method of Coordination. See eg, R Dehousse, 'The Open Method of Coordination: A New Policy Paradigm?' (2003) 3 *Les Cahiers Européens de Sciences Po* 1.

to report locally devised and implemented solutions to a central clearing house; (ii) an obligation to subject the design *and* effects of local solutions to peer review by other participating actors, including both regulatory peers and stakeholders; and even (iii) a penalty default instrument, which can discipline recalcitrant actors who fail to exercise discretion, do so opportunistically or otherwise obstruct the implementation of local solutions.

Despite such formal instruments, experimentalist regulation is not ordinarily implemented through litigation, given that it does not rely on rule enforcement through judicial techniques of interpretation and precedent or traditional judicial remedies. However, as we will see, the courts can play a supporting role for experimentalist governance through review standards that encourage the acknowledgement of uncertainty and incorporate the peer accountability mechanisms mentioned above. Moreover, experimentalist governance does not require specific institutional formats. Instead, experimentalist regime must incorporate mechanisms that perform the functions discussed above, including those of defining framework goals, tailoring and reporting of local solutions, as well as peer review and monitoring of such solutions. Finally, experimentalist governance is recursive. Given that actors are expected to learn from their own and the implementation experience of others, such learning allows for existing rules and even framework objectives to be continuously revised in the light of experience.

As a result, authors have been able to identify experimentalist frameworks in very different policy fields, ranging from food safety and financial regulation to data privacy and rights protection. The EU has been an important forum for studying experimentalist frameworks precisely because in the face of uncertainty and polyarchy, regulatory alignment to establish the internal market has proceeded through flexible forms of harmonisation (with the 'directive' as a paradigm example), but also through the formalisation of reporting obligations (from early on) and peer review frameworks (more recently), all circumscribed by a dialogic EU-national framework of judicial remedies.[70]

Despite experimentalist governance architectures having been detected in many policy fields in the EU,[71] at first blush the relevance of this regulatory model for EU competition law may seem limited. After all, the implementation of EU competition law has traditionally been highly centralised, being described as the EU's 'first supranational policy'.[72] As discussed earlier, the centralisation of competition law in the hands of the Commission reflected both the role competition was to play in building the common market and the absence of strong national competition enforcement traditions. But despite such history of supranational centralisation, greater legal scope for experimentalist implementation of EU

[70] *cf* M Tushnet, 'Dialogic Judicial Review' (2008) 61 *Arkansas Law Review* 205.
[71] See the contributions in Sabel and Zeitlin (eds) (n 60).
[72] L McGowan and S Wilks, 'The First Supranational Policy in the European Union: Competition Policy' (1995) 28 *European Journal of Political Research* 141.

competition law[73] was created by a set of institutional reforms – initiated by the Commission – as part of the modernisation package that came into force at the time of the expansion of the EU to include 10 new Member States, mostly from Central and Eastern Europe, in 2004. Given the fact that many new Member States had little or no recent history of either competitive markets or competition law, it was perhaps surprising that the centrepiece of the modernisation package was a decentralisation of the enforcement system. Namely, apart from the Commission, the NCAs were empowered to enforce EU competition law (in addition to their responsibility of applying national competition law).[74] The modernisation reforms did not involve any substantive changes in the legal and doctrinal framework of EU competition law, and involved no attempts to consolidate and codify the existing principles or precedents that had been developed by the EU Commission and the courts in applying the Treaty articles, nor any attempt to define or stabilise the goals of EU competition law.

Instead of any attempts at substantive consolidation to ensure compliance and coherence in a more diverse union, the principal reforms of the Modernisation Regulation focused on inter-institutional obligations in the relationship between the Commission and the NCAs as well as on competition enforcement techniques. For the purposes of the argument presented in the book, we may highlight the following features of the reforms, as they would go on to play an important role in the experimentalist account of EU competition law:

- the formalisation of the European Competition Network (ECN) as a forum for the accommodation of decentralised enforcement and mutual consultation between the Commission and the NCAs, which had previously operated largely informally;[75]
- the formalisation of an obligation to report draft decisions under EU competition law by the NCAs to the Commission and the members of the ECN;[76]
- the formalisation of the previously informal mechanism of peer consultation among the Commission and NCAs with respect to proposed competition decisions through the establishment of the Advisory Committee on Restrictive Practices and Dominant Positions;[77]
- the abandonment of the informal clearance procedure for interfirm arrangements that might violate Article 101(1), while making the Article 101(3)

[73] Y Svetiev, 'Networked Competition Governance in the EU: Delegation, Decentralization, or Experimentalist Architecture?' in Sabel and Zeitlin (eds) (n 60).

[74] Council Regulation (EC) 1/2003 of 16 December 2002 on the implementation of the rules on competition laid down in Articles 81 and 82 of the Treaty [2003] OJ L1/1, art 3 (hereinafter 'Modernisation Regulation' or 'Regulation 1/2003').

[75] Modernisation Regulation, Recital 15; Commission Notice of 27 April 2004 on cooperation within the network of competition authorities [2004] OJ C101/43.

[76] Modernisation Regulation, art 11(4).

[77] ibid art 14.

exceptions on the basis of balancing of anti-competitive effects with legitimate justifications of such arrangements directly applicable;[78]

- the formalisation of the procedure for closure of cases through remedial commitments provided by the defendant undertaking to address identified competition concerns, thereby replacing the previously informal practice of consensual case resolution.[79]

On the one hand, decentralised responsibility for enforcing EU competition law, including an enhanced role for the NCAs, together with the formalisation of obligations of reporting and peer review, may lead to a transformation of competition law towards an experimentalist tool for locally contextualised market regulation, as described above.[80] On the other hand, much of the contemporaneous and subsequent commentary reflected scepticism about the Modernisation Regulation ushering in a more decentralised elaboration of *substantive* EU competition law.[81] Overwhelmingly, commentators saw the Regulation and the ECN as mechanisms through which to relieve the Commission from having to enforce EU competition law across (a much larger) union, while allowing it to maintain tight control over its substantive content.[82] Charging NCAs to apply the common EU competition law articles together with an economic framework for their interpretation[83] could turn them into the Commission's local agents, reducing the significance of national traditions in regulating competition and markets.[84] The possibility for competition law to be hybridised with a variety of (particularly local) public policy objectives would be reduced by the fact that NCAs were not empowered to apply Article 101(3) administratively. According to this view, the networking and reporting obligations were seen as mechanisms to ensure the Commission's overall control over the enforcement and evolution of EU competition law and to guard against the risks of fragmentation and incoherence.[85] This effect was to be further enhanced by the granting of formal instruments of hierarchical control by the Commission, including the power to take over a case from a NCA and the explicit prohibition on national regulatory *and* judicial decisions that were inconsistent with those of the Commission.[86]

[78] ibid art 1(2).
[79] ibid art 9.
[80] Svetiev (n 73).
[81] D Geradin, 'Competition between Rules and Rules of Competition: A Legal and Economic Analysis of the Proposed Modernization of the Enforcement of EC Competition Law' (2002) 9 *Columbia Journal of European Law* 1, 1.
[82] Eg, A Riley, 'EC Antitrust Modernisation: The Commission Does Very Nicely – Thank You! Part One: Regulation 1 and the Notification Burden' (2003) 24 *European Contract Law Review* 604.
[83] Gerber (n 37).
[84] S Wilks, 'Agency Escape: Decentralization or Dominance of the European Commission in the Modernization of Competition Policy?' (2005) 18 *Governance* 431.
[85] Sauter (n 24) 152, 156.
[86] Modernisation Regulation, art 16.

V. The Scope Conditions for Experimentalist Governance in Competition Law

As the above discussion suggests, institutional architectures may be ambiguous.[87] Mechanisms involving reporting, monitoring and peer review can be used for hierarchical control just as much as for experimentalist discipline over local implementation. In the remainder of this book, we will seek to demonstrate the experimentalist potential of the above mechanisms and to provide evidence about their use consistently with an experimentalist logic, as well as to point to ways in which their experimentalist potential can be more fully realised. But in a first step, we need to demonstrate the salience of the scope conditions of uncertainty and polyarchy for the implementation of competition law.

A. Strategic Uncertainty

Strategic uncertainty as a scope condition for experimentalist governance points to the difficulty of specifying or selecting the instruments (or means) through which to achieve desirable policy outcomes (or ends). Such uncertainty can arise from different sources and can provide a spur for decision-makers to pursue differentiated experimentalist solutions. Throughout the following chapters, we will seek to highlight sources of uncertainty faced by decision-makers in confronting competition and market regulatory problems, the extent to which such uncertainty is openly acknowledged and how it can result in the formulation of experimentalist mechanisms.

For chiefly analytical purposes, we can identify three sources of uncertainty in implementing competition law as a tool to deliver market outcomes consistent with policy objectives, which we might term conceptual, predictive and interaction uncertainty. While these three sources are in fact closely related in any specific case, there is at least some analytical purchase in distinguishing them at the outset so as to connect them to familiar competition law debates.

Conceptual uncertainty may arise due to doubts about the very meaning of market competition and, consequently, the reasons for promoting competitive rivalry as a policy objective. Competitive rivalry can be defined in many ways, including in terms of the concentration of markets or their contestability, by the degree of cross-border transactions or by the degree of business autonomy in setting prices or other decision-making, to name but a few. All of these conceptions of competitive rivalry may be appealing, though none is clearly preferred

[87] Svetiev (n 73); B Rangoni, 'Architecture and Policy-Making: Comparing Experimentalist and Hierarchical Governance in EU Energy Regulation' (2019) 26 *Journal of European Public Policy* 63.

to the others from a policy perspective, either theoretically or empirically. The kind of rivalry that competition policy should pursue would thus seem to depend on the goals that we assign to competition law, which accounts for long-standing and largely inconclusive debates about the appropriate goals of competition law.[88] Adopting an economics-oriented approach does not resolve this problem to the extent that it does not provide us with an optimal market structure that competition policy should target. If the textbook model of perfect competition is neither feasible nor desirable, concepts such as 'workable competition' only re-state the problem that business conduct and rivalry are beneficial if they promote 'good' market outcomes.[89]

Predictive uncertainty may be understood as uncertainty about the effects of observed market conduct on policy-relevant market outcomes, as well as about the effects of any enforcement remedy implemented through competition law. Even if we narrow the objective of competition law, such as to allocative efficiency or consumer welfare,[90] enforcers face uncertainty about the reliability of rules or analytical tools with which to gauge effects of conduct, especially if such effects are not immediately appreciable in the market. Likely effects may be assessed contextually on a case-by-case basis, but such enforcement depends on the availability of reliable predictive tools linking conduct and context to effects. In aiming to predict price or output effects, economists can build quite sophisticated models of demand and strategic interaction, though these are often based on extrapolation either from other markets or from observed past conduct in the market under consideration and assumptions of rational behaviour.[91] Two factors that generate predictive uncertainty are heterogeneity across industries and dynamic change within industries. Heterogeneity means that differences in conditions, such as the basis of competition in different markets, as well as different national or even local economic circumstances, may lead to different effects of similar species of business conduct. Rapid technological change or business model innovation are sources of market dynamism, potentially radically altering the competitive

[88] *cf* I Lianos, 'Some Reflections on the Question of the Goals of EU Competition Law' (2013) *CLES Working Paper Series* 3/2013.

[89] S Sosnick, 'A Critique of Concepts of Workable Competition' (1958) 72 *Quarterly Journal of Economics* 380. As has been argued, such a concept does not 'fill any gap in existing theories of market behavior' and was 'an outgrowth of a public policy need'. See RL Knox, 'Workable Competition and Public Policy' (1967) 1 *Antitrust Law and Economics Review* 41, 48; C Veljanovski, 'EC Merger Policy after GE/Honeywell and Airtours' (2004) 49 *Antitrust Bulletin* 153.

[90] These concepts are not in themselves necessarily clear and unambiguous. See GJ Werden, 'Consumer Welfare and Competition Policy' in J Drexel et al (eds), *Competition Policy and the Economic Approach* (Cheltenham, Edward Elgar, 2011) 11: 'discourse on competition policy often uses the term "consumer welfare" but rarely is clear about its meaning or role'.

[91] As observers have noted, just as the economics-based analytical categories for gauging competitive effects stabilised in antitrust practice, they became less useful in analysing novel problems in dynamic markets. See D Coyle, 'Discussion on "Competition Economics and Antitrust in Europe"' (2006) 21 *Economic Policy* 786, 787.

landscape or the basis of competition. Moreover, going beyond price to consider attributes such as product quality and innovation as relevant market effects only exacerbates the analytical burden on competition decision-makers.[92]

Finally, interaction uncertainty relates to uncertainty about the effects of competition interventions (however we define the goals of competition policy) on non-competition (or non-economic) objectives, as well as on the legal and regulatory instruments that pursue such objectives.[93] Business conduct that has an impact on competitive rivalry could have consequences for objectives such as safety in product markets, security of supply and affordability in food or energy markets, or – as discussed above – financial stability in financial markets. Strategies to cope with such interactions might include developing a hierarchy of enforcement objectives[94] or creating mechanisms to redirect problems that involve policy trade-offs to political – rather than regulatory – actors.[95] However, as in the above examples and as we will observe in Chapter 2 (in the context of competition law and data protection or sustainability), these strategies are not always either feasible or desirable, particularly if we care about both effective problem-solving and the social legitimacy of competition enforcement.[96]

The foregoing typology of different sources of uncertainty is intended to provide conceptual clarity about the complexity that besets competition law enforcement as an instrument that applies transversally to many different markets. As we will observe in the following chapters, in analysing specific market conduct, a competition decision-maker is likely to face all of these sources of uncertainty simultaneously. Both legal and technocratic approaches to the decision-making task may incentivise the concealment of uncertainty by arguing either that existing rules cover impugned conduct (even if novel) or that expert modelling reliably forecasts the effects of such conduct. By contrast, an experimentalist decision-making framework aims to encourage open acknowledgement of uncertainty as a precondition for regulatory discretion, but subject to the experimentalist accountability disciplines discussed above, including peer review, stakeholder participation and continuous recursive revision.

[92] See, eg, J Drexl, 'Real Knowledge is to Know the Extent of One's Own Ignorance: On the Consumer Harm Approach in Innovation-Related Competition Cases' (2010) 76 *Antitrust Law Journal* 677.

[93] Sauter (n 24) 75, has argued that in order to maintain its coherence and legitimacy, EU competition law should be focused on economic objectives to the exclusion of broader public policy objectives.

[94] G Monti, 'Article 81 EC and Public Policy' (2002) 39 *Common Market Law Review* 1057.

[95] G Majone, 'State, Market, and Regulatory Competition in the EU: Lessons from the Integrating World Economy' in A Moravcsik (ed), *Centralization or Fragmentation? Europe Facing the Challenges of Deepening, Diversity and Democracy* (New York, Council of Foreign Relations, 1998) 97–98, 117.

[96] Competition agencies and courts must decide cases that are presented to them, and their decisions may have either immediate or delayed impacts on a variety of policy objectives, including unintended consequences, particularly if they are uncoordinated with other more specialised regulatory instruments.

B. Polyarchy and the Limits of Coercive Enforcement

Polyarchy is the second scope condition for experimentalist governance. The experimentalism literature treats polyarchy as a multipolar distribution of power whereby 'no single actor has the capacity to impose her own preferred solution without taking account of the views of others'.[97] As Sabel and Zeitlin explain, in the absence of a multi-polar distribution of power, one actor is dominant and 'the powerful impose outcomes, rather than pursuing them cooperatively with others'.[98] Polyarchy seems an apt description of the multi-actor and multi-level rule-making and enforcement processes in the EU.[99] A polyarchic distribution of power might explain, for example, why the Commission may have been unable to impose a particular substantive vision of competition law policy as part of the modernisation reforms. It may also explain specific efforts at the accommodation of strongly held national policy preferences in specific competition interventions by the Commission.[100]

For the purposes of this book, the second scope condition also captures the intuition about the difficulties in imposing hierarchical regulatory solutions, which has been recognised in the market regulation literature more generally.[101] These difficulties include the costliness of monitoring business conduct, gathering market information relevant for understanding the significance and effects of such conduct, as well as designing, implementing and supervising effective remedies. As Gunningham and Kagan point out:

> If socio-legal research has taught us anything, it is that legal coercion is expensive and difficult. Law can rarely hope to be meaningful and effective without the cooperation, indeed the normative accord, of the vast majority of populations it hopes to control.[102]

The costliness of coercive enforcement by the Commission is one likely explanation for the decision to decentralise enforcement responsibilities on to the NCAs in the Modernisation Regulation. But it may also suggest a limited capability by the Commission to impose its own preferred model of competition enforcement on the NCAs. Further, the difficulties of coercive enforcement are also salient for all regulatory agencies, including both NCAs and national regulatory authorities (NRAs),

[97] Sabel and Zeitlin, 'Learning from Difference' (n 60) 280.

[98] CF Sabel and J Zeitlin, 'Experimentalism in the EU: Common Ground and Persistent Differences' (2012) 6 *Regulation and Governance* 410, 412.

[99] O Gerstenberg and C Sabel, 'Directly Deliberative Polyarchy: An Institutional Ideal for Europe?' in C Joerges and R Dehousse (eds), *Good Governance in Europe's Integrated Markets* (Oxford, Oxford University Press, 2002).

[100] See, eg, JG Backhaus and R Hansen, 'Resale Price Maintenance for Books in Germany and the European Union: A Legal and Economic Analysis' in A Marciano and JM Josselin (eds), *From Economic to Legal Competition: New Perspectives on Law and Institutions in Europe* (Cheltenham, Edward Elgar, 2003).

[101] See generally I Ayers and J Braithwaite, *Responsive Regulation: Transcending the Deregulation Debate* (Oxford, Oxford University Press, 1992).

[102] N Gunningham and RA Kagan, 'Regulation and Business Behavior' (2005) 27 *Law and Policy* 213.

which in turn may necessitate collaboration with target undertakings and other market stakeholders.[103] As Braithwaite has argued, the regulatory state promoted concentrated markets – including through laxer antitrust enforcement – not only because of the efficiency of mass production,[104] but also because a decentralised economy is largely unregulable: 'the regulatory reach of contemporary capitalism would be impossible without the lumpiness of a commerce populated by big businesses that can be enrolled to regulate smaller businesses'.[105]

Throughout the book, we will explore how the interaction of the above two scope conditions affects the use of competition law as a tool for regulating markets in the EU. The combination of uncertainty and the difficulties associated with coercive enforcement limits the ability of actors to impose hierarchical solutions, creating scope for devolved and collaborative problem-solving: between the EU Commission and NCAs, between NCAs and other specialised regulators, and between enforcement authorities at all levels and target undertakings (as well as other affected third parties).

Chapter 1 focuses on the decentralised and networked enforcement regime introduced by the Modernisation Regulation, and the role of the ECN. Going beyond the legal provisions that define the governance architecture, we will draw on available practice to illustrate how the ECN has been used as a mechanism for experimentalist rule-making and enforcement. We will also aim to examine the extent to which the Commission's supervisory powers under the Regulation can be understood as a hierarchical control mechanism as opposed to an experimentalist penalty default. Finally, the chapter will focus on the operation of the NCAs by arguing that recent legislative interventions on the powers of the NCAs may enhance their experimentalist capabilities by protecting the scope conditions for experimentalism and providing NCAs with experimentalist enforcement tools. The creation of multi-function market regulatory authorities in some Member States will also be explored, as a mode of both managing regulatory regime interactions and promoting experimentalist problem-solving.

Chapter 2 focuses on the techniques that have been used by the Commission and NCAs in enforcing competition law vis-a-vis target undertakings to understand whether they are legalistic, technocratic or experimentalist. At the theoretical level, we will highlight how the mechanisms of experimentalist governance, inspired by the product and process design disciplines of pragmatist firms, rationalise a number of developments in regulatory theory. At the same time, we will observe how the formalisation of the tool for negotiated case resolution through commitments in the Modernisation Regulation creates scope for a problem-solving orientation in competition enforcement by sidestepping the retrospective characterisation

[103] ibid.

[104] AD Chandler, Jr, *The Visible Hand* (Cambridge, MA, Harvard University Press 1993).

[105] J Braithwaite, 'The Regulatory State' in RAW Rhodes et al (eds), *Oxford Handbook of Political Science* (New York, Oxford University Press, 2009) 223–26.

of conduct and focusing on remedial formulation and adjustment. Both the formal design and the use of this tool in competition enforcement incorporate the experimentalist mechanisms of dynamic adjustment, stakeholder participation and monitoring of implementation. Later on in the chapter, we will identify how competition enforcement in dynamic markets (such as internet search), as well as in cases that involve interaction with non-competition objectives (such as data protection and sustainability), can be rationalised from an experimentalist perspective even when the authorities use coercive violation-based techniques. In particular, in such cases competition law can act as a diagnostic tool[106] that identifies problems in the operation of the competitive market mechanism, as well as deficiencies in specialised regulatory regimes.

In Chapter 3 we turn to the question of accountability mechanisms in experimentalist governance and the use of peer review. The chapter draws on the EU and transnational governance literatures to identify different functionalities of peer review in transnational governance and to highlight the extent to which they are compatible with experimentalist peer review. Further, it explores the formalisation of peer review mechanisms in EU competition law and sectoral market regulation. Finally, we will identify how different peer review mechanisms in EU competition law may be assembled together into an experimentalist regime,[107] as well as pointing to certain deficiencies in their operation from an experimentalist perspective.

Chapter 4 focuses on the role of courts in an experimentalist architecture for competition enforcement and market regulation, both through judicial review and through civil damages litigation. It has sometimes been suggested that the review standards for violation decisions fashioned by the EU courts may appear both uneven and not well settled. We will argue that the courts' approach is not incompatible with an experimentalist framework, in that they neither completely defer to expertise, nor do they seek to discipline discretion through probabilistic frameworks under conditions of uncertainty. While the light-touch review standard for commitment decisions does encourage their use to stimulate more open acknowledgement of uncertainty, the courts would require an enforcement authority to motivate its decision to opt for a commitment resolution. This chapter will also demonstrate how courts can lean on peer-review frameworks to enhance their oversight of regulatory authorities through dialogic review standards, such as conditional deference, and by enhancing the interaction of multiple review frameworks applicable in the same case.

Chapter 5, the final substantive chapter, reviews the evolution of international antitrust cooperation, including in the light of the EU's efforts to both stimulate

[106] *cf* M Piore and A Schrank, *Root-Cause Regulation: Protecting Work and Workers in the Twenty-First Century* (Cambridge, MA, Harvard University Press, 2018).

[107] C Overdevest and J Zeitlin, 'Assembling an Experimentalist Regime; Transnational Governance Interactions in the Forest Sector' (2014) 8 *Regulation and Governance* 22.

the adoption of competition law by other jurisdictions and to formulate an international antitrust instrument. As a result, the International Competition Network (ICN) has been created as a largely informal forum for transnational cooperation and learning focused on the goal of voluntary convergence. As the chapter will show, the salience of the scope conditions of uncertainty and the limits of hierarchy has created pressures for the evolution of the role of the ICN in an experimentalist direction, including by interacting cooperation mechanisms from different transnational forums such as the Organisation for Economic Co-operation and Development (OECD) Competition Committee, the Intergovernmental Expert Group (IGE) on Competition Law and Policy of the United Nations Conference on Trade and Development (UNCTAD) and a host of regional networks for antitrust cooperation. Review of such efforts will disclose that the formalisation of experimentalist mechanisms may require the formation of clusters of shared enforcement context, whereby member authorities face mutually salient implementation problems, so that the exercises of reporting, peer review and implementation monitoring can be meaningful.

Finally, in the Conclusion, we will revisit the aspects of contemporary market regulation that might suggest that an experimentalist evolution of competition law is normatively desirable, both within the EU and beyond. In that context, we will seek to distinguish experimentalist governance from governance models that rely on coordinated controlled experimentation, while also pointing to techniques through which the efficacy of experimentalist governance may be evaluated. We will also identify possible limitations and roadblocks to a fuller elaboration of experimentalism in EU market regulation, including through the emergence of Eurosceptic and populist governments, and the incorporation of national particularities in competition and regulatory law that appear contrary to consensus EU templates. The aim is to underscore that the contestation of consensus rules is entirely consistent with experimentalism, though attempts to limit participation in the formulation, implementation and monitoring of local solutions may not be.

Before turning to Chapter 1, it is worth noting a few clarifications about the scope, orientation and methodological approach of this book. First, it is worth emphasising that the argument presented in the book does not hinge on a claim that the modernisation of competition enforcement in the Modernisation Regulation, or subsequently, was purposely designed to formalise an experimentalist governance regime.[108] As we will see in the following pages, some

[108] Even strictly as a matter of chronology, the first writings about the emergence of experimentalism were published after Regulation 1/2003 was either envisaged or promulgated. See Sabel and Zeitlin (n 60); Sabel and Zeitlin (eds) (n 60); Svetiev (n 73); Y Svetiev, 'Antitrust Governance: The New Wave of Antitrust' (2007) 38 *Loyola University Chicago Law Journal* 593. Dorf and Sabel's work on democratic experimentalism appeared in 1998, though principally with reference to the US: MC Dorf and CF Sabel, 'A Constitution of Democratic Experimentalism' (1998) 98 *Columbia Law Review* 267. As such, this book does not explore the intention of the drafters.

of the new tools of enforcement and cooperation may have been intended to overcome the problem of uncertainty, while others may have been intended as tools for enhancing hierarchical control at the centre. The experimentalism literature suggests that where the scope conditions of radical uncertainty and polyarchy are present, actors aiming for effective problem-solving may develop experimentalist mechanisms spontaneously.[109] This can be done by using and adapting existing regulatory instruments into tools for experimentalist learning, although, as we will see, there are limits to such spontaneous emergence in the absence of a deliberate experimentalist orientation.

Second, as a matter of both scope and method, the aim of the book is not to test the experimentalism hypothesis by demonstrating a perfect fit between the modes of implementing competition law (or market regulation) and the experimentalist governance model. Instead, I aim to show how different elements of the competition and market regulatory frameworks, which may have been incorporated for a variety of different technocratic or political reasons, have been or can be used in an experimentalist way. As such, the book will draw on the formal provisions of the legislative frameworks for competition enforcement and market regulation, actual decision-making practice and interviews with enforcement officials at the EU and national levels. The interviews were mainly used to identify relevant practice examples and highlight areas where uncertainty and polyarchy are salient for enforcers, as well as to gain an insight into how officials plug into and perceive their own role in the studied EU frameworks.

Third, as a normative matter, the object of this book is to demonstrate that experimentalism is a desirable governance architecture that promotes diversification while coping with uncertainty and interdependence, without undermining the unity of EU law or fundamental normative commitments to rule of law or rights protection. Moreover, another object is to suggest that experimentalism is a feasible model, which repurposes existing mechanisms without requiring radical reforms. As such, the book will also identify areas where the experimentalist infrastructure appears to be incomplete or where actors have failed to take advantage of the scope for experimentalist solutions, so as to highlight how relatively modest changes in enforcement practice or even modes of justification would reinforce experimentalism.

[109] Sabel and Zeitlin (n 98) 412; G de Búrca, 'Stumbling into Experimentalism: The EU Antidiscrimination Regime' in Sabel and Zeitlin (eds) (n 60).

1

Networks and Hierarchy

Completing an Experimentalist Architecture?

I. The ECN as a Convergence Network?

As discussed in the Introduction, being the EU's 'first supranational policy',[1] competition law was a powerful centralised mechanism of market regulation in the hands of the EU Commission. Given its sole responsibility for the enforcement of the Treaty competition articles, subsequently enhanced by the power to vet mergers, the Commission could use competition law – though traditionally a tool of market *regulation* – for the task of market *integration*. In pursuit of market integration, centralisation and uniformity are often seen as important to prevent undermining the EU law compact by either denying market access or just making it more burdensome. More broadly, the pressure towards the harmonisation of common rules for regulating national markets is typically motivated by a transaction costs rationale: common rules eliminate barriers to trade by reducing the compliance costs for business to operate across the internal market. Such a rationale reflects the fact that – at least in the early period – business was regarded as a principal motor of market integration through seeking opportunities to serve cross-border customers or establish cross-border operations. In fact, what we identified as the shallow idea of the 'internal market' as the interpenetration of market activity – placing importance on the 'nationalities' of supplier and customer – continues to this day to be used as a metric of success in achieving market integration.[2]

However, the harmonisation of rules and uniformity through their centralised application is in tension with the experimentalist notions of tailoring regulatory instruments to the local context, as well as learning from diversity in implementation, albeit in pursuit of common policy goals. Moreover, if harmonisation is seen to unambiguously reduce transaction costs for cross-border activity, the

[1] L McGowan and S Wilks, 'The First Supranational Policy in the European Union: Competition Policy' (1995) 28 *European Journal of Political Research* 141.

[2] MP Mariani, 'From Market Fragmentation to Market Integration in the EU Insurance Industry: Can EU Regulation Unify What is Separate at Birth?' (2017) 42 *European Law Review* 657 (indicating that the Commission measures progress in building the internal market by counting up cross-border transactions and establishment).

EU law principle of subsidiarity may be largely neutered in the regulation of the internal market.[3] The harmonisation impulse can thereby make less visible the diversity of goals, as well as instruments, in national public regulation or private business practices. This appears to be at the heart of growing complaints about the competitive strictures of EU internal market law.[4] Such concerns apply perhaps even more strongly to EU competition law as a transversal tool, which can be technocratically enforced in a way that may not easily accommodate a variety of public interest justifications, particularly of a non-economic nature.[5] Moreover, the net of EU competition law has been cast widely to ensnare all kinds of market-related conduct by loosening the 'boundary conditions' of its application, including the definition of an undertaking engaged in any economic activity and the threshold of cross-border effects,[6] particularly in the light of the liberalisation or privatisation of public functions (whereby public interest objectives are delivered through the market) and technological change in transport and communications (easing potential cross-border entry).

Given its history as a centripetal force, one key question we have already identified is whether the modernisation reforms instigated by the Commission in the run-up to the eastern enlargement of the EU created the scope for a devolved and experimentalist elaboration of EU competition law as a market regulatory tool. The devolution of responsibilities for implementing *EU law* (in addition to national law) to Member State authorities – instead of simply enhancing the enforcement capabilities of the Commission – was a unique approach in which EU competition enforcement somewhat diverged from the US.[7] Such an arrangement provided potential for adjusting EU competition law and policy to local conditions and priorities, within an EU that was ever more heterogeneous by comparison to the original six-member Community. Greater national responsibility for case handling combined with reporting and review obligations create opportunities for disciplined divergence, comparison and learning both by the Commission from NCAs, and by the NCAs from each other.

[3] This was in essence the EU Commission's argument in *British American Tobacco* that in the context of market regulation on the basis of the internal market power in art 114 TFEU, the subsidiarity principle has little or no relevance (Case C-491/01 *British American Tobacco (Investments) and Imperial Tobacco* ECLI:EU:C:2002:741 [176]). While the Court did not accept the broad proposition, it did hold that the market integration 'objective cannot be sufficiently achieved by the Member States individually and calls for action at Community level, as demonstrated by the multifarious development of national laws in this case', thereby neutering the practical bite of subsidiarity. See also Case C-84/94 *UK v Council* [1996] ECR I-5755 [47].

[4] See A Somek, 'Europe: Political, Not Cosmopolitan' (2014) 20 *European Law Journal* 142; M Bartl, 'The Way We Do Europe: Subsidiarity and the Substantive Democratic Deficit' (2015) 21 *European Law Journal* 23.

[5] eg, G Monti and J Mulder, 'Escaping the Clutches of EU Competition Law: Pathways to Assess Private Sustainability Initiatives' (2017) 42 *European Law Review* 635.

[6] W Sauter, *Coherence in EU Competition Law* (Oxford, Oxford University Press, 2016).

[7] See, eg, F Cengiz, *Antitrust Federalism in the EU and the US* (Abingdon, Routledge, 2012).

A number of authors have at least implicitly recognised the desirability of devolved implementation as a source of variability and tailoring in EU competition policy. However, these authors have also suggested that such an outcome was always unlikely[8] and that it has not been observed in practice (in light of the unwillingness of the Commission to relinquish its policy-shaping monopoly).[9] Moreover, both practitioners and authors also worried that devolution and divergence carried risks of incoherence and fragmentation through non-uniform application, thereby undermining both rights of defence and the rule of law.[10]

Examining key features of the legal architecture introduced by the Modernisation Regulation could lend support to the view that the ECN was institutionalised as a mechanism of hierarchical control by the Commission. In particular, the Regulation contains a number of both formal and informal mechanisms of control for the Commission vis-a-vis NCAs and even national courts. Based on the discussion of the scope conditions for experimentalist governance in the Introduction, arguably the legal design of the Regulation discloses sensitivity to the problem of the limits of hierarchy – and thereby the need to enhance the reach of EU enforcement through the NCAs – without much sensitivity to the problem of uncertainty about how to use competition law instruments to deliver desired policy outcomes.

The formal mechanisms of uniformity and control include the harmonising effect of having EU law applied by national actors,[11] as well as the prohibition of national (court or authority) decisions that are inconsistent with those of the Commission. The Commission's ability to impose its own preferred view, including in specific cases, was apparently enhanced by the power to take over and itself decide a case handled by a responsible NCA, as well as its monopoly on declaring EU competition law inapplicable to defined conduct.[12] In addition to the informal bonds of professionalism, reputation and trust that may result from agency networking,[13] the Commission was granted other soft mechanisms through

[8] A Riley, 'EC Antitrust Modernisation: The Commission Does Very Nicely – Thank You! Part One: Regulation 1 and the Notification Burden' (2003) 24 *European Competition Law Review* 604; A Riley 'EC Antitrust Modernisation: The Commission Does Very Nicely – Thank You! Part Two: Between the Idea and the Reality: Decentralisation under Regulation 1' (2003) 24 *European Competition Law Review* 657; S Wilks, 'Agency Escape: Decentralization or Dominance of the European Commission in the Modernization of Competition Policy?' (2005) 18 *Governance* 431.

[9] *cf* G Monti, 'Independence, Interdependence and Legitimacy: The EU Commission, National Competition Authorities, and the European Competition Network' (2014) *EUI Department of Law Research Paper*, 2014/01.

[10] Sauter (n 6); G Monti, 'Managing Decentralized Antitrust Enforcement: *Toshiba*' (2014) 51 *Common Market Law Review* 261.

[11] The harmonisation effect of empowering national actors to apply EU law enhances the already observed spontaneous harmonisation of national competition laws to the EU template over time. See FV Waarden and M Drahos, 'Courts and (Epistemic) Communities in the Convergence of Competition Policies' (2002) 9 *Journal of European Public Policy* 913.

[12] Modernisation Regulation, art 10.

[13] *cf* G Majone, 'The New European Agencies: Regulation by Information' (1997) 4 *Journal of European Public Policy* 262.

which to influence decision-making by NCAs and national courts, including the obligation of reporting draft decisions to the Commission, as well as the ability for the Commission to provide comments to both NCAs and national courts before they formulate final decisions. Finally, the peer review mechanism[14] through the Advisory Committee on Restrictive Practices and Dominant Positions (ACRPDP) provided only a soft consultative framework of oversight over the Commission's decision-making under EU law, particularly given the non-binding nature of the Committee's opinions.

Statements by the Commission and even by some NCAs in the run-up to and even after the modernisation reforms, emphasised the role of the ECN as a vehicle for coordination that would ensure consistency, coherence or uniformity within the context of the decentralised enforcement of EU competition law. In the White Paper setting out the modernisation agenda, the Commission identified the risk that the 'decentralised application of the competition rules' could undermine the consistent and uniform application of the rules and 'stand in the way of the maintenance of conditions of competition that are consistent throughout' the EU. Both the conflicts rules in Regulation 1/2003, as well as the information, reporting and cooperation obligations, were identified as tools that could ensure the consistent and uniform application and the 'preservation of the unity of competition policy' by the Commission, including through its use of the infringement procedure.[15]

Along similar lines, the 2004 Cooperation Notice characterised the ECN as a 'forum for discussion and cooperation' in the enforcement of EU competition law and the 'basis for the creation and maintenance of a common competition culture in Europe'.[16] The Notice dedicated an entire chapter to the topic of the 'consistent application of EC competition rules', again with specific reference to the rules of convergence, reporting and pre-emption in Regulation 1/2003. However, at the same time, the (political) Joint Statement of the Council and the Commission on the Functioning of the ECN contains the following (somewhat Delphic) point about the Commission's exercise of its new powers:

> The Commission, as the guardian of the Treaty, has the ultimate *but not the sole* responsibility for developing policy and safeguarding efficiency and consistency. Therefore, the instruments of the Commission on the one hand and of the NCAs on the

[14] Modernisation Regulation, art 14. While the Advisory Committee is not formally part of the ECN, given that it is made up of officials from all EU competition authorities, it may be regarded as an aspect of the networked governance architecture for EU competition enforcement. Apart from Commission decisions, like some of the other EU networked bodies that provide peer review functions in market regulation, the Advisory Committee can also consider decisions by the NCAs applying EU law, pursuant to art 14(6) of Regulation 1/2003.

[15] European Commission, 'White Paper on Modernisation of the Rules Implementing Articles 85 and 86 of the EC Treaty' (1999) 99/027, para 104.

[16] Commission Notice 2004/C of 27 April 2004 on cooperation within the Network of Competition Authorities [2004] OJ C101/43, para 1.

> other hand are not identical. The additional powers the Commission has been granted to fulfil its responsibilities will *be exercised with the utmost regard for the cooperative nature* of the Network. (Emphasis added)[17]

The theme of consistent application also emerges in the subsequent reports on the operation of the Modernisation Regulation and the ECN. Both the five-year and ten-year report affirmed in identical terms that the 'EU competition rules have to a large extent become "the law of the land" for the entire EU',[18] not least because the NCAs have become a key pillar of their application.[19] While the five-year report identified the ECN as 'an innovative model of governance for the implementation of Community rules',[20] the ten-year report characterises it as 'increasingly important to ensure coherent enforcement and to allow stakeholders to benefit from a more level playing field'.[21]

These reports also addressed the question of further convergence in rules and enforcement procedures. Consistent with the harmonisation and transaction cost savings perspective, the five-year report points out that 'the divergence of standards regarding unilateral conduct was commented on critically by the business and legal communities which consider that diverging standards fragment business strategies that are typically formulated on a pan-European or global basis'.[22] The ten-year report lauds a substantial convergence in rules *and* their application, while noting subsisting divergences as areas for 'further progress', including the differing institutional positions of the NCAs, as well as divergent national procedures and sanctions.[23] The latter were not harmonised by the Modernisation Regulation and were left subject to the general EU law principles of equivalence and effectiveness, as well as soft law guidance through a number of ECN Recommendations on enforcement.[24]

In light of the legal architecture and its subsequent operation, Sauter synthesises the academic and policy consensus about networked competition governance by characterising the ECN as a 'policy network with elements of cooperation and hierarchy'.[25] He suggests that the ECN is not just a forum for information exchange, but a 'policy network' which is more than a coordination mechanism for

[17] Joint Statement of the Council and the Commission on the Functioning of the Network of Competition Authorities, https://ec.europa.eu/competition/ecn/joint_statement_en.pdf.

[18] Commission, Communication from the Commission to the European Parliament and the Council, Report on the functioning of Regulation 1/2003 COM (2009) 206 final, para 42 (hereinafter 'Five-year report'); Commission, Communication from the Commission to the European Parliament and the Council, Ten Years of Antitrust Enforcement under Regulation 1/2003: Achievements and Future Perspectives COM (2014) 453 final, para 23 (hereinafter 'Ten-year report').

[19] Ten-year report, para 23.

[20] Five-year report, para 42.

[21] Ten-year report, para 23.

[22] Five-year report, para 22.

[23] Ten-year report, paras 24–25.

[24] ibid paras 30–31.

[25] Sauter (n 6) 170.

enforcement activity as it ensures consistency and systemic cohesion in relation to common goals.[26] As such, the ECN is seen to favour convergence and systemic coherence,[27] and the goals of effectiveness and consistency over 'promoting policy experiments at [the] national level in a pattern of decentralization', consistent with the still 'dominant objective of promoting the internal market'.[28]

According to this view, the elements of pre-emption and oversight in the Modernisation Regulation ensure that the Commission is *primus inter partes*. Thus, while recognising that the Commission does not invoke the powers of pre-emption and override, NCA and national court decisions are said to be taken in the 'shadow of pre-emption' by the Commission.[29] In other words, the Commission need not use the powers of override (as it does not appear to); the mere threat of their use is sufficient for other actors to decide in a manner consistent with the outcome preferred by the Commission.[30]

II. Detecting Experimentalism in Light of Institutional Ambiguity

While the foregoing discussion may suggest quite limited scope for experimentalism in the aftermath of Regulation 1/2003, one difficulty in understanding whether the EU competition framework may be characterised as experimentalist or convergence-oriented stems from the fact that, as already foreshadowed, similar institutional forms can play different functions in different governance architectures.

In what follows, my first objective is to add conceptual clarity in distinguishing experimentalism in market regulation from other apparently similar governance architectures. My second objective is principally methodological, namely to point to the kinds of evidence that can be used to distinguish the practice of experimentalist competition law from some descriptively similar, but operationally distinct, governance architectures in market regulation.

Take, for example, the role of the regulatory network. In the EU law and governance literature, the networking of regulatory authorities or the creation of networked EU-level agencies has been identified as a key feature of 'new governance' arrangements.[31] Trubek and Trubek distinguish legal regulation, which

[26] ibid 148–49.

[27] D Gerber, 'Two Forms of Modernization in European Competition Law' (2008) 31 *Fordham Journal of International Law* 1235 (arguing that the focus on economic goals and methodologies of assessing anti-competitive effects would provide a common language ensuring consistency of enforcement by all ECN members).

[28] Sauter (n 6) 170.

[29] ibid 154, 263.

[30] ibid 170.

[31] See generally the contributions in G de Búrca and J Scott (eds), *Law and New Governance in the EU and the US* (Oxford, Hart Publishing, 2006).

relies on detailed rules and judicial enforcement, from new governance, which relies on 'alternative methods to solve problems and affect behaviour', while recognising that these 'concepts mask real complexities and empirical variation'.[32] In a similar vein, the incorporation of a regulatory network does not tell us much about its role, as regulatory networks can perform different functions in different governance frameworks.

Regulatory networks can be used in informal governance as a way of attenuating the costs of coercive and uniform enforcement of common rules rather than managing uncertainty. Drawing on Majone's view of competition law and policy as a technocratic form of market regulation, the networking of regulators can build common bonds of professional reputation, peer pressure and common purpose.[33] Such bonds through networking and socialisation facilitate voluntary opting into best enforcement practices by national authorities, without the Commission having to supervise their work on an ongoing basis, which would be a burdensome exercise for a resource-constrained authority. Reporting obligations can aid informal convergence by making the actions of different network members mutually observable.[34] Formal powers of pre-emption and override can also facilitate voluntary convergence by creating a 'shadow of hierarchy'.[35]

By contrast, while not necessarily an essential institutional feature, a regulatory network can aid experimentalism by providing a forum for monitoring, peer review and deliberation about the reasons and effects of divergent solutions in pursuing commonly identified goals. As such, experimentalist regulatory networks serve the function of managing uncertainty, apart from alleviating the constraints of hierarchical enforcement by a central actor, such as the Commission. In order to manage uncertainty, experimentalism treats lower unit discretion as not only inevitable, but also desirable. However, lower unit discretion in experimentalist governance is combined with a set of hard obligations, such as the obligation to report interventions, as well as to subject them to peer review both of their design (*ex ante*) and of their effects (*ex post*). In addition, participants in an experimentalist network also re-examine and revise common rules and objectives in light of the experience of different actors with their implementation. Apart from formal reporting and peer review of enforcement efforts, the recursive rule-revision function can be bolstered by incorporating sunset clauses that automatically trigger the re-examination of existing instruments in light of implementation experience.

[32] DM Trubek and LG Trubek, 'New Governance and Legal Regulation: Complementarity, Rivalry and Transformation' (2006) 13 *Columbia Journal of European Law* 539, 543.

[33] Majone (n 13).

[34] Y Svetiev, 'The Limits of Informal International Law: Enforcement, Norm-Generation and Learning in the International Competition Network' in J Pauwelyn, R Wessel and J Wouters (eds), *Informal International Law-Making* (Oxford, Oxford University Press, 2012) 271.

[35] On the shadow of hierarchy, see A Héritier and D Lehmkuhl, 'The Shadow of Hierarchy and New Modes of Governance' (2008) 28 *Journal of Public Policy* 1.

Finally, hierarchical instruments can also be incorporated into the regulatory architecture for experimentalist governance, for example, to act as a check on lower-level units' abusing or failing to exercise discretion to tailor local solutions, failing to cooperate with stakeholders or becoming captured by particular stakeholder interests.[36] In such circumstances, experimentalist governance can default to a hierarchical top-down solution by way of a penalty. Compared to the shadow of hierarchy notion, the penalty default mechanism in experimentalist governance takes seriously the interaction of the scope conditions of uncertainty and the limits of hierarchy. Under such conditions, the central actor is incapable of either devising or imposing a preferred optimal solution due to the combination of uncertainty, the lack of local knowledge and the costliness of coercive enforcement and monitoring. Thus, rather than being the preferred optimal solution from the point of view of the central actor (such as the Commission), the experimentalist penalty default is a solution that leaves all involved actors unambiguously worse off.[37]

In other words, if networked enforcement of EU competition law takes place in the shadow of (the Commission's) hierarchy, this means that the Commission has a preferred view on the outcomes in the cases decided by the NCAs, and the NCAs in turn seek to shadow that outcome to avoid being corrected. If networked enforcement has an experimentalist character, then the Commission may not even have a preferred view on the outcomes of individual cases, due to uncertainty and a lack of administrative capabilities to analyse all such cases. The hierarchical default only occurs by way of a penalty for the abuse or failure to take advantage of the discretion granted to tailor locally appropriate solutions. But the hierarchical default is not in any sense optimal: it is a less preferred solution for all involved, including the Commission as the central actor.

On the one hand, a key insight of the experimentalism literature is that the penalty default mechanism is far less demanding for a central actor, such as the Commission, in terms of monitoring cases across the EU, developing its own view on preferred outcomes and monitoring if such outcomes are in fact implemented by NCAs. On the other hand, both the penalty default and the shadow of hierarchy solutions typically do not need to be implemented by the central actor in order to have the desired effect on the lower-level units. Therefore, the mere fact that the Commission does not frequently invoke its pre-emption and override powers can be consistent with both a shadow of hierarchy and an experimentalist account of the operation of the network.

[36] CF Sabel and J Zeitlin, 'Experimentalism in the EU: Common Ground and Persistent Differences' (2012) 6 *Regulation and Governance* 410, 413–14 (a penalty default as a 'freestanding punitive power' that can be invoked by a hierarchical authority 'when selfish and short-sighted interests prevent actors from pursuing explorations that are likely to prove mutually beneficial and public-regarding').

[37] TA Börzel, 'Experimentalist Governance in the EU: The Emperor's New Clothes?' (2012) 6 *Regulation and Governance* 378, 380–81 ('penalty default' is defined as the threat to engage in hierarchical decision-making 'that is disruptive and produces dysfunctional results').

This presents a methodological challenge for distinguishing whether networked governance combined with powers of pre-emption and override is being used as a tool for informal convergence or for experimentalist governance. Reviewing the text of NCA decisions does not necessarily establish whether an authority is merely seeking to shadow the Commission's preferred outcome in a case or is experimenting with a more tailored solution to cope with uncertainty. One way to empirically distinguish these two hypotheses is to proceed inferentially by seeking to reconstruct the implicit interaction between different actors.[38] An alternative approach is to conduct an in-depth study of decision-making practice and the factors that influence a specific decision of a national authority. Such an approach requires an understanding of the type and extent of uncertainty involved in specific cases, the degree of constraint imposed by existing precedents, as well as the actual or perceived capability of the Commission to monitor the approach adopted by a NCA and to intervene in the specific case.

Apart from the general monitoring that the Commission can engage in through the notified investigations by the NCAs and their proposed decisions via the ECN, the Commission is also granted a more active power to provide its own views on specific cases to both NCAs and national courts under Articles 11(5) and 15(3) of the Modernisation Regulation. Whether and the way in which such powers are used may provide evidence about the extent to which the Commission seeks to and is able to control national competition decision-making. To the extent that such power is used actively and the Commission frequently provides directions that indicate its preferred outcome in the case, which the responsible national actor follows, this would be persuasive evidence that the ECN creates a shadow of hierarchy, steering national decision-making towards the Commission's preferred outcomes rather than learning from difference.

While the exchanges between the Commission and the other NCAs, including on specific cases, take place on a regular basis, albeit more informally, the exchanges with national courts are typically formalised in amicus opinions. The Commission's power to provide its own comments on the application of EU competition law before national courts does not appear to be used very frequently.[39] An examination of the substance of the Commission's amicus briefs can reveal that such interventions may be consistent with an experimentalist framework, such

[38] For example, in interviews with NCA officials, they typically do not seem concerned about the possibility of the Commission exercising its power to take over a case if it is dissatisfied with the approach being adopted.

[39] Sauter (n 6) 179–80. Based on data from the ten-year report on Regulation 1/2003, the Commission submitted amicus briefs to national courts in only 13 cases, while in twice as many cases, national courts requested the Commission's view pursuant to art 15(1). See Commission Staff Working Document, 'Ten Years of Antitrust Enforcement under Regulation 1/2003' SWD (2014) 230/2, para 248. However, see also K Wright, 'The European Commission's Own "Preliminary Reference Procedure" in Competition Cases?' (2010) 16 *European Law Journal* 736.

as in cases where national divergences can result in opportunities for regulatory arbitrage undermining networked competition enforcement.[40] Alternatively, in some cases, there is greater substantive uncertainty about the competitive significance and likely effects of impugned conduct. In such cases, the amicus opinions may contain general references to the state of existing precedent, while still leaving considerable scope for tailored local decision-making,[41] compared to cases where there is little uncertainty about anti-competitive effects.[42]

Finally, interviews with national officials also suggest that the review of implementation experience, including of specific decisions and remedies adopted by NCAs, often takes place in fora that have been created within the ECN, such as the working groups,[43] whose operations and role in policy and decision-making may be less visible, particularly for scholarly legal research.

In the remainder of this chapter, we will examine some of the centrifugal and centripetal forces delimiting the scope for experimentalist elaboration of EU competition law through combining networked implementation, recognition of uncertainty with the formalisation of procedures for review, and recursive revision of remedies and common rules. We will focus on the evolution of enforcement procedures at the national level, the evidence of national divergence on substantive issues and the institutional design of competition authorities. At all times, the aim will be to demonstrate the impetus for experimentalist solutions and the extent of their adoption, as well as to point to (typically modest) institutional reforms that would complete an experimentalist framework.

III. Enforcement Institutions, Techniques and Procedures

National procedural autonomy in competition enforcement is an important source for sustaining implementation diversity, particularly in the face of the expanded

[40] The Commission has submitted briefs on issues relevant to the problem of regulatory arbitrage. Sauter, (n 6) 180–84, points to briefs on whether cartel fines are tax deductible for defendants, on when the limitation period is triggered for private actions following on from a public finding of infringement, as well as on the use of leniency application materials in private damage actions. These are the types of issues that can make competition proceedings in some Member States less onerous and more attractive for undertakings, potentially undermining the scope for experimentalist use of networked enforcement.

[41] ibid 185–86 (briefs with respect to the prohibition of internet sales within a selective cosmetics distribution network and with respect to selective rules for the motor vehicle distribution networks).

[42] ibid (negotiated reductions of beef slaughterhouse capacities). See European Commission, 'Antitrust: Commission Welcomes Court Ruling in Irish Beef Case', https://ec.europa.eu/commission/presscorner/detail/en/MEMO_08_728.

[43] F Cengiz, 'Multi-level Governance in Competition Policy: The European Competition Network' (2010) 35 *European Law Review* 660.

scope of application of EU competition law by NCAs and courts, as well as the spontaneous harmonisation of national substantive rules to the EU template.[44] As we will see in more detail in Chapter 2, a particularly important aspect of procedural autonomy is national remedial law, because it is through remedial design and monitoring that the otherwise elastic competition law rules have their eventual effects in the market. As such, continued emphasis by the Commission on the harmonisation of national enforcement procedures and remedies may suggest further consolidation and convergence over experimentation and contextualisation, although, as we will see, the interpretation of the evidence is more ambiguous.

In a speech in the run-up to the tenth anniversary of the Modernisation Regulation and the formalisation of the ECN, the then Director-General of Competition at the EU Commission observed:

> [Regulation 1/2003] left it to the Member States to determine the institutional set-up of their enforcement systems. They could opt for administrative, judicial, or mixed systems. The regulation also left Member States the freedom to determine their own procedures and sanctions. Apart from a general obligation on Member States to ensure effective enforcement, these matters are not regulated or harmonised by EU law.[45]

He went on to add that differences in national procedures 'can negatively affect competition enforcement' in the EU and that, as such, from its inauguration, the ECN recognised the benefits of increased convergence 'regarding procedures and the sanctioning of infringements' and 'has been working on a purely voluntary basis to align procedures and sanctions'.

Following a public consultation (in light of the aforementioned reports on the functioning of the ECN), the Commission pushed beyond the voluntary approach to procedural convergence to propose a directive to make NCAs more effective enforcers.[46] The key focus of the ECN+ Directive is to ensure that in 'cases of parallel application of national competition law and Union law … NCAs have the same guarantees of independence, resources, and enforcement and fining powers necessary to ensure that a different outcome is not reached'. Consequently, this legislation introduced a set of obligations designed to ensure: (i) the independence and budgetary autonomy of the NCAs; (ii) that each NCA possesses a minimum set of enforcement tools and powers; and (iii) a degree of harmonisation of the provisions for levying and collecting fines across Member States to

[44] Y Svetiev, 'Networked Competition Governance in the EU: Delegation, Decentralization or Experimentalist Architecture?' in CF Sabel and J Zeitlin (eds), *Experimentalist Governance in the European Union: Towards a New Architecture* (Oxford, Oxford University Press, 2010).

[45] A Italianer, 'The ECN, Convergence and Enforcement of EU Competition Law: Achievements and Challenges', speech delivered at the European Competition Day (Vilnius, 3 October 2013).

[46] Council Directive (EU) 2019/1 of 11 December 2018 to empower the competition authorities of the Member States to be more effective enforcers and to ensure the proper functioning of the internal market [2019] OJ L11/3, Recital 3 (hereinafter 'ECN+ Directive').

prevent undertakings from either escaping liability or re-organising their activities in the internal market in jurisdictions with lower fines. As we will see, these procedural provisions are entirely consistent with an experimentalist elaboration of competition law.

The ECN+ Directive guarantees for NCA independence require that officials are able to exercise their functions independently and without 'taking any instructions from government or any other public or private entity', though a government may issue 'general policy rules' that are not related to specific proceedings or sector inquiries.[47] With respect to the staffing of NCAs, the Directive requires that the decision-making body members be 'selected, recruited or appointed according to clear and transparent procedures laid down in advance in national law' and provides protections from dismissal for such members for reasons related to their performance of their duties.[48] Finally, the Directive obliges the Member States to ensure that NCAs 'have a sufficient number of qualified staff and sufficient financial, technical and technological resources … necessary for the effective performance of their duties',[49] although without defining the appropriate qualifications of officials responsible for case analysis or decision-making.

On the one hand, enhancing the autonomy of NCAs from domestic political control may be seen as a tool to reinforce a narrowly technocratic vision of competition law and policy in the local implementation of EU and national competition law.[50] This would be consistent with Majone's view of competition enforcers as expert trustees of the efficient operation of markets who can be legitimately insulated from political influence because of the technocratic nature of their decision-making, while leaving distributive and policy trade-offs in the domain of political decision-making.[51]

In the preparatory materials for the promulgation of the ECN+ Directive, the concerns about threats to NCA independence were explained as follows:

> Measures taken to undermine the independence of the NCAs or to limit their resources necessarily emanate from the Member States themselves … restrictions on independence can be motivated by the desire to exercise greater control over decision-making by the authority. A government's ability to apply influence or pressure on a NCA may result in political considerations prevailing over sound competition enforcement based on legal and economic arguments, to the detriment of companies operating in the internal market.[52]

[47] ibid art 4(2).
[48] ibid art 4(3) and (4).
[49] ibid art 5(1).
[50] See, eg, ibid Recital 17 (NCA independence 'should be strengthened in order to ensure the effective and uniform application of Articles 101 and 102 TFEU').
[51] Majone (n 13).
[52] European Commission, 'Proposal for a directive of the European Parliament and of the Council to empower the competition authorities of the Member States to be more effective enforcers and to ensure the proper functioning of the internal market' COM(2017) 142 final, 5–6.

Discussing the importance of independence, a former Director-General of Competition observed that NCAs should be impartial, in the sense that their decisions 'should be free from external influence' and 'solely … based on the application of competition rules, supported by legal and economic arguments' and neutral, in the sense of not advantaging or disadvantaging businesses 'based on ownership or nationality'. Further, they should 'function without the threat of interference from political authorities and vested interests', thus being 'unbound by political or business or other ties'.[53]

It should be noted that, apart from entrenching a technocratic conception of competition law and policy, the rationales offered for guaranteeing NCA independence may also be seen to protect the scope conditions for experimentalist governance. If government officials – or corporate executives for that matter – could interfere with or provide instructions to NCA officials on how to decide cases, such officials of executives would be tempted to impose their own preferred solutions to competition problems, even in the face of uncertainty about the effects of particular conduct in the competitive landscape, rather than engaging in collaborative experimentalist problem-solving. As Sabel and Zeitlin explain:

> [I]n the absence of strategic uncertainty, actors are convinced that they know how to pursue their ends, so joint exploration of possibilities is superfluous … In the absence of polyarchy, one actor is dominant, or there is a struggle for dominance, and the powerful prefer to impose outcomes, rather than pursue them cooperatively with others.[54]

As such, prohibiting direct interventions or instructions from either public or private actors would maintain the problem-solving orientation of NCAs, as well as other (private and public) actors, consistent with experimentalism. But absolute independence is neither possible nor desirable: even technocrats need input to make decisions. If NCAs have adequate mechanisms through which to obtain input from relevant market stakeholders when deciding cases and fashioning remedies (a point to which we will return in Chapters 2 and 3), NCAs can engage in experimentalist problem-solving precisely if they are protected from attempts by public or private actors to impose specific preferred outcomes.

One aspect of the harmonisation of enforcement mechanisms pursued through the ECN+ Directive is the requirement that all NCAs adopt a leniency programme granting immunity and fine reductions for information leading to the detection and prosecution of secret cartels.[55] A number of the provisions in

[53] Alexander Italianer, 'The Independence of National Competition Authorities' (Competition Conference – Best Practice in Investigations, Vienna, 12 December 2014), https://ec.europa.eu/competition/speeches/text/sp2014_08_en.pdf.

[54] CF Sabel and J Zeitlin, 'Experimentalism in the EU: Common Ground and Persistent Differences' (2012) 6 *Regulation & Governance* 410, 412.

[55] Article 17, which leaves it up to the Member States and their authorities to decide whether such leniency programmes should be instituted for competition violations other than secret cartels.

Chapter VI of the Directive establish harmonised or minimum requirements for national leniency programmes and, at least to some extent, mirror the provisions of the ECN's Model Leniency Programme (MLP).[56] The MLP was jointly developed by the members of the ECN in 2006, shortly after the coming into force of the Modernisation Regulation, to ensure that in a world of parallel enforcement competences, cartel participants are not discouraged from applying for leniency.[57] officials of the Commission's DG Competition described the MLP as an example of the ECN being used for 'policy reflexion beyond the legal obligations' of the Modernisation Regulation.[58] Drawing on the experience of running leniency programmes by the Commission and some NCAs, the MLP provided a set of key elements and considerations to be taken into account for developing a leniency programme at the Member State level.

In prior work,[59] I have argued that the MLP could be regarded as an example of experimentalist elaboration of an enforcement mechanism, since it allowed substantial freedom of tailoring at the national level. Given that the object of leniency programmes is to uncover secret cartels, there is little uncertainty faced by the NCAs (or undertakings for that matter) about the characterisation of the substantive (cartel) conduct as an anti-competitive violation. However, there would be some predictive uncertainty about how to structure a leniency mechanism so as to incentivise the reporting of cartels as early as possible and thereby to also even destabilise the formation of cartels. After all, the Commission's first attempt to develop a leniency programme was judged not to be a great success in achieving its defined objectives.[60] Further, the MLP also identified the problem of interaction uncertainty, suggesting that a uniform mechanism across the Member States was inappropriate given 'the variety of legislative frameworks, procedures and sanctions' across the Member States.[61] Thus, apart from identifying some elements (which based on existing knowledge may be necessary for an effective programme), the MLP suggested that NCAs develop 'further detailed provisions' which suit their procedural and enforcement regime or 'to provide for a more favourable treatment of its applicants' if this was considered necessary 'to ensure effective enforcement'.[62] Moreover, the MLP was to be reviewed in light of the experience of the ECN members through a sunset clause mechanism, whereby after two years, 'the state of convergence of the leniency programmes of ECN members will be assessed'.[63]

[56] European Competition Network, 'Explanatory Notes to the ECN Model Leniency Programme' (2012), https://ec.europa.eu/competition/ecn/mlp_revised_2012_en.pdf.

[57] K Dekeyser and M Jaspers, 'A New Era of ECN Cooperation: Achievements and Challenges with Special Focus on Work in the Leniency Field' (2007) 30 *World Competition* 3, 22.

[58] ibid 3.

[59] Svetiev (n 44).

[60] Dekeyser and Jaspers, 'A New Era of ECN Cooperation' (2007).

[61] Svetiev (n 44) 104.

[62] Explanatory Notes to the ECN Model Leniency Programme, https://ec.europa.eu/competition/ecn/mlp_revised_2012_en.pdf, para 8.

[63] ibid para 31.

The MLP Review Report examined key contentious elements of this enforcement tool, such as the scope of leniency, the types of applicants excluded from immunity, the marker system, the possibility of summary applications and of oral submissions, and the conditions for leniency.[64] While the Report focused on substantive rather than formal convergence in leniency programmes, it provided the basis for a revision to the MLP, which draws on the *experience* of NCAs operating leniency programmes, including an assessment of the effects of certain provisions, as well as the identification of provisions regarded as necessary.[65] It is precisely this experimentalist process of formulating objectives and provisional rules, reviewing the experience of the implementation of such rules, so as to provide a basis for their further revision that led to the eventual legislative entrenchment of Chapter VI of the ECN+ Directive.

Notwithstanding the mandatory language of Chapter VI, the ECN+ Directive allows room for choice and local tailoring to the Member States,[66] as well as specifically calling for the exercise of discretion by the NCAs.[67] Apart from the fact that Chapter VI imposes only minimum requirements, it is also worth noting that the mere existence of a leniency programme does not prevent an NCA from using other enforcement techniques even for cartels.

The ECN+ Directive contains other aspects of procedural harmonisation, chiefly mandating that Member States make available certain enforcement mechanisms to their NCA. Article 12, for example, mandates that NCAs are able to take a decision by accepting remedial commitments offered by the undertaking that resolve the authority's competition concerns. The provision shadows Article 9 of the Modernisation Regulation, which following its introduction became a very important tool for case closure by the Commission, despite the fact that it was originally envisaged that it would have a relatively limited scope. Note that apart from ensuring its availability, the ECN+ Directive does not mandate a preference for the use of such a tool vis-a-vis others. As will be further discussed in Chapter 2, the use of negotiated remedies can be an important mechanism for the experimentalist implementation of competition law, as negotiated remedies are oriented at problem-solving rather than retrospective characterisation of conduct, are jointly designed by the authority and the undertakings with input from market stakeholders, and allow for dynamic adjustment through the monitoring of effects. While the ECN+ Directive does not seek to standardise the use of commitments,[68] it does

[64] European Competition Network, 'ECN Model Leniency Programme: Report on Assessment of the State of Convergence' (2006), https://ec.europa.eu/competition/ecn/model_leniency_programme.pdf.

[65] ibid [7], [29] (termination of cartel activities), [41] (multiple applications) and [50] (discovery orders in civil proceedings).

[66] ECN+ Directive, arts 21(5) and 23(3).

[67] ibid art 21(2).

[68] Practice discloses divergences in the use of commitment-like instruments by the NCAs, including both the kinds of cases where such instruments are appropriate and the modalities of implementation and monitoring. See CD Ehlerman and M Marquis, *European Competition Law Annual 2008: Antitrust Settlements under EC Competition Law* (Oxford, Hart Publishing, 2010); H Schweitzer,

mandate that the equivalent national procedures incorporate the mechanisms for monitoring and adjustment.[69]

As such, the ECN+ Directive ensures a minimum *range* of implementation tools available to NCAs, which could only enhance their ability to experiment with different modalities for competition enforcement.[70] It is true that under the ECN+ Directive, there are provisions that would harmonise certain procedural tools across the Member States, such as with respect to the levying and collection of fines. While fines are not a particularly experimentalist remedy (a point explored in more detail in Chapter 2), a possible concern when building an experimentalist architecture is that procedural divergences between the sanctioning regimes in different jurisdictions may inadvertently create opportunities and incentives for regulatory arbitrage by encouraging undertakings to localise in specific jurisdictions.[71] Even if the NCAs are free to experiment with different enforcement tools that could effectively identify and remedy anti-competitive conduct, such arbitrage opportunities can undermine the scope for local experimentation. As such, a degree of harmonisation to attenuate arbitrage and relocation incentives is entirely consistent with preserving and stimulating an experimentalist architecture, including the networked authorities' ability to take advantage of that architecture for learning through diverse approaches and implementation instruments.

IV. Substantive Competition Law: Shadowing the Commission or Innovating?

Experimentalist market regulation places the onus on responsible lower-level actors, such as the NCAs as well as undertakings, to adopt tailored and innovative mechanisms for implementation in the face of uncertainty. As we will elaborate in subsequent chapters, an experimentalist approach requires responsible authorities to candidly acknowledge the uncertainties underlying any enforcement effort and to use both stakeholder input and regulatory networks to jointly evaluate the design and the ongoing effects of an intervention. The plasticity of the rules and

'Commitment Decisions in the EU and in the Member States: Functions and Risks of a New Instrument of Competition Law Enforcement within a Federal Enforcement Regime', *e-Competitions Bulletin*, Special Issue on Commitment Decisions, 2 August 2012, https://ssrn.com/abstract=2101630.

[69] ECN+ Directive, art 12(1) (input from market stakeholders), art 12(2) (monitoring implementation) and art 12(3) (power to re-open proceedings in the light of material changes in fact).

[70] Similarly, the Commission and the ECN have also sought to ensure that enforcement capabilities of the NCAs are maintained and strengthened, even in the face of fiscal tightening in many Member States. This argument has been raised in the face of Member State initiatives to merge competition and market regulatory authorities to which we will return.

[71] *cf* V Fleischer, 'Regulatory Arbitrage' (2010) 89 *Texas Law Review* 227.

their fact-intensive application allow flexibility for NCAs to localise their enforcement efforts[72] rather than simply blindly following precedents or shadowing the Commission, but a key question is whether they actually do so.

Consistent with the view that the ECN is a technocratic club that tends to entrench the Commission's perspective on competition policy, one knowledgeable observer surmises a general impression that: 'There is no widespread notion that regulatory competition and intellectual leadership outside DG Comp is regularly displayed within the ECN.'[73] As noted earlier, interviews with NCA officials suggest that there is considerable space for both autonomy and contestation on the part of NCAs. Thus, officials from different NCAs suggested that even in deciding cases pursuant to EU law, national case teams typically are not concerned about triggering disagreements with the Commission, let alone the possibility that the Commission would use its power to relieve the authority of a case due to such disagreement. The latter appears to be regarded as a remote possibility by national officials, not least because of the capacity constraints on the Commission to monitor and decide all such cases by itself. In a similar vein, interviewed officials have also suggested that in the deliberations of the Advisory Committee – focusing on draft Commission decisions – some NCAs often present perspectives on the case that are different from those of the Commission and seek to influence the DG Competition's approach.

Furthermore, at a prominent EU competition law gathering focused on competition enforcement challenges in dynamic technology markets,[74] the President of the Bundeskartellamt (BKA), the German competition authority, appeared to endorse an experimentalist model for the elaboration of competition law and policy through the ECN. As a regulator involved in complex competition litigation, the BKA President acknowledged that his initial position towards experimentalism was sceptical, while pointing out that he has come to recognise the potential offered by an experimentalist approach in EU competition law within the framework of the ECN. On this view, an experimentalist framework within the ECN avoids the risk of an inconsistent application of EU competition law, while allowing participating authorities to benefit from mutual learning and exchange.

[72] O Brook, 'Struggling with Article 101 (3) TFEU: Diverging Approaches of the Commission, EU Courts, and Five Competition Authorities' (2019) 56 *Common Market Law Review* 121.

[73] Sauter (n 6) 158. Interestingly, however, in its contemporaneous 2015 ranking of competition authorities, the Global Competition Review ranked the German, UK and French authorities ahead of the Commission's DG Competition. See Global Competition Review Enforcement Ranking 2015, https://globalcompetitionreview.com/benchmarking/rating-enforcement-2017/1144939/star-ratings. Admittedly, such rankings need not necessarily reflect intellectual leadership.

[74] A Mundt, 'The EU's Response: The ECN and the Case for Experimentalist Enforcement', speech delivered at the 12th Global Competition Law Centre Annual Conference on 'Dynamic Markets and Dynamic Enforcement: Which Competition Policy for a World in Flux?' (Brussels, 26–27 January 2017), https://www.coleurope.eu/system/tdf/uploads/event/gclc_-_2016_annual_conference_final_program_1.pdf?file=1&type=node&id=35740&force (notes by Riccardo Haupt).

Such comments were made in the context of discussing cases in dynamic digital markets presenting challenges, including considerable uncertainty about the competitive significance of novel business models and the limits they present for purely territorial enforcement.

A prominent example invoked by the BKA President that has attracted attention was the EU-wide enforcement conducted by NCAs against the use of Most Favoured Nation (MFN) contractual clauses by online hotel booking platforms such as Booking.com and Expedia. The use of similar clauses had already been subject to scrutiny by competition authorities in other markets.[75] Pursuant to such contractual clauses, the supplier (in this case a hotel) guarantees to offer its best price to the platform counterparty. The competitive assessment of MFN clauses has presented difficulties in both traditional and digital markets. Such clauses may provide benefits to consumers (including price transparency and reduction of transaction costs), though they may also give rise to anti-competitive effects.[76] Such clauses can reduce competition among online travel booking platforms and discourage the entry of new platforms. MFN clauses remove price and availability of hotel rooms as elements of competition and reduce incentives for online platforms to compete on the fees charged to hotels, as lower prices must then be extended to incumbent platforms. At the same time, MFN clauses also have an economic justification in protecting the investment by the intermediary for building a reliable platform and reducing free-riding.[77] Without the MFN clauses, customers may use the platform to get information about the provider's services, but finalise the transaction on the hotel supplier's own website for a lower price. If the platform cannot recoup its investments due to such free riding, it has no incentive to invest in providing and improving the quality of its service.

In formulating an enforcement response to this problem, the EU authorities within the ECN faced two challenges. On the one hand, Fletcher and Hviid point out that there had been both considerable policy debate about the appropriate treatment of such clauses, where the economic literature was 'new and still developing'.[78] On the other hand, hotel reservation platforms, such as Booking.com operate across different jurisdictions. Despite the cross-border nature of the operations, the Commission did not take over the investigation itself. Instead, the ECN was used to appoint lead authorities that would investigate the case, thereby avoiding the duplication of activities, while allowing other interested NCAs to be informed and contribute to the process through the formation of an *ad hoc*

[75] See *US v Apple Inc* 952 F Supp 2d 638 (SDNY 2013), affirmed in *US v Apple Inc* 791 F3d 290 (2d Cir 2015); and *E-Books* (Case COMP/39.847) Commission Decision 1/2003 [2013] OJ C112/9.

[76] A Fletcher and M Hviid, 'Broad Retail Price MFN Clauses: Are They RPM "at its Worst"?' (2016) 81 *Antitrust Law Journal* 65, 69.

[77] A Ezrachi, 'The Competitive Effects of Parity Clauses on Online Commerce' (2015) 11 *European Competition Journal* 448.

[78] Fletcher and Hviid, 'Broad Retail Price MFN Clauses' (2016) 69–70.

working group.[79] In addition to cooperating in the investigation and evaluation of the case, the NCAs also coordinated the adoption of a remedy. The proposed commitments were subject to market testing as well as discussion and feedback from other NCAs before final revised commitment remedies were accepted by the NCAs for Italy, France and Sweden.[80] The joint remedy narrowed the scope of the MFN clauses so that they only apply to prices and other conditions publicly offered by hotels through their own direct online sales channels, while also allowing hotels to manage the room availability themselves.

In contrast to the above joint commitments, a subsequent decision by the German BKA additionally prohibited the application of even the narrower MFN clauses in booking platform contracts with hotel suppliers.[81] The decision included a remedial injunction requiring the removal of MFN clauses for hotels in Germany. Procedurally, in an earlier case against a German online travel platform (upheld by the Düsseldorf Higher Regional Court), the use of MFN clauses was prohibited generally as an infringement of Article 101.[82] Substantively, the BKA's economic assessment of the effects of MFN clauses appeared to be sceptical about the significance of the free-riding argument in the context of online booking platforms, as well as about the likelihood of hotels offering lower prices via other platforms if their online prices were higher. The BKA also seemed to place greater emphasis on protecting hotels' pricing freedom.

In light of the uncertainty about the effects of the impugned MFN clauses and the adopted remedies in a novel and evolving marketplace, the Commission together with 10 NCAs[83] also instituted a monitoring mechanism for the sector, including to assess the effects of the remedial measures adopted in the Booking.com cases. A monitoring report issued in 2016 was based on a uniform electronic questionnaire sent to market stakeholders, including a sample of 16,000 hotels in the 10 participating Member States, as well as 20 online travel agents, 11 metasearch websites and 19 large hotel chains.[84] The report concluded that both types

[79] See Ezrachi, 'The Competitive Effects of Parity Clauses on Online Commerce' (2015) 510. See also G Cipolla, 'Hotel Online Booking Sector: The Commitments of Booking and the Most Favored Nation Clauses. A Case Conducted in Cooperation with Other National Competition Authorities' (2015) 3 *Italian Antitrust Review* 178.

[80] French Competition Authority (Autorité de la concurrence), Decision 15-D-06 of 21 April 2015; Italian Competition Authority (Autorità Garante della Concorrenza e del Mercato), Decision of 21 April 2015; and Swedish Competition Authority (Konkurrensverket) Decision 596/2013 of 15 April 2015.

[81] German Competition Authority (Bundeskartellamt), Decision B 9–121/13 of 22 December 2015.

[82] German Competition Authority (Bundeskartellamt), Decision B 9–66/10 of 20 December 2013. Both France and Austria also limited the use of MFN clauses through legislative change. See ECN, *Report on the Monitoring Exercise Carried out in the Online Hotel Booking Sector by the EU Competition Authorities in 2016*, https://ec.europa.eu/competition/ecn/hotel_monitoring_report_en.pdf, 4–5.

[83] These included the Belgian, Czech, French, German, Hungarian, Irish, Italian, Dutch, Swedish and UK national authorities.

[84] ECN, *Report on the Monitoring Exercise*, para 5.

of remedies restricting the scope of MFN clauses more narrowly (the trilateral Italian-French-Swedish solution) as well as more broadly (as per the German solution) generally improved conditions for competition and led to greater choice for consumers. Moreover, based on the monitoring results, the ECN members also 'agreed to keep the online hotel booking sector under review and to re-assess the competitive situation in due course', allowing 'the sector more time to make full use of the measures that have already been taken'. Finally, in light of this experience, the ECN instituted an 'early warning system' allowing consideration of 'ongoing cases that raise novel issues at the earliest possible stage'.[85]

The BKA's investigation of Facebook was another prominent case involving a ubiquitous networking platform mentioned by the BKA President in the context of his endorsement of experimentalism. Even before the BKA's action, Facebook had been subject to investigations by different authorities both within and outside the EU. A notable feature of the BKA's investigation was the novel theory of abusive conduct, based on Facebook's contractual terms for the collection of user data. Focusing specifically on the interaction of the regulatory regimes for competition enforcement and data protection, in opening its investigation, the BKA observed:

> There is an initial suspicion that Facebook's conditions of use are in violation of data protection provisions. Not every law infringement on the part of a dominant company is also relevant under competition law. However, in the case in question Facebook's use of unlawful terms and conditions could represent an abusive imposition of unfair conditions on users. The [BKA] will examine, among other issues, to what extent a connection exists between the possibly dominant position of the company and the use of such clauses.[86]

The notion that violation of data protection rules may give rise to a competition law violation was the culmination of research and consultation activities conducted by the BKA in seeking to identify appropriate responses to novel concerns presented by digital platforms, including two-sided platforms and zero-price services. Such activities included the creation of a think-tank of competition enforcers, economists and legal experts, and the subsequent publication of a working paper outlining the competitive concerns and possible solutions identified by the think-tank.[87] Moreover, following the publication of the BKA working paper, the BKA

[85] ECN, *Outcome of the Meeting of ECN DGs on 17-02-2017*, https://ec.europa.eu/competition/antitrust/ECN_meeting_outcome_17022017.pdf. Ezrachi reports Commissioner Vestager's view that 'the Booking.com cases have been a "learning experience"' and a demonstration of how EU competition law can intervene earlier in new markets. See Ezrachi (n 77) 515, quoting Matthew Newman: 'Vestager says Booking.com case shows EU should intervene earlier in new markets.'

[86] Bundeskartellamt, 'Bundeskartellamt Initiates Proceedings Against Facebook on Suspicion of Having Abused its Market Power by Infringing Data Protection Rules', 2016, https://www.bundeskartellamt.de/SharedDocs/Meldung/EN/Pressemitteilungen/2016/02_03_2016_Facebook.html.

[87] Bundeskartellamt, 'Digital Economy', www.bundeskartellamt.de/EN/Economicsectors/Digital_economy/digital_economy_node.html.

worked with the French Autorité de la concurrence, releasing a joint paper on competition enforcement in digital markets.[88]

We will return to the question of the analytical and remedial approach in the Facebook case in Chapter 2, but one notable aspect for the present purposes is the BKA's (as well as other NCAs') intellectual leadership in deciding to incorporate privacy or data protection concerns into competitive analysis. In this respect, the BKA was 'tak[ing] a different approach from that adopted … by the EU Commission' up to that point, whereby the Commission had treated data protection and competition law as separate regulatory regimes targeted to achieve different regulatory objectives.[89] The German think-tank working paper concluded that 'new digital products and business models as well as the special characteristics of digital markets have created new challenges for competition policy and enforcement', specifically suggesting that the assessment of digital platforms under economic and antitrust aspects often requires that 'the platform side which uses the platform for free' be included in the assessment. The working paper went on to observe that prior case law did not recognise 'free platform use as a market', an approach that 'is no longer adequate' given the novel interdependencies presented by the digital economy.[90] While the German BKA's approach in the Facebook case may not amount to an endorsement of a wholesale switch towards a multi-goal competition policy, it does point towards the diagnostic use of competition law to identify shortcomings in the operation of the competitive market mechanism in the digital economy, and even the failures or inadequacies of targeted regulatory regimes for consumer protection or data protection.

V. Experimentalism and Institutional Design

Authors who have questioned the BKA's approach in the Facebook investigation, including in particular its consideration of data protection implications in performing the competitive analysis, have warned that such an approach may threaten the analytical purity and coherence of competition law.[91] Such analytical purity could

[88] Bundeskartellamt, 'Competition Law and Data', 10 May 2016, www.bundeskartellamt.de/SharedDocs/Publikation/DE/Berichte/Big%20Data%20Papier.pdf;jsessionid=E705766DBE18A0DD8F2D5AE08DF97661.1_cid387?__blob=publicationFile&v=2.

[89] G Schneider, 'Testing Art. 102 TFEU in the Digital Marketplace: Insights from the Bundeskartellamt's Investigation against Facebook' (2018) 9 *Journal of European Competition Law and Practice* 213, 214.

[90] Also notable in this respect were the ensuing amendments to the German statute on restraints of competition, including consideration of access to competitively relevant data, network effects and innovation-driven competitive pressure in the assessment of dominance. See ibid 215 (discussing BGB IS 1416, 1 June 2017, modifying Gesetz gegen Wettbewebbeschränkunge).

[91] M Maggiolino and G Colangelo, 'Antitrust über Alles: Whither Competition Law after Facebook?' (2019) 42 *World Competition* 355; A Ezrachi, 'Sponge' (2017) 5 *Journal of Antitrust Enforcement* 49, 50: 'Differences, in one's understanding of the ends of competition law often transform into a "purity battle" – the claim that competition analysis has been polluted by some, and that a pure approach, as propagated by others, would deliver better, optimal results.'

be polluted either by incorporating non-competition objectives into the mandate of competition authorities or by explicitly interacting competition law with other market regulatory regimes.

By contrast, Ezrachi has highlighted 'the porous and absorbent characteristics of competition law'[92] both in general and with specific reference to EU competition law. Thus, he has argued that 'competition law, like other legal disciplines, is a social construct and stems from the domestic foundations and values of each jurisdiction' so that it is shaped by different social realities, experience, or levels of economic development.[93] Further, EU competition law itself has pursued 'a multitude of different aims, including the promotion of efficiency and consumer welfare, the protection of market structure and economic freedom, and market integration'.[94] Thus, it was not 'designed as a hermetically sealed discipline' and continues to be influenced by a variety of economic and social objectives, giving it a 'sponge'-like character.[95] However, at the same time, he acknowledges that the sponge-like character of competition law, as well as the permeability of the technocratic barrier provided by economic analysis of the competitive effects of conduct, can lead to concerns about the politicisation and instrumentalisation of competition law, including to advance specific political agendas, industrial policies or protectionist measures.[96]

The definition of the mandate of competition enforcement authorities and the possibility of bringing within their purview a broader range of policy objectives have obvious implications for the design of competition enforcement authorities, as well as their relationship and interaction with other (targeted) regulatory regimes. In the run-up to the promulgation of the ECN+ Directive, an EU Commission official observed that 'Member States are free to choose the institutional set up of their competition authorities'.[97] As was discussed earlier, a key aspect of the ECN+ reforms was to entrench the independence and appropriate funding for the NCAs. And yet in an academic report to the European Parliament in the run-up to the promulgation of the ECN+ Directive, Cengiz suggested that – at least at that time – there were no notable examples where the lack of independence of an NCA had 'jeopardised effective enforcement of EU competition rules'. The report noted that the independence of NCAs did not appear to be problematic, at least as far as the law was concerned in any jurisdiction.[98] Moreover, the report also concluded that while there was variation in the size and budget of different NCAs, such variation

[92] Ezrachi, 'Sponge' (2017) 50.
[93] ibid 51.
[94] ibid 52.
[95] ibid 53.
[96] ibid 72–73.
[97] Italianer, 'The Independence of National Competition Authorities' (2014).
[98] The report noted only the exception of Estonia, where the NCA was connected to the executive. The concern about political interference has greater salience more recently in some Member States, a point to which we will return in the Conclusion.

seemed to reflect differences in market size rather than 'varying commitment to competition law enforcement'.[99]

However, in the period leading up to the promulgation of the ECN+ Directive, a number of Member States implemented measures for the re-organisation of national agencies responsible for market regulation, including competition, consumer and sectoral regulators. One important reason for such initiatives was fiscal pressure in various Member States, which in turn led to concerns about adequate funding to ensure the efficacious enforcement by the national authorities. A number of Member States, including the Netherlands, Spain, Finland and the UK, re-structured their competition enforcement authorities so as to merge a number of market regulatory functions under a single roof. Such re-organisation of national authorities through the amalgamation of different mandates had been criticised by the Commission, for example, in the case of Spain, as potentially undermining the independence, powers and enforcement capabilities of the competition authority.[100]

But quite apart from any fiscal and cost-cutting considerations, such authority mergers had also been justified as an exercise in purposeful institutional innovation in market regulation. For example, in describing the creation of the integrated Authority for Consumers and Markets in the Netherlands, Ottow argues that:

> [T]he new combination opens the way for institutional innovation, thus preventing or at least reducing the risks of regulatory and competition silos and of capture. In addition, greater coordination of the new authority's interpretations of legislation and interventions can promote cross-fertilization between the different areas of the law. Improved integration of the different areas is also possible, without any need for complicated external coordination mechanisms between separate entities. As well as merging the three organizations in the Dutch case, those responsible have also made efforts to start thinking strategically as to how functions can be combined and integrated under the same roof.[101]

The traditional division of labour between sectoral, competition and consumer protection authorities is based on the distinction of regulation as an *ex ante* ongoing activity of *oversight* of undertakings as opposed to competition (and even consumer protection) law, which involves *ex post* adversarial *enforcement* to combat violations. The *ex ante* conception of sectoral regulation posits that such regulation is a substitute discipline in markets where there is insufficient competitive rivalry or where there were obstacles (such as asymmetric information) to the

[99] F Cengiz, 'An Academic View on the Role and Powers of National Competition Authorities: Background to the ECN Plus Project' (2016) European Parliament Study IP/A/ECON/2016-06.

[100] MC Neff, 'La Creación de la CNMC:¿ Qué Lecciones Cabe Extraer para el Futuro?' (2019) 21 *Revista Española de Control Externo* 69, 85; IF Alonso, 'Independent Audiovisual Regulators in Spain: A Unique Case in Europe' (2016) 10 *International Journal of Communication* 359, 365–66 (discussing infringement proceedings in the Spanish case); interview with Spanish competition official (Madrid, July 2015).

[101] AT Ottow, 'Erosion or Innovation? The Institutional Design of Competition Agencies: A Dutch Case Study' (2014) 2 *Journal of Antitrust Enforcement* 25, 27.

disciplining power of competition on market actors. For example, in what were identified as natural monopoly markets, the entities responsible for production and distribution were owned and/or comprehensively and continuously regulated by the state, including key aspects of service delivery such as price, quantity and quality,[102] necessitating both technical and economic expertise as well as ongoing relationships with the regulated entities. Once competition is introduced as a potential disciplining force in such markets, competition authorities maintain competitive rivalry by prosecuting anti-competitive arrangements or abuses of power of incumbent players.

Yet, as Brousseau and Glachant argue, post-liberalisation 'network industries are characterized by strong coordination needs' because of a 'combination of long-term investments with the risks of systemic failures'. As such, in their view, the role of regulators is simultaneously 'to attempt to ensure both a sufficient coordination among actors to guarantee an efficient performance of the industry, and to promote competition to guarantee the long term dynamic of innovation and redistribution of welfare gains to the various stakeholders'.[103] As we will discuss in more detail in Chapter 2, experimentalist market governance dissolves the *ex ante*/*ex post* distinction in regulatory activity so as to manage uncertainty about the effects of market conduct on different policy goals, thereby also eliding the distinction between technocratic and political decision-making.[104] Precisely because of the need to 'access critical information and knowledge',[105] experimentalist market regulators require the combination of interdependent mechanisms for diagnosis, stakeholder participation and monitoring of remedial effects.

First, diagnostic tools are an essential element of experimentalist market governance for the purpose of identifying problems, preferably already in their incipience. Competition authorities rely on market surveillance activities, including market studies, as well as complaints from market stakeholders (competitors or clients) as the sources of information about problem detection. As such, incorporating a consumer protection mandate can be one method of enhancing the diagnostic capabilities of a competition authority.[106] The Dutch Autoriteit Consument & Markt (ACM), for example, developed an integrated consumer complaints online portal ConsuWijzer, which provides tools enabling consumers

[102] J Braithwaite, 'The Regulatory State' in RAW Rhodes et al (eds), *The Oxford Handbook of Political Institutions* (Oxford, Oxford University Press, 2006) 230; H Schweitzer, 'Services of General Economic Interest: European Law's Impact on the Role of Markets and of Member States' in M Cremona (ed), *Market Integration and Public Services in the European Union* (Oxford, Oxford University Press, 2011) 60.

[103] E Brousseau and J Glachant, 'Regulators as Reflexive Governance Platforms' (2011) 12 *Competition and Regulation in Network Industries* 194, 195.

[104] *cf* DA Crane, 'Technocracy and Antitrust' (2007) 86 *Texas Law Review* 1159.

[105] Brousseau and Glachant (n 103) 196.

[106] Experimentalist governance is in part inspired by disaster-avoiding regulatory systems, which use apparently minor problems or failures in performance to identify deeper malfunctions through persistent questioning and root cause analysis, a point to which we return in ch 2.

'to resolve problems themselves', while also aiding enforcement activity by providing the ACM with 'real time information about the markets it oversees'.[107] Since all consumer questions are registered, the portal is said to generate 'valuable intelligence' about market operation problems, which can be combined to bolster other top-down[108] and bottom-up[109] tools of problem detection. Similarly, the ACM relies on information exchanges with other market regulatory authorities and public agencies as an important source of diagnostic information about potential market problems.[110]

Second, experimentalist governance relies on stakeholder participation in both the design and monitoring of adopted remedies. Consistent with their traditional law-enforcement mandate, competition authorities may prefer simple remedies (such as fines or cease and desist injunctions), compliance with which is apparently easier to verify, given that they have limited resources for the monitoring of remedial effects. However, the incorporation of a sectoral regulator under the same roof – or cooperation with a sectoral regulator – can enhance the monitoring capabilities of a competition agency to enable it to engage in experimentalist interventions. For example, the creation of the merged ACM in the Netherlands followed a collaboration between the former competition (NMa) and telecommunications authority (OPTA), whereby the NMa had diagnosed a problem in the review of a merger, while the access remedy imposed was to be monitored by OPTA.[111]

In describing the synergies resulting from the merged authority in the Netherlands, a former head of the ACM has emphasised the benefits of using 'joint teams, with experts from the regulatory and the competition side', enabling the new authority to work 'more swiftly'.[112] Moreover, with respect to substantive enforcement, he points out that changes in markets themselves, including the 'shifting boundaries between content and infrastructure', may require 'structural changes among regulators'. And even in the absence of formal re-organisation, the development of new data-based business models has necessitated a 'fresh look on the application of competition rules' based on 'contacts with the Dutch data protection agency'.[113]

[107] C Fonteijn, 'The Importance of Innovation in the Detection of Anticompetitive Practices' in J Almunia et al (eds), *New Frontiers of Antitrust 2014* (Brussels, Groupe Larcier, 2014) para 55.

[108] The ACM has used ConsuWijzer complaints about online real estate sales together with a market study in real estate services to remedy identified problems with operations of an online real estate portal: ibid para 56.

[109] The ACM has used web-crawlers, such as Coosto, to monitor social media, including blogs and Twitter: ibid para 57.

[110] ibid paras 64–69.

[111] See D Hesseling and T Vermeulen, 'Access to Networks through Competition Law: The Case of KPN – Reggefiber' (2011) 13 *Network Industries Quarterly* 14, 15.

[112] C Fonteijn, speech at the IBA Conference (Amsterdam, 6 June 2016), https://www.acm.nl/nl/publicaties/publicatie/15872/Speech-Fonteijn-bij-the-IBA-Conference-Amsterdam.

[113] ibid. Article 4(2)(c) of the ECN+ Directive provides that in competition decision-making, the NCAs shall 'neither seek nor take any instructions from any government or other public or private entity when carrying out their duties'. A prohibition on taking 'instruction' does not seem to prevent collaboration and consultation.

It follows that the merger of different functionalities of market regulation can be one way to retool existing institutions in aid of experimentalist governance. In a recent contribution on 'root-cause regulation', which, as we will see, has affinities with experimentalist governance, Piore and Schrank have argued that narrowly specialised authorities find it difficult to respond to the problems of uncertainty and unintended consequences in volatile market environments.[114] A narrow definition of goals, as well as the reliance on rules or narrowly focused expertise by functionally specialised regulators, produces bureaucratic rigidity and an inability to cope with business conduct that has not previously been encountered (particularly where such conduct has potentially both beneficial and pernicious consequences).[115] Generalist market regulators, by contrast, are more likely to be problem-oriented and – not circumscribed by a narrow mandate – explicitly consider the effects and potential trade-offs on different regulatory objectives, thereby treating apparent violations as symptoms, looking for their root causes and tailoring regulatory interventions to the heterogeneous environments in which different firms operate.[116]

The combination of an effects-oriented market regulation together with broad stakeholder-participation and effects-monitoring mechanisms can make experimentalist competition authorities suitable venues for the integration of tasks and policy mandates. Apart from integrating or merging regulatory tasks under a single roof, Piore and Schrank[117] also suggest that a similar effect can be achieved through the creation of problem-oriented collaborative platforms between agencies with different mandates.[118]

VI. Conclusion

This chapter has focused on the question whether the ECN together with other provisions of Regulation 1/2003 and the ECN+ Directive can be seen as mechanisms for imposing uniformity and convergence in competition enforcement or of experimentalist governance. While much of the analysis, both by the Commission and the scholarly commentary, identifies the ECN as a vehicle for consistency and coherence, we have sought to show why the ECN structure does not impede – and can in fact promote – experimentalist learning from difference. Moreover, even

[114] MJ Piore and A Schrank, *Root-Cause Regulation: Protecting Work and Workers in the Twenty-First Century* (Cambridge, MA, Harvard University Press, 2018) (comparing the narrowly specialised labour market regulation in the US with the Franco-Latin system of general labour inspectorates).

[115] ibid 12.

[116] ibid 11, 153.

[117] ibid 159.

[118] See Y Svetiev, 'European Regulatory Private Law: From Conflicts to Platforms' in KP Purnhagen and P Rott (eds), *Varieties of European Economic Law and Regulation* (Cham, Springer, 2014); *cf* Ezrachi (n 77) 20.

the ECN+ Directive, passed under the guise of procedural harmonisation, simply expands the scope of implementation mechanisms available to NCAs and, as we will see in the next chapter, ensures the availability of collaborative and dynamic implementation tools that are more conducive to experimentalist enforcement. The emergence of differentiated enforcement exercises within the ECN may point to efforts to not only permit, but also exploit remedial divergences in aid of mutual learning. Importantly, this goal also requires retooling the enforcement architecture so as to ensure that differentiated enforcement strategies neither cancel each other out (by being mutually inconsistent) nor create opportunities for arbitrage that undermine the networked experimentalist enforcement of EU competition law.

Such observations lead us to the question about the sources for divergence in enforcement practices that can lead to mutual learning from difference. Given the textual convergence of competition laws, common or standardised analytical frameworks for deciding cases, ongoing interaction through the ECN, stable epistemic communities, convergent procedural and remedial mechanisms for enforcement,[119] we may well ask whether there are any residual sources of difference. After all, a common form of mutual learning may be described as mimesis – imitating what others are doing and thereby benefiting from the safety of the crowd. The preceding discussion suggests at least three sources of difference in competition enforcement and market regulation practices, which could guard against a regulatory monoculture and provide sources of divergence to sustain experimentalism in competition law:

- Differences in pre-established enforcement practices and routines of national authorities may reflect pre-existing precedents or the legal and constitutional context in which an authority operates. Legal or constitutional constraints affect the ways of using certain enforcement techniques, such as negotiated remedies or leniency applications, as well as the kinds of cases in which they can be used.[120]
- Differences in the underlying environments in which national authorities operate, such as the levels of development and sophistication of markets, in turn necessitate tailoring the use of competition law as a market regulatory tool.[121] The literature on the varieties of capitalism recognises that variability in the institutions of economic coordination leads to local specificities and

[119] Ezrachi (n 77).

[120] See Schweitzer (n 68) on the use of commitments.

[121] A Svetlichnii and M Botta, 'Article 102 TFEU as a Tool for Market Regulation: "Excessive Enforcement" against "Excessive Prices" in the New EU Member States and Candidate Countries' (2012) 8 *European Competition Journal* 473 (in small markets impervious to entry, competition law may be used to control exploitation through excessive pricing).

advantages in production and distribution and specific regulatory responses.[122] Experimentalism recognises that variability in local economic institutions can generate tailoring; however, it also recognises that deeply entrenched path dependences may suggest a fairly limited scope for beneficial mutual learning,[123] a point to which we will return in both Chapter 2 and the Conclusion.

- Divergence can also result from a conscious and cognitive shift towards generating differentiation either in enforcement or in institutional design as a source of experimentalist learning in regulating markets. Such a shift may require de-emphasising harmonisation and convergence as the ultimate goal of regulatory cooperation in competition enforcement and market regulation in the EU and a more open embrace of uncertainty in the face of the limits of technocratic knowledge.

[122] PA Hall and D Soskice, *Varieties of Capitalism: The Institutional Foundations of Comparative Advantage* (Oxford, Oxford University Press, 2001); J Snell, 'Varieties of Capitalism and the Limits of European Economic Integration' (2011) 13 *Cambridge Yearbook of European Legal Studies* 415.

[123] G Herrigel and J Zeitlin, 'Alternatives to Varieties of Capitalism' (2010) 84 *Business History Review* 667.

2

Experimentalism and the Choice of Enforcement Technique

Chapter 1 focused on the operation of the ECN as the infrastructure for the shared enforcement of EU competition law, which can also provide a framework for experimentalist tailoring of competition policy based on mutual learning through monitoring and peer review of local solutions. This chapter focuses on the techniques used by authorities at both EU and national levels to implement competition law from an experimentalist governance perspective. It is worth highlighting that the two scope conditions for experimentalist governance – (1) uncertainty about identifying and remedying anti-competitive conduct and (2) the limits of hierarchically imposing a preferred solution – are salient not only for the relationship between authorities in the ECN, but also for the relationship between competition (or regulatory) authorities and their target undertakings. As a result, in cases in which competition authorities face uncertainty about selecting means to achieve desired objectives, an overall experimentalist architecture would entail that their enforcement orientation shifts from a rule-enforcement (or legalistic) to a problem-oriented approach.[1] Experimentalist enforcement techniques are outcomes-oriented, as well as recursive through monitoring and peer review of implementation outcomes. To illustrate the argument, section V will focus on the relevance of experimentalism in cases involving novel business conduct in digital markets, as well as business coordination initiatives to pursue sustainability objectives.

I. From Rule-Enforcement to Problem-Solving in Market Regulation

Analysing the choice of implementation techniques for public agencies, Sparrow distinguishes between service delivery agencies (education, health or public transport), social regulation agencies that protect society from a variety of harms

[1] MK Sparrow, 'Joining the Regulatory Fold' (2012) 11 *Criminology & Public Policy* 345.

(pollution, crime or unsafe products) and economic regulation agencies that focus on the healthy functioning of markets (by preserving competition or controlling restrictive trade practices).[2] He has argued that given the nature of their tasks, social regulation agencies have innovated towards a broader range of compliance-management and behaviour-modification instruments compared to more traditional law enforcement techniques because they need to 'invent alternative methods for influencing behaviors that may be harmful but not illegal'.[3]

According to Sparrow, there are a few features of social regulation that allow such authorities to shift towards problem-solving techniques. First, social regulatory agencies deal with entities and persons who are identifiable upfront, with whom they have ongoing relationships, as opposed to searching for persons unknown and at large for committed violations, who, in turn, seek to avoid detection and circumnavigate control.[4] Further, their risk-control orientation leads social regulators to focus on 'identifying and suppressing specific harms', including 'emerging and unfamiliar ones' that do not necessarily match existing rules, operational structures and enforcement methods.[5] Such orientation in the face of uncertainty requires exploring diverse structural relationships with private parties so as to further the public goals of risk control or harm reduction.[6]

Both enforcement authorities and regulatory agencies pursue their mandate by developing and enforcing obligations that constrain the behaviour of their targets, backed up by the coercive power of the state.[7] Under the legal model of regulation, enforcers focus on procuring compliance with existing law, while the 'expert model of regulation', according to Sparrow, focuses on harm reduction. The legal enforcement model of regulation is seen to promote legal certainty and to more adequately constrain administrative discretion; however, the reliance on pre-existing rules and practices to guide enforcement can hamper regulatory efficacy. Such reduced efficacy results if there is a poor fit of existing rules and precedents with emerging and as yet unfamiliar types of conduct, and due to the more limited scope for regulators to innovate in developing novel techniques for harm reduction.[8] 'Wicked' regulatory problems spur governance experiments away from the legal mode of regulation, because they present the need to cope with 'complexity, uncertainty and heterogeneous interactions', which may also create 'difficult problems of co-ordination' of regulatory activity.[9] The combined problems of uncertainty as to the effects of conduct and the difficulty of monitoring

[2] ibid.
[3] ibid 350.
[4] ibid 348.
[5] ibid 350, 355.
[6] ibid 354.
[7] ibid 345.
[8] ibid 350.
[9] G Capano, J Rayner and AR Zito, 'Governance from the Bottom up: Complexity and Divergence in Comparative Perspective' (2012) 90 *Public Administration* 56, 57.

target entities and implementing remedies may lead to efforts at innovation in regulatory approaches, broadening participation in regulatory interventions, as well as the sharing of authority among regulators.[10]

According to Sparrow, competition law as a form of market regulation is not typically seen to focus on harm reduction, as it aims instead to ensure 'the healthy functioning of markets'. Moreover, on this view, the objective of market regulation is 'to preserve competition, efficient market function, and fair trade practices within one specific industry (e.g., transportation, utilities, communications, or financial services)'.[11] Along similar lines, the ordoliberal approach, which has been influential in the evolution of EU competition law, views competition law as providing a neutral framework of *ex ante* rules within which the exercise of contractual autonomy and market competition jointly discipline market actors.[12] While favouring regulation and strong competition law enforcement, ordoliberals were suspicious of both the exercise of discretion by public authorities and their engagement in 'experimental' economic policy more generally.[13]

In light of the foregoing observations, as Crane has pointed out, traditionally competition enforcement has been based on the 'crime-tort' model, which involves the application of established rules to identify defined violations as the basis of antitrust liability and a preference for one-off remedies such as fines, injunctions or damages.[14] At least one of the core functions of competition authorities – the detection and punishment of hardcore cartels – fits neatly into Sparrow's description of enforcement activity focused on searching for persons unknown responsible for committing well-defined offences who seek to conceal their activities to avoid detection. Yet even within that ambit, we observe that opportunities for learning about the means through which to uncover clandestine cartels – while maintaining other public objectives related to the rule of law and rights protections – can trigger experimentalist frameworks, such as the Model Leniency Programme discussed in Chapter 1.

Outside of the apparently safe ground of facially pernicious anti-competitive practices, other practices, such as vertical restraints along different levels of the supply chain, dominant firm conduct and mergers present different challenges for traditional enforcement. They are often not clandestine, and may have *ex ante* indeterminate competitive significance. In order to address them through the

[10] *cf* J Freeman and J Rossi, 'Agency Coordination in Shared Regulatory Space' (2012) 125 *Harvard Law Review* 1131.

[11] ibid; Sparrow (n 1) 349.

[12] D Gerber, 'Ordoliberalism: A New Intellectual Framework for Competition Law' in D Gerber, *Law and Competition in Twentieth-Century Europe: Protecting Prometheus* (Oxford, Oxford University Press, 2001) 240.

[13] M Siems and G Schnyder, 'Ordoliberal Lessons for Economic Stability: Different Kinds of Regulation, Not More Regulation' (2014) 27 *Governance: An International Journal of Policy, Administration, and Institutions* 377, 384–85.

[14] DA Crane, *Institutional Structure of Antitrust Enforcement* (Oxford, Oxford University Press, 2011) 13.

crime-tort model of enforcement, it is necessary to identify specific criteria that make practices pernicious either in themselves (irrespective of consequences) or because they point ineluctably to negative market effects. Different antitrust systems have sought to develop formal violation criteria, including price-setting across organisational boundaries, other limits on business autonomy, territorial or other vertical restrictions, benchmark tests for anti-competitive pricing as well as structural parameters, such as market share thresholds or other indicators of market power. However, such form-based criteria for identifying competition violations have been contested, either as not necessarily targeting pernicious conduct or because the conduct they target can have pro-competitive or other beneficial consequences in heterogeneous market contexts.[15]

As elaborated in Chapter 1, different sources of uncertainty about the likely effects of both conduct and remedies make it difficult to settle upon the 'essential' criteria mapping onto anti-competitive conduct across different jurisdictions as well as different markets, particularly dynamic ones. This would suggest that market practices, as well as competition remedies, should be assessed principally by reference to their effects.[16] In an effects-based competition policy, competition agencies need not be principally focused on enforcing existing rules or precedents. They may instead seek to diagnose and remedy potential harm from business conduct, which may in turn lead such agencies to adopt problem-solving as opposed to law enforcement techniques.[17]

II. The Transformation of EU Competition Enforcement: Legalism or Experimentalism?

The original enforcement design for implementing EU competition policy was a mixture of legalist and expert approaches to market regulation. For example, with respect to anti-competitive agreements, Article 101(1) provides the benchmark rule of prohibition of anti-competitive agreements affecting the internal market, including a set of examples illustrating the scope of the rule. To the extent that the prohibition on restraints on competition may be over-inclusive, Article 101(3) provides an outlet based on the assessment of the potential effects of impugned restraining practices. Granting the Commission a monopoly on the application of Article 101(3) reflected confidence in its ability – as a technocratic body entrusted to act as a guardian of the Community interest – to accurately assess

[15] J Vickers, 'Abuse of Market Power' (2005) 115 *Economic Journal* F244.

[16] ibid.

[17] This discussion draws on Y Svetiev, '(Re-)Joining the Regulatory Fold? Problem-Solving Innovations in Competition Enforcement' in J Drexel and FD Porto (eds), *Competition Law as Regulation* (Cheltenham, Edward Elgar, 2015).

ex ante the competitive significance and likely effects of proposed arrangements. Such an enforcement approach balanced the objectives of providing legal certainty to undertakings with the flexibility of coping with potentially beneficial and even innovative arrangements. The *ex ante* notification regime required competition officials at the Commission to exercise their powers prospectively and make the assessment about the effects of arrangements (including novel ones) before they were implemented by the parties.

In practice, since such a task is challenging both analytically and in terms of workload – virtually any interfirm contract or arrangement restrains competition to some degree – the Commission did not typically deliver finalised assessments of the compatibility of notified arrangements under Article 101. Instead, the main technique was the development of bureaucratic tools for caseload management, including safe harbours from prosecution via *de minimis* rules, block exemptions and informal comfort letters. Such tools can be open (at least in principle) to *ex ante* economic input about market effects, but they privilege legal certainty, while also limiting learning by the enforcement authority as well as innovation by firms. For example, safe harbour instruments limit business' innovation incentives because undertakings have a strong reason to seek to take advantage of safe harbours, for example, by using 'blessed' rather than novel contractual terms.[18] At the same time, safe harbour instruments or comfort letters may also limit the reasons for the competition authority to engage in ongoing monitoring of the actual implementation of interfirm arrangements.[19] Striking a balance in favour of legal certainty and stability of business practices may be appropriate in a relatively stable market environment, but it becomes more costly in more volatile dynamic environments. Uncertainty about demand, production and distribution techniques increases the need for firms to innovate business practices, which in turn reduces the reliability of pre-existing templates for 'safe' collaboration.

This discussion provides the background against which to examine the changes in enforcement approach and technique in the aftermath of the Modernisation Regulation. With respect to the enforcement of Article 101, the Regulation removed the Commission's monopoly to provide 'exemptions' under Article 101(3), so that this provision was to be directly applicable in competition enforcement

[18] I Forrester, 'The Modernization of EC Competition Law' (1999) 23 *Fordham International Competition Law Journal* 1028; J Drexl et al, 'Comments of the Max Planck Institute for Intellectual Property, Competition and Tax Law on the Draft Commission Block Exemption Regulation on Research and Development Agreements and the Draft Guidelines on Horizontal Cooperation Agreements' (2010) Max Planck Institute for Intellectual Property, Competition and Tax Law Research Paper No. 09-06, https://ssrn.com/abstract=1695421.

[19] Both scholars and practitioners questioned the utility of the *ex ante* notification regime both for identifying harmful practices and for useful learning by the enforcer. See D Neven, P Papandropoulos and P Seabright, *Trawling for Minnows: European Competition Policy and Agreements between Firms* (London, Centre for Economic Policy Research (CEPR), 1998); *cf* W Sauter, *Coherence in EU Competition Law* (Oxford, Oxford University Press 2016) 163 (expressing doubts about whether the volume of notifications was indeed a burden for the Commission).

proceedings, including before national courts. Such a shift heralded a departure from an administrative (*ex ante*) clearance approach towards self-evaluation by the undertakings together with *ex post* enforcement by competition authorities and courts, as had previously been in place for Article 102.

As was mentioned in the Introduction, some commentators saw the foregoing transformation in enforcement technique as a shift away from administrative control towards litigation, including private antitrust litigation. Such a shift was said to reduce the relative certainty provided by an *ex ante* clearance regime. While it enhances business autonomy, growing reliance on *ex post* litigation could also increase the levels of litigiousness and create instability for business.[20] Writing from a varieties of capitalism perspective, Wigger and Nölke suggested that there is no single optimal set of means and procedures of competition enforcement; instead, they argued that the choice between *ex ante* regulatory versus *ex post* litigation approaches must be made on the basis of institutional complementarities in specific variants of capitalism. An increase in litigation together with a narrowing of the substantive law towards short-term effects on economic efficiency or consumer welfare (as opposed to administrative balancing of multiple objectives) would increase instability for business and undermine the comparative advantage of Rhenish capitalism in high-skill/high-technology products sustained by incremental innovation and long-term investment.[21] The transformation, in their view, was pushed by the Commission and would end up benefiting the Commission, the legal profession (which would benefit from the growing emphasis on business self-assessment) and shareholder interests.[22]

Along similar lines, Kelemen argued that the modernisation reforms in the enforcement of competition law were an instance of emergent 'Eurolegalism' as a regulatory technique. Competition law was a market regulatory tool in which this European variant of the American legalistic regulatory style was being consolidated, through 'more coercive legal enforcement, more rights claims, and a growing judicial role in shaping policy'.[23] While national patterns of market regulation in the Member States traditionally relied on informal, cooperative and more opaque procedures, American 'regulation through litigation' was characterised by detailed and prescriptive rules, adversarial approaches to enforcement and dispute resolution, and the reliance on courts for both active judicial review of administrative action and private litigation over regulatory policies.[24] Kelemen has

[20] A Wigger and A Nölke, 'Enhanced Roles of Private Actors in EU Business Regulation and the Erosion of Rhenish Capitalism: The Case of Antitrust Enforcement' (2007) 45 *Journal of Common Market Studies* 495: 'the business community could count on a high degree of legal certainty and public support for the pursuit of long-term strategies'.

[21] ibid 500.

[22] ibid 502.

[23] RD Kelemen, *Eurolegalism: The Transformation of Law and Regulation in the European Union* (Cambridge, MA, Harvard University Press, 2011) 5, 18.

[24] ibid 6–7. On the limits of regulating markets through litigation, see generally WK Viscusi (ed), *Regulation through Litigation* (Washington DC, Brookings Institution Press, 2002).

argued that the spread of Eurolegalism does not reflect a preference for regulation through litigation by Europeans, who might see this variant of enforcement as both repugnant and inconsistent with the pre-existing institutional set-up of social control, but was being 'induced' by the process of EU integration.[25] Eurolegalism was propelled by the EU institutions due to internal political economy considerations rather than a desire to emulate US practice. Moreover, it was taking root in the EU notwithstanding national institutional impediments and resistance to such a legalistic regulatory style.[26]

Eurolegalism as an account of the evolution of competition law and market regulation in Europe seems generally inconsistent with experimentalism and Kelemen makes two further observations that strengthen this perception. First, he dismisses the claim that EU regulation is relying on new modes of governance through flexible, informal and cooperative mechanisms. He suggests that new governance techniques are to be regarded as red herrings, being tools with limited significance and effectiveness that distract from the consolidation of Eurolegalism. Since the EU does not provide an 'institutional environment conducive to the use' of flexible instruments, they are relegated to peripheral areas, rather than being core competences, such as regulating the internal market.[27] Second, Kelemen argues that the diversity in the legal institutions and cultures among the various EU Member States does not act as a constraint on the consolidation of Eurolegalism as regulatory technique. National differences, in his view, crumble under the pressures of economic liberalisation and political fragmentation, leading to growing judicial activism as well as an expansion of the legal services industry. As such, the foregoing set of developments would combine with the rights-based approach to economic and social regulation consolidated in EU law to reinforce adversarial legalism, notwithstanding pre-existing national divergences in both legal institutions and regulatory technique.[28]

In the case of competition law, Kelemen pointed to at least three factors that would enhance the consolidation of Eurolegalism at both the EU *and* the national levels. First, the shift from *ex ante* administrative clearance to full reliance on direct effect for the enforcement of both Articles 101 and 102, including at the national level, further strengthens regulation through litigation. Second, CJEU cases such as *Courage*,[29] declaring the existence of an individual right of action for

[25] ibid 7–8.

[26] But see HW Micklitz, 'The Visible Hand of European Regulatory Private Law: The Transformation of European Private Law from Autonomy to Functionalism in Competition and Regulation' (2009) 28 *Yearbook of European Law* 3.

[27] ibid; Kelemen, *Eurolegalism* (2011) 30–31.

[28] ibid 33. Compare Gerstenberg's experimentalist account suggesting that interaction with EU law upgrades national procedural law: O Gerstenberg, 'Constitutional Reasoning in Private Law: The Role of the CJEU in Adjudicating Unfair Terms in Consumer Contracts' (2015) 21 *European Law Journal* 599.

[29] Case C-453/99 *Courage Ltd v Bernard Crehan and Bernard Crehan v Courage Ltd and Others* [2001] ECR I-06297.

violation of EU competition law under EU law, would encourage private actions for antitrust remedies, including compensation. Private litigation typically is not propitious to balancing various policy goals,[30] but requires simple rules based on a defined criterion, such as short-term price effects.[31] Finally, the growing need for firms both to self-assess their compliance with the competition law norms and to defend themselves in civil suits[32] would further stimulate growth in the legal services industry as one crucial component *and* driver of Eurolegalism.[33]

III. The Use of Commitments in EU Competition Enforcement

While any overall assessment is necessarily partial and tentative, the enforcement of competition law since the coming into force of the Modernisation Regulation does not suggest an unrelenting consolidation of a self-sufficient legalist mode of market regulation.[34] On the public enforcement side, the trend most noted in the literature at least in the aftermath of the Modernisation Regulation was a growing use of the (cooperative) Article 9 procedure for negotiated remedial commitments in resolving antitrust cases without an adversarial determination of a violation either by the Commission or by a court. This tool has also been increasingly used by the NCAs, and, as we saw, the ECN+ Directive seeks to ensure commitments are available to the NCAs. While private enforcement was never predicted to pick up immediately, but 'in time',[35] despite some uptick in private litigation (particularly in some jurisdictions),[36] it cannot be said that private antitrust actions are a key driver of the enforcement and the substantive content of competition policy in any of the Member States, certainly anywhere near to the extent they historically have been in the US.[37] On the contrary, private actions at the national level

[30] Kelemen (n 23) 147.

[31] ibid 169.

[32] ibid 174.

[33] ibid 19 (where the EU exerts authority, 'prescriptive regulations, judicial controls and legions of lawyers follow').

[34] For a broader overview of enforcement developments in market regulation at the EU and national levels, see H Micklitz and A Wechsler (eds), *The Transformation of Enforcement: European Economic Law in a Global Perspective* (London, Hart/Bloomsbury Publishing, 2016), suggesting widespread innovations in enforcement tools, typically not relying on traditional litigation.

[35] Kelemen (n 23) 17.

[36] See, eg, Germany (A Bach and C Wolf, 'Germany: Private Antitrust Litigation', *Global Competition Review*, 20 July 2016, https://globalcompetitionreview.com/insight/the-european-middle-eastern-and-african-antitrust-review-2017/1067842/germany-private-antitrust-litigation) and the Netherlands (W Knibbeler et al, 'Netherlands: Private Antitrust Litigation', *Global Competition Review*, 22 July 2016, https://globalcompetitionreview.com/insight/the-european-middle-eastern-and-african-antitrust-review-2017/1067852/netherlands-private-antitrust-litigation).

[37] See generally A Jones, 'Private Enforcement of EU Competition Law: A Comparison with, and Lessons from, the US' in M Bergström, M Iacovides and M Strand (eds), *Harmonising EU Competition Litigation: The New Directive and Beyond* (Oxford, Hart Publishing, 2016).

often involve actions following on public enforcement efforts, even after the EU legislator promulgated a new directive with the aim of stimulating private antitrust litigation.[38]

To focus on the commitments instrument, Article 9 involves undertaking(s) investigated for violations of Article 101 or 102 offering remedial commitments, thereby avoiding a full adversarial process before the Commission leading up to a violation finding. Following this route effectively limits the extent of judicial review of the decision before the EU courts. It seems that rather than 'biting back' and using judicial review more aggressively,[39] competition defendants have frequently opted for cooperation and resolution through negotiated remedies, effectively forfeiting the possibility of judicial review. In principle, Article 9 of Regulation 1/2003 does not exclude judicial review of a commitment decision (given that it produces a decision with binding effects), but antitrust defendants proposing – and agreeing to – commitments may understandably be unlikely to resort to judicial review. Moreover, where a third party affected by a commitments decision has sought review of such decisions, the CJEU declared that they were subject to a very light-touch review, not least because of their voluntary nature.[40] Practising lawyers and legal academics noted that the growing reliance on negotiated remedies in the absence of formal findings of liability leads to a paucity of legal precedents about what kind of conduct violates the competition provisions, undermining the 'struggle for competition law' and thereby even the rule of law itself.[41] In the face of the growing resort of commitments-based enforcement at both the EU and the national levels, authors and commentators even called for rebalancing towards the ordinary Article 7 violation determinations.[42]

Given the prominent role of negotiated remedies within experimentalist governance, it is worth pointing out that it may be possible to reconcile the use of commitment decisions with the adversarial legalism account of the evolution of EU competition policy. To the extent that Eurolegalism is a variant of the American form of regulation through litigation, some have argued that the use of commitments may be understood as the transplant of the litigation settlement

[38] See Council Directive 2014/104/EU of 26 November 2014 on certain rules governing actions for damages under national law for infringements of the competition law provisions of the Member States and of the European Union [2014] OJ L349/1. The Directive seems to be calibrated to preserve the scope and integrity of public enforcement, including flexible enforcement tools, as will be discussed in more detail in ch 4.

[39] Kelemen (n 23) 159. Such an expectation was fuelled by a number of merger cases in the early 2000s in which the then Court of First Instance rebuffed the reliability of the Commission's showing of likely economic effects on the evidence and economic analysis.

[40] Case C-441/07 P *European Commission v Alrosa Company Ltd* [2010] ECR I-05949.

[41] FWV Papp, 'Best and Even Better Practices in Commitment Procedures after *Alrosa*: The Dangers of Abandoning the "Struggle for Competition Law"' (2012) 49 *Common Market Law Review* 929.

[42] P Lugard and M Mollman, 'The European Commission's Practice under Article 9 Regulation 1/2003: A Commitment-a-Day Keeps the Court Away?' (2013) 3 *CPI Antitrust Chronicle* 1, 11: 'the pendulum may have swung too far out'.

mechanism frequently used by the US Department of Justice in antitrust and other areas of market regulation, including in securities or pharmaceuticals markets.[43] This type of resolution of alleged violations typically involves a negotiated amount of payment (in lieu of a fine) by the defendant, as well as a mechanism such as a deferred prosecution agreement that sets out obligations on the defendant that – if satisfied – will avoid formal prosecution.[44] Resolution through settlement is typically seen to ensure transaction costs savings both for the defendant company and the enforcer by avoiding formal adversarial proceedings and court review. For the impugned undertaking, a negotiated resolution without litigation also reduces the costs of uncertainty that can weigh upon its activities and reputation, both with customers and suppliers, and in capital markets.[45]

The use of commitments can also be consistent with a consolidation of a legalist mode of competition enforcement if such a resolution is viewed as a form of lenience through a low-stakes resolution as opposed to a legal sanction. For example, in Ayers and Braithwaite's account of responsive regulation, authorities resort to an enforcement pyramid to steer compliance by regulated entities. On such a view, informal suasion, discretionary leniency (such as a warning) or low-powered remedies (without sanctions) can be used by enforcers when violations are first detected or minor, so as to encourage corporate compliance, saving coercive sanctions through litigation and fines for persistently non-complying entities and serious violations.[46]

The problem with the above accounts is that they do not match well onto either the formal provisions governing the commitments procedure or the practice of how they have been used by the Commission. For example, the Modernisation Regulation suggests that resort to Article 9 is not appropriate in a case where a fine can be imposed. Thus, if there is a relatively clear violation of the competition rules by an undertaking, a fine would be appropriate, unless perhaps the violation was relatively minor. However, a substantial proportion of the cases that have been decided through the commitments procedure can hardly be described as minor or insignificant. Moreover, the obligations that have been assumed

[43] See, eg, G Georgiev, 'Contagious Efficiency: The Growing Reliance on US-Style Antitrust Settlements in EU Law' (2007) 4 *Utah Law Review* 971; P Choné, S Saïd and A Vialfont, 'On the Optimal Use of Commitment Decisions under European Competition Law' (2014) 37 *International Review of Law and Economics* 169.

[44] The growing use of consent decrees has also raised concerns among US antitrust scholars. See H First, 'Is Antitrust "Law"?' (1995) 10 *Antitrust Law Journal* 9; AD Melamed (1995) 'Antitrust: The New Regulation' (1995) 10 *Antitrust Law Journal* 13; DH Ginsburg and JD Wright, 'Antitrust Settlements: The Culture of Consent' in N Charbit et al (eds), *William E Kovacic: An Antitrust Tribute – Liber Amicorum (Vol I)* (New York, Institute of Competition Law, 2012).

[45] H Schweitzer, 'Commitment Decisions under Article 9 of Regulation 1/2003: The Developing EC Practice and Caselaw' in C Ehlermann and M Marquis (eds), *Antitrust Settlements under EC Competition Law, European Competition Law Annual 2008* (Oxford, Hart Publishing, 2010) 548.

[46] See, eg, I Ayres, and J Braithwaite, *Responsive Regulation: Transcending the Deregulation Debate* (Oxford, Oxford University Press, 1992).

by undertakings through commitments have involved extensive and intrusive behavioural and even structural modifications, so that it is difficult to think of them as low-powered or lenient remedies. In fact, as some authors have pointed out, a number of these decisions appeared to push the boundaries of the application of existing competition law principles. Commitment decisions have been used to re-organise and re-structure, as well as introduce competition in segments of markets typically subject to regulation, such as electricity and gas.[47] As such, by adopting a forward-looking and competition-enhancing enforcement stance through voluntary commitments, EU competition authorities (at EU and national levels) may become the new regulators, with competition law as a new form of regulation.[48]

IV. Commitment Decisions and Experimentalism

It is, of course, possible to use commitments as a technocratic regulatory tool if the competition authority has clearly defined objectives and can identify the preferred means through which to pursue these objectives. As such, the commitment decision could be a type of regulatory contract,[49] which clearly sets out the specific obligations the undertaking is supposed to implement. If the desired objectives and the conduct sought from the regulated undertaking are relatively well-defined and clear, the authority's choice between a negotiated or litigated enforcement technique is a calibration of the carrot and the stick approaches to procuring desired compliance, consistent with Ayers and Braithwaite's enforcement pyramid idea.

Alternatively, if the competition agency is operating subject to uncertainty and its ability to enforce coercively is constrained, the object of the implementation of a negotiated remedy may not be to procure compliance, but to jointly learn about how to solve identified problems. The fact that an Article 9 remedy is jointly designed by the authority and the undertaking, affording a more flexible approach to specifying and adjusting obligations, makes it an appropriate means for experimentalist enforcement to cope with the conceptual uncertainty (about the type of rivalry we seek to promote in a particular market and for what purpose), predictive uncertainty (about the likely effects of impugned conduct)

[47] See generally M Sadowska, *Committed to Reform? Pragmatic Antitrust Enforcement in Electricity Markets* (Cambridge, Intersentia, 2014) (arguing that competition law enforcement was used to achieve regulatory objectives in sectors where the Commission failed to push through more ambitious sectoral legislative reforms).

[48] J Drexl and FD Porto (eds), *Competition Law as Regulation* (Cheltenham, Edward Elgar, 2015). For developments in national enforcement practices, see E Lachnit, *Alternative Enforcement of Competition Law* (The Hague, Eleven International Publishing, 2016).

[49] *cf* VP Goldberg, 'Regulation and Administered Contracts' (1976) 7 *Bell Journal of Economics* 426.

and interaction uncertainty (as to the potential unintended consequences of an adopted remedy).

To understand the role that commitments-based enforcement plays in experimentalist governance, it is useful to point out that the inspiration for experimentalist governance as a regulatory architecture comes from a set of pragmatist disciplines formalised by firms in the formulation of business strategy under conditions of uncertainty.[50] These disciplines have been termed pragmatist because they lead to constant questioning and self-doubt about established practices of production and distribution through joint design, benchmarking, error-correction and detection and root-cause analysis.[51]

Through benchmarking for product design, the firm surveys the solutions developed by others in solving the same or similar problems, so as to identify a set of existing designs, as well as potential improvements. Error detection, by contrast, seeks to identify internal disruptions in production and problems in product design so as to remedy them quickly. The process of error-correction is aided by diagnostic tools, including 'just-in-time' production and root-cause analysis. Just-in-time production acts as a diagnostic technique because, in the absence of inventories, the firm must immediately identify and correct any identified problems in its production process.[52] Root-cause analysis seeks to direct attention away from the proximate cause[53] of a product failure or production breakdown to identify misconnections in the overall production system, including by identifying such misconnections across existing divisional boundaries within the firm or with collaborators outside the firm.

Finally, joint design ensures that the product design process within the firm proceeds simultaneously with the design of component parts (or complementary products) by collaborating firms (such as suppliers) or even through input from customers. The discipline of simultaneous design can speed up the modification of provisional product prototypes by generating further error-correction information in real time and by re-examining – rather than taking for granted – assumptions about the existing relationships among component parts. The initial design process is refined through iterated modification and ongoing consultation

[50] See WH Simon, 'Toyota Jurisprudence: Legal Theory and Rolling Rule Regimes' in G de Búrca and J Scott (eds), *Law and New Governance in the EU and the US* (Oxford, Hart Publishing, 2006); MC Dorf and CF Sabel, 'A Constitution of Democratic Experimentalism' (1998) 98 *Columbia Law Review* 267.

[51] CF Sabel, 'A Real Time Revolution in Routines' in C Hecksher and P Adler (eds), *The Firm as a Collaborative Community* (Oxford, Oxford University Press, 2006) 106–56.

[52] Y Svetiev, 'Antitrust Governance: The New Wave of Antitrust' (2007) 38 *Loyola University Chicago Law Journal* 593, 645.

[53] Root-cause analysis can be implemented through the 'five whys?' technique, suggesting a sequence of questions to focus beyond the symptomatic cause of the identified problem to trace problems backwards through the production process. See Simon, 'Toyota Jurisprudence' (1998) 50, 53: 'when root cause analysis discovers violations of established norms, it does not stop. It goes on to consider whether the violations are symptomatic of some background condition that might be improved'.

and contribution from both employees and collaborators, including component suppliers or customers. Such an iterated process is also intended to identify multiple potential designs because under rapid and unpredictable shifts in the market, it is unwise to commit exclusively to a single product design version.[54]

In seeking to highlight how these pragmatist disciplines used by the firm can inform experimentalist legal and regulatory thinking, Simon points out that the pragmatist production system:

> (1) emphasises the goals of learning and innovation (rather than of dispute resolution and the vindication of accepted norms); (2) combines the normative explicitness associated with formal rules with the continuous adjustment to particularity associated with informal norms (no dialectic of rules and standards); (3) treats normative decision making in hard cases as presumptively collective and interdisciplinary (rather than the heroic labour of a solitary professional); (4) fosters a style of reasoning that is intentionally destabilising of settled practices (rather than harmonising or optimising); and (5) attempts to bracket or sublimate issues of individual and retrospective fairness or blame.[55]

As both Simon[56] and Ford[57] recognise, experimentalist governance shares common features with a number of new models of regulatory governance that have been developed in practice and theorised in the literature. Such regulatory models, either explicitly or often implicitly, aim to develop coping mechanisms for regulators in the face of the scope conditions of uncertainty and limits of hierarchy that beset regulatory action. Ford groups these theories as models of 'flexible regulation', which neither aim to develop comprehensive *ex ante* rules under conditions of uncertainty nor to comprehensively enforce them in the marketplace.[58] Flexible regulation relies on regulatory strategies that are more context-sensitive, iterative and nimble, as well as polycentric in the sense of porous to input from a broader range of actors beyond regulators and regulated target entities. Despite such commonalities, the boundaries between these flexible models continue to be contested.[59] In that sense, experimentalist governance may be seen to incorporate or rationalise a number of regulatory techniques relying on contextualisation, collaboration and adaptation, while at the same time providing a particular formal framework for aggregating information from implementation, making such implementation knowledge explicit and incorporating it into recursive rule-making.[60]

[54] Svetiev (n 52) 646.
[55] Simon (n 50) 38.
[56] ibid 37.
[57] C Ford, *Innovation and the State: Finance, Regulation, and Justice* (Cambridge, Cambridge University Press, 2017).
[58] ibid 83.
[59] ibid 18–19.
[60] ibid 95.

One variant of flexible regulation, for example, is principles-based or outcomes-oriented regulation.[61] Where an authority is able to specify the outcomes or results a regulatory intervention should achieve, but cannot specify the means to achieve them,[62] it can proceed by specifying a set of principles or objectives that guide the regulated undertaking in its formulation of corporate strategy. As such, the principles or outcomes so defined may be assimilated to the commonly agreed-upon objectives to be pursued by lower-level actors in experimentalist governance. However, experimentalism supplements the principles or outcomes-based approach by requiring formal mechanisms for monitoring and peer review of implemented solutions and achieved results (including through input by affected third parties). Monitoring and review can identify the need for adjustment either of the specific measures adopted by a lower-level unit, such as a target corporation, or even of the higher-level objectives or principles of the regulatory regime.

As such, experimentalism also incorporates regulated undertakings in the regulatory enterprise,[63] so that they become one of the lower-level actors to whom discretion is granted to select appropriate means sensitive to their own context to pursue regulatory objectives.[64] However, one *quid pro quo* for such firm-level discretion and for the absence of coercive enforcement by the agency is the need for undertakings to develop internal processes and protocols to promote the achievement of regulatory objectives, as envisaged in theories of management-based regulation[65] and meta-regulation.[66] Meta-regulation relies on undertakings putting in place 'appropriate systems and oversight mechanisms' for their internal activities. At the same time, the evaluation of the appropriateness and efficacy of such internal systems is no easy task for the regulator (or a court for that matter).[67] In order to be able to engage in the task of evaluating internal control systems meaningfully, an agency would require regular input from affected third parties and stakeholders.[68] Again, the experimentalist approach may suggest that a public

[61] ibid.

[62] E Rubin, 'The Myth of Accountability and the Anti-administrative Impulse' (2004) 103 *Michigan Law Review* 2073, 2131.

[63] *cf* T Prosser, *The Regulatory Enterprise: Government, Regulation, and Legitimacy* (Oxford, Oxford University Press, 2010).

[64] CF Sabel and J Zeitlin, *Experimentalist Governance in the EU: Towards a New Architecture* (Oxford, Oxford University Press, 2010); CF Sabel and WH Simon, 'Contextualizing Regimes: Institutionalization as a Response to the Limits of Interpretation and Policy Engineering' (2011) 110 *Michigan Law Review* 1265.

[65] C Coglianese and D Lazer, 'Management-Based Regulation: Prescribing Private Management to Achieve Public Goals' (2003) 37 *Law and Society Review* 691.

[66] C Parker, *The Open Corporation: Effective Self-Regulation and Democracy* (Cambridge, Cambridge University Press, 2002).

[67] N Gunningham, 'Environment Law, Regulation and Governance: Shifting Architectures' (2009) 21 *Journal of Environmental Law* 179, 190.

[68] *cf* N Gunningham and P Grabosky, *Smart Regulation: Designing Environmental Policy* (Oxford, Oxford University Press, 1998); Ayers and Braithwaite, *Responsive Regulation* (1992) 92 (bringing third parties into the regulatory process).

authority should encourage undertakings to pursue differentiated strategies for promoting regulatory goals that can be subject to monitoring, peer review, comparison and benchmarking.[69] In competition law and market regulation, the experimentalist approach entails stimulating multiple regulatory solutions by different firms or even a plurality of possible evolutions of the market itself.[70]

In sum, experimentalist governance does involve defining desired objectives and delegating the task of devising mechanisms to promote such objectives to lower-level units, including undertakings or associations of undertakings. However, an experimentalist authority would be concerned if all regulated undertakings adopt the same or similar mechanisms to advance the defined objectives. Experimentalist governance relies on input from affected third parties, but not just in rule-making or remedial design; it also imposes formal obligations of monitoring, input and peer review of the implementation of adopted solutions. As such, experimentalism is responsive or recursive, but through adjusting adopted remedies, rather than escalating from informal and non-coercive tools towards punitive ones. The obligation to make implementation information explicit and transparent is used to revise adopted remedial solutions and, through the identification of unintended consequences, may also lead to the revision of the framework goals of the regulatory regime. As such, compared to some flexible regulation models, experimentalism avoids reliance on informal suasion in private conversations between agencies and undertakings, aiming instead for 'maximally formalised flexibility'.[71]

Turning back to the Article 9 commitments procedure, the consensus of commentators is that the EU legislator provided this procedure to replace the largely informal approach for case resolution that had been previously employed by the Commission to avoid full violation findings.[72] Whatever the original intent of the Commission (as initiator) and the EU legislator,[73] both the text of

[69] Thus, Ford's account of the failure of principles-based models of financial regulation in the run-up to the financial crisis points to insufficient granularity and contestability of the principles, the absence of adequate monitoring of self-regulation, as well as the herd behaviour of financial institutions seeking to mimic their peers, not least due to competitive pressures, rather than developing differentiated strategies for financial resilience. See generally Ford, *Innovation and the State* (2017).

[70] Y Svetiev, 'The EU's Private Law in the Regulated Sectors: Competitive Market Handmaiden or Institutional Platform?' (2016) 22 *European Law Journal* 659; Y Svetiev and G Tagiuri, 'The Opportunities and Dislocations of Technological Change: EU Law as a Coping Mechanism?' (2018) 24 *Columbia Journal of European Law* 612.

[71] AJ Cohen, 'Governance Legalism: Hayek and Sabel on Reason and Rules, Organization and Law' (2010) *Wisconsin Law Review* 357, 365.

[72] In fact, art 9 reflects a broader shift in the Regulation away from purely informal mechanisms, given the objective of moving away from the informal comfort letters used by the Commission in response to art 101 TFEU notifications.

[73] Commentators suggested that the Commission itself did not expect art 9 to be used extensively. See H Schweitzer, 'Commitment Decisions under Article 9 of Regulation 1/2003' (2010) 551 ('unusual and rare').

Article 9 and the actual practice of implementing commitments-based remedies may be seen to disclose elements of experimentalist governance:

- Article 9 seeks to formalise non-adversarial case resolution and subject it to discipline. Experimentalist governance disavows informal implementation, whether by way of suasion or settlement. Where informal resolution leads to closure of cases through settlement, lack of transparency can be inimical to experimentalist learning by doing, which requires participation of affected stakeholders in remedial design and monitoring effects.[74]
- Article 9 focuses the negotiations between the agency and the investigated undertaking on the question of remedial formulation to address potential harms, rather than the existence of a violation. Excluding the possibility of negotiated penalty payments also reinforces the focus on joint problem-solving in such negotiations.
- The remedial solutions under Article 9 are proposed by the investigated undertaking and also have to be agreed to by the Commission. Thus, the commitments mechanism provides an invitation to the undertaking to reformulate corporate strategy in a way that attenuates competition concerns. As such, the mechanism provides a disruptive moment for strategy formulation by the undertaking(s) investigated.
- The Modernisation Regulation provides formal mechanisms for external input into Article 9 case resolution,[75] including both review of the decision by the Advisory Committee, composed of representatives of the other competition agencies in the EU, and 'market testing' of the remedial proposal through input by affected third parties.[76]
- The text of Article 9 does not provide a specific monitoring mechanism for the implementation of commitment remedies, defaulting to the presumption that the Commission's DG Competition staff are responsible for ensuring compliance with the commitments. In practice, however, the Commission has resorted to the use of monitoring trustees to supervise the implementation of commitment remedies under Article 9. Such monitoring trustees provide a complaint and dispute resolution infrastructure for affected stakeholders in

[74] Knowledgeable observers estimated that under the former Regulation 17/62, up to 90 per cent of cases before the Commission were subject to some type of informal resolution. See I van Bael and J Bellis, *Competition Law of the European Community* (The Hague, Kluwer Law International, 2005), 1136.

[75] It follows that unlike purely informal comfort letters or settlements, art 9 commitments should not be characterised as 'consensus privately negotiated'. See I Forrester, 'Creating New Rules? Or Closing Easy Cases? Policy Consequences for Public Enforcement of Settlements under Article 9 of Regulation 1/2003' in Ehlermann and Marquis (eds) (n 45) 639.

[76] Article 27(4). While art 7 violation decisions are also subject to Advisory Committee review, there is no equivalent to the formal market testing of remedies following a violation finding. On the experimentalist role of these mechanisms of peer review, see ch 3.

the course of remedial implementation and thus for the tracking of the effects of the remedy in the market.

- Article 9 also provides a revision mechanism of commitment remedies. Article 9(2) allows for a decision to be re-opened in cases where the undertaking has provided false, incomplete or misleading information in negotiating the commitments (as a form of penalty default discouraging strategic information provision by the undertaking). Importantly, a commitments-based decision – unlike a violation decision – can be re-opened to respond to market dynamics, in particular where 'there has been a material change in any of the facts on which the decision was based' (Article 9(2)(a)).[77]

Finally, it should be recalled that Recital 13 of Regulation 1/2003 provides that commitment decisions are inappropriate in cases 'where the Commission intends to impose a fine'. An experimentalist reading of this instruction suggests that the Article 9 mechanism can be used in cases where the pre-existing law or techniques of market analysis do not clearly point to the presence or absence of a violation due to anti-competitive effects.[78] To cope with this problem, experimentalist use of commitments can afford three principal advantages. The first is the tendency to avoid final closure in the case.[79] Such an approach blurs the distinction between the *ex ante* and *ex post* world (relative to the time of observing the conduct and taking the decision) and thus attenuates two constraints of the hierarchical enforcement approach: the limits of the knowledge of the final decider (the agency or court)[80] and the risk of strategic presentation of evidence by the defendant undertaking(s). Second, experimentalist mechanisms aim to broaden participation in the problem-solving effort, but channel such input towards deliberation on implementing solutions that attenuate harmful effects, rather than retrospective characterisation of conduct or prospective assessment of the likelihood of such effects. Finally, the combination of non-closure with participative monitoring means that experimentalist solutions can respond to the effects of the adopted remedy that were unforeseen or unintended at the time that the decision was taken.

[77] Decisions involving commitments with long-term effects have included sunset provisions for adjustment in response to observed effects. See, eg, Commission Decision of 11 October 2007, Case COMP/B-1/37.966 – *Distrigaz*, paras 30, 36 (proceedings to be re-opened if industrial users 'demonstrate that there is good cause, which has not yet been examined'); Commission Decision of 11 August 2010, Case COMP/39.386 – *Contrats Long Terme France (EDF)* (re-examination of the remedies to take place in response to market or national regulatory developments).

[78] Consistently with this interpretation, Recital 39 of the ECN+ Directive clarifies that 'commitment decisions are not appropriate in the case of secret cartels, in respect of which NCAs should impose fines'.

[79] This is why experimentalism offers an attractive alternative for selecting enforcement technique in an effects-based competition policy, where the full relevant effects of the impugned conduct are not observable at the time of having to take a decision.

[80] CF Sabel and O Gerstenberg, 'Constitutionalising an Overlapping Consensus: The ECJ and the Emergence of a Coordinate Constitutional Order' (2010) 16 *European Law Journal* 511, 526, where the authors highlight the 'no final decider' feature of experimentalist decision-making.

V. Experimentalism and the Choice of Enforcement Technique

In the remainder of the chapter, we will examine the choice of enforcement technique in cases that may appear to be appropriate for an experimentalist approach to market regulation due to the combined presence of the scope conditions of uncertainty and polyarchy. In particular, first, we will focus on competition agencies dealing with the regulation of digital platforms presenting novel problems that have not been faced before in highly dynamic market settings, whereby rapid technological change leads to volatility in business models, market boundaries and bases of competition. Second, we will focus on more traditional market settings in which anti-competitive effects may be easier to foresee, but where competitive rivalry or market structure may impact broader public interest goals, which may not be seen as strictly competition-related. The discussion will draw on EU and national practice in order to illustrate how the presence of the scope conditions can lead to assemblages of an experimentalist regime, while also identifying possible constraints upon the emergence of experimentalist solutions.

A. Regulating Platforms

Ever since the multiple and drawn-out Microsoft antitrust cases pursued in the US, EU and other jurisdictions through the early 2000s,[81] the concentration of information and communication technology (ICT) markets and the subsequent emergence of platforms for search, social media and e-commerce, such as Google, Facebook and Amazon, has been an important focus both for competition agencies and for public debate.[82] At least based on their size and market share, the new internet behemoths have raised concerns about dominance and the openness and contestability of digital markets. In particular, the concentration of data, combined with network effects that engender winner-take-all markets, has led to concerns that the position of such firms cannot be dislodged, possibly entrenching them as the permanent gatekeepers of the digital world.[83]

Some have argued that the entrenchment of new digital giants reflects a failure of competition law enforcement, including antitrust regulators being

[81] See, eg, D Geradin and JG Sidak, 'European and American Approaches to Antitrust Remedies and the Institutional Design of Regulation in Telecommunications' in SK Majumdar, I Vogelsang and ME Cave (eds), *Handbook of Telecommunications Economics Volume II* (Amsterdam, Elsevier Science, 2005); C Ahlborn and DS Evans, 'The *Microsoft* Judgment and its Implications for Competition Policy towards Dominant Firms in Europe' (2009) 75 *Antitrust Law Journal* 1.

[82] See, eg, R Pollock, 'Is Google the Next Microsoft? Competition, Welfare and Regulation in Online Search' (2010) 9 *Review of Network Economics* 1446.

[83] T Wu, *The Curse of Bigness* (New York, Columbia Global Reports, 2018).

asleep at the wheel and failing to update competition law methods to the digital world.[84] Some authors suggest that many of the economics-based methodological tools for antitrust analysis are not useful and lead to significant underenforcement in the digital space.[85] Such concerns have led to radical proposals, including the breaking-up or nationalisation of the tech giants,[86] or the creation of specialised regulatory regimes assimilating these platforms to public utilities.[87] However, none of these proposals provides a magic bullet that can simultaneously promote a multitude of public policy objectives. The history of utility regulation or nationalisation shows that such interventions are not strategy-proof and may lead to substantial static and dynamic efficiency losses.[88] Similarly, even if break-ups of the tech giants may seem appealing, in practice they may be quite difficult to implement and sustain, given the fluidity of product and market boundaries in the digital economy. As Shapiro has argued, economies of scale and network effects in the technology sector may lead these markets to 'drift back toward winner-takes-most anyhow'.[89] Finally, as Braithwaite has argued, given the limits and costs of hierarchical compliance monitoring and enforcement by the state, a decentralised economy can be largely ungovernable.[90] Having business, including big business, as part of the regulatory framework, through its oversight of corporate supply chains, assists the task of regulation.

Others, by contrast, have argued that digital technology markets are contestable, with very low barriers to entry, given the idea that competition in the digital world is only 'a click away' and that many of today's giants began life as relatively small start-ups. Given such conditions, these authors argue that platform owners have incentives to be good stewards of their platform and to continue to innovate

[84] ibid.

[85] See, eg, LM Khan, 'Amazon's Antitrust Paradox' (2016) 126 *Yale Law Journal* 710 (arguing that the US antitrust framework is 'unequipped to capture the architecture of market power in the modern economy').

[86] See, eg, N Srnicek, *Platform Capitalism* (Cambridge, Polity, 2016); N Srnicek, 'We Need to Nationalise Google, Facebook and Amazon: Here's Why', *The Guardian*, 30 August 2017, https://www.theguardian.com/commentisfree/2017/aug/30/nationalise-google-facebook-amazon-data-monopoly-platform-public-interest; J Taplin, *Move Fast and Break Things: How Facebook Google and Amazon Cornered Culture and Undermined Democracy* (Boston, Little Brown, 2017).

[87] FA Pasquale, 'Dominant Search Engines: An Essential Cultural and Political Facility' in B Szoka and A Marcus (eds), *The Next Digital Decade: Essays on the Future of the Internet* (Washington DC, TechFreedom, 2011).

[88] See generally DF Spulber, *Regulation and Markets* (Cambridge, MA, MIT Press, 1989); DF Spulber, 'Deregulating Telecommunications' (1995) 12 *Yale Journal on Regulation* 25.

[89] C Shapiro, 'Antitrust in a Time of Populism' (2018) 61 *International Journal of Industrial Organization* 714, 744.

[90] J Braithwaite, 'The Regulatory State' in RAW Rhodes et al (eds), *The Oxford Handbook of Political Institutions* (Oxford, Oxford University Press, 2006) 230. Following this argument, the constraints on hierarchical monitoring of decentralised production and distribution makes the digital ecology 'unregulable', given phenomena such as pirating copyrighted works, proliferation of fake news or manipulation of product and service reviews, without the platform acting as a regulatory actor.

so as to keep users satisfied.[91] Moreover, concerns have also been expressed about the ability of competition enforcers to design, implement and supervise adequate antitrust remedies under conditions of uncertainty and the limits of hierarchy in fast-moving digital markets.[92]

In between the alarmist and the pollyannaish, writing in the aftermath of the Microsoft litigation and seeking to synthesise a set of emergent perspectives on the relationship between platform owners and the suppliers (and users) of platform applications, Farrell and Weiser highlight that platform owners do have an incentive to be good stewards of the platform infrastructure and to stimulate openness and innovation among the suppliers of functionalities on their platform.[93] After all, platforms only derive value by bring together different applications and users. As such, a platform owner benefits from innovation and diversity in the functionalities that make the platform more attractive to users.

On the one hand, a platform owner may integrate downstream functionalities into the platform itself so as to improve the user experience in accessing such functionalities on its platform. On the other hand, Farrell and Weiser also point out that platform owners' incentives to integrate into downstream functionalities may be inefficient. Inefficient integration can be the result of the incompetence of the incumbent platform (in not appreciating the benefits of downstream diversity and innovation), but also due to uncertainty faced by an incumbent platform about the future competitive or regulatory environment,[94] as well as concerns that a downstream application or functionality may come to commoditise the platform given the fluidity of market boundaries and the ease with which information-based technology is reprogrammable to different purposes.[95]

The concern about inefficient platform integration is further aggravated by the fact that the digital production environment is deeply collaborative and networked. It involves intimate information-sharing between platforms and developers of downstream functionalities, creating a risk of opportunistic conduct by platform owners. In particular, the platform owner can learn sufficiently from relationships with such developers to enable it 'to integrate in the downstream market

[91] See, eg, RH Bork and JG Sidak, 'What Does the Chicago School Teach about Internet Search and the Antitrust Treatment of Google?' (2012) 8 *Journal of Competition Law & Economics* 663.

[92] See, eg, M Ammori and L Pelican, 'Competitors' Proposed Remedies for Search Bias: "Neutrality" and Other Proposals' (2012) 15 *Journal of Internet Law* 1.

[93] J Farrell and PJ Weiser, 'Modularity, Vertical Integration, and Open Access Policies: Towards a Convergence of Antitrust and Regulation in the Internet Age' (2003) 17 *Harvard Journal of Law and Technology* 85, 95.

[94] ibid 105–19.

[95] The argument captures Christensen's idea that incumbent companies can be disrupted by niche competitors who originally serve a small and underserved segment of the market, allowing them to develop capabilities that ultimately undermine the incumbents. See CM Christensen, ME Raynor and R McDonald, 'What is Disruptive Innovation?' (2015) 93 *Harvard Business Review* 44. If it is difficult for an incumbent to disrupt itself, one alternative is to snuff out nascent threats.

and eliminate the value of the investments of the downstream collaborators'.[96] In the face of such potential for 'network failure',[97] which reduces the incentives for innovation through collaboration, the task of competition enforcement may be to promote the creation of structures for governing platform collaborations, which have strong affinity with experimentalist governance architectures.[98]

i. Digital Search

The above set of challenges in implementing competition law vis-a-vis digital platforms was evident in the EU Commission's *Google Shopping* case. Google's conduct impugned in the case may be characterised as a set of product improvement decisions that reduced traffic from Google's generic search results to online comparison shopping websites. First, Google's amendment of the algorithm for generic search results to downgrade websites with non-original derivative content (plausibly justified to promote higher-quality search results) led to a demotion in the rankings of online comparison websites.[99] Second, Google incorporated a specialist shopping search box to respond to user product searches. The shopping box was prominently displayed on the first results page and linked to Google's own comparison shopping tool, and was not subject to demotion by the general search algorithm.[100] As such, the combined effect of its conduct could be characterised as a form of downstream integration by Google, favouring its own specialised search tool at the expense of existing suppliers of online comparison shopping tools.

For the purposes of the present discussion on the selection of enforcement technique, we will focus on a few key aspects of the case and the ultimate resolution approach pursued by the Commission. First, as a number of authors pointed out, not least because of the novelty of the market and impugned practice, it was difficult to fit Google's conduct within either the specific terms of Article 102 or the existing precedents and doctrines developed by the EU Commission and courts on the forms of abuse of a dominant position. As such, commentators queried whether Google had notice that its conduct constituted an abuse of dominance violation consistent with the principle of legality.[101] Second, even if the focus

[96] Svetiev (n 52) 655. See also M Jennejohn, 'The Private Order of Innovation Networks' (2016) 68 *Stanford Law Review* 281; Khan, 'Amazon's Antitrust Paradox' (2016).

[97] A Schrank and J Whitford, 'The Anatomy of Network Failure' (2011) 29 *Sociological Theory* 151 (distinguishing network failures from more traditional forms of market failure).

[98] Compare Svetiev (n 52) 663–67 with RJ Gilson, CF Sabel and RE Scott, 'Contracting for Innovation: Vertical Disintegration and Interfirm Collaboration' (2009) 109 *Columbia Law Review* 431.

[99] Case AT.39740 – *Google Search (Shopping)*, 27 June 2017, C(2017) 4444 final [358].

[100] ibid [379].

[101] See, eg, P Akman, 'The Theory of Abuse in Google Search: A Positive and Normative Assessment under EU Competition Law' (2017) *University of Illinois Journal of Law Technology and Policy* 301; A Renda, 'Searching for Harm or Harming Search? A Look at the European Commission's Antitrust Investigation against Google' (CEPS Special Report No 118, September 2015), https://www.ceps.eu/ceps-publications/searching-harm-or-harming-search-look-european-commissions-antitrust-investigation.

was to be purely on the anti-competitive effects of Google's conduct, there were challenges in establishing such effects. On the one hand, the established economics-based tools for assessing both dominance and competitive constraint were not applicable to the search context, not least due to fluid product and technological boundaries and the fact that Google's service was provided to users without charge. On the other hand, even if there was potential for reduction in traffic for other online comparison shopping suppliers, this does not conclusively establish net harm to final users, particularly also because Google's decisions could be regarded as a product improvement, which could have benefited users.[102]

Finally, whatever the merits of an abuse of dominance claim based on the impugned conduct, remedial design and implementation also presented significant challenges. There was no simple normative principle that could be developed to mandate neutral or organic search.[103] Even if a set of criteria could be developed to implement such a normative principle, hierarchical supervision of compliance was made difficult by the frequent changes to the algorithm that Google implements to improve search results.[104] Moreover, any such remedy could constrain the evolution of search engine algorithms, which are in any event not neutral (because they seek to order the internet space for users) and are inherently dynamic, since they are driven by the broader internet ecology.[105]

During its investigation, the EU Commission initially entertained a set of commitment-based remedies proposed by Google pursuant to Article 9.[106] In light of the discussion above on the problems of uncertainty and remedial design, this would seem to be an appropriate case for using the commitments procedure. However, after all Google's remedial proposals were rejected in the market testing procedure and subsequent to a change in the responsible Commissioner, the Commission made a formal violation decision under Article 7, resulting in the largest ever fine imposed on a single undertaking. Commissioner Vestager synthesised the Commission's approach by acknowledging that 'Google is a wonderful company … and they have brought us innovation that has changed

[102] The difficulty in establishing anti-competitive effects was the basis for the peremptory conclusion of the US Federal Trade Commission (FTC) in its investigation of the same conduct. See Statement of the Federal Trade Commission Regarding Google's Search Practices in the Matter of Google Inc, FTC File Number 111-0163, 3 January 2013: 'Google's display of its own content could plausibly be viewed as an improvement in the overall quality of Google's search product' without 'sufficient evidence that Google manipulates its search algorithms to unfairly disadvantage vertical websites that compete with Google-owned vertical properties.'

[103] M Lao, '"Neutral" Search as a Basis for Antitrust Action?' (2013) 26 *Harvard Journal of Law and Technology* 1.

[104] M Ammori and L Pelican (n 92).

[105] Renda (n 101) 14–17.

[106] The first set of commitments was submitted to the Commission on 3 April 2013, the second set of commitments on 21 October 2013 and the third set of commitments on 31 January 2014. European Commission, Commission decision of 27 June 2017 relating to a proceeding under Article 102 of the Treaty on the Functioning of the European Union and Article 54 of the EEA Agreement (*Google Search (Shopping)* (n 99) para 17).

our lives', but underlining that the decision is 'about legal behaviour that [Google] should and can correct'.[107]

Despite this observation, the Commission, albeit implicitly, acknowledged that the findings underlying its decision were subject to considerable uncertainty. First, on the establishment of anti-competitive effects, the decision went to great lengths to demonstrate that Google's algorithm and display changes led to traffic diversion from other comparison shopping sites and even in favour of Google's own tool.[108] While such a finding may be diagnostically indicative of a possible problem of foreclosure, the Commission recognised that it was not conclusive. The Commission's effects analysis relied on the proposition that it was sufficient to establish some likelihood of effects such as foreclosure, higher prices for customers or reduced innovation, without disclosing any methodologies through which such effects could be predicted (as had been the case earlier in *Microsoft*).

Second, on the question of whether users might value Google's decision as a product quality improvement, which is to be balanced against potential exclusionary effects, the Commission's decision acknowledges that there may be heterogeneity between different types of final users and their ability and knowledge to interpret Google's search results display. Thus, the decision points out that: 'Google did not inform users that the Product Universal was positioned in its general search results pages using different underlying mechanisms than those used to rank generic search results.' With respect to Google's shopping unit, the Commission pointed out that 'the "Sponsored" label may suggest that different positioning mechanisms are used', but that such 'information is likely to be understandable only by the most knowledgeable users'.[109] This may be viewed as another diagnostic finding that the competitive market disciplines on Google's conduct are weakened by users' insufficient knowledge in interpreting the search output display.

Given the lack of fit between the impugned conduct and existing doctrines on abuse, as well as uncertainty about anti-competitive effects, an experimentalist enforcement technique may be seen as appropriate in the face of the above diagnostic findings.[110] While the ultimate violation decision combined with a heavy

[107] S Amaro and S Sedgwick, 'Google Still a "Wonderful" Company, Says EU's Top Antitrust Enforcer after $2.7 Billion Fine', *CNBC*, 2 September 2017, https://www.cnbc.com/2017/09/02/ambrosetti-forum-google-still-a-wonderful-company-says-eus-top-antitrust-enforcer-after-2-point-7-billion-fine.html; M Vestager, 'Making the Most of Europe's Strengths' (Ambrosetti Forum, Villa d'Este, 2 September 2017), https://ec.europa.eu/commission/commissioners/2014-2019/vestager/announcements/making-most-europes-strengths_en.

[108] In this respect, the decision also acknowledged the heterogeneity of user behaviour across national markets. Differences in these diagnostic effects were identified across different national markets, though they were not highlighted as significant. Similarly, the decision acknowledges the dynamism of the market, pointing out that merchant platforms may already be transforming e-commerce.

[109] *Google Search (Shopping)* (n 99) [536].

[110] Y Svetiev, 'Settling or Learning: Commitment Decisions as a Competition Enforcement Paradigm' (2014) 33 *Yearbook of European Law* 466.

fine appears to adopt an anti-experimentalist stance, a closer look suggests that the Commission's approach can be consistent with an experimentalist approach to regulating digital platforms via competition law.

Focusing on the substantive remedy, the injunction is said to follow a principles or outcomes-based approach by providing a set of 'guiding principles as to the scope of an acceptable remedy'.[111] Acknowledging the scope conditions of uncertainty and the limits of hierarchy, the decision pointed out that there may be more than one way to remedy the identified problem and left it up to Google to select the appropriate means for doing so.[112] The overarching principle of the remedy, akin to the regulation of infrastructure owners in utility markets, is that of equal treatment, whereby any selected measure must 'ensure that Google treats competing comparison shopping services no less favourably than its own comparison shopping service within its general search results pages'.[113]

As discussed earlier, a principles-based approach to regulatory problem-solving can be consistent with experimentalism, provided that it also incorporates mechanisms for monitoring, peer review of different measures and their effects through stakeholder input, as the basis for revising both Google's adopted measures and the overall objectives of the remedy in light of experience. The limits on the experimentalist implementation of the principles-based remedy proposed by the Commission stem from two factors. The first limit arises out of the procedural context of an Article 7 violation decision, which means that the remedy is not jointly designed, including with participation from affected parties. Further, the adversarial posture of Article 7 may lead to more minimalist efforts by Google, with more limited scope for joint monitoring and recursive adjustment in the remedy, a point to which we will return in Chapter 4. The second limit stems from the principle that the same measure is to be adopted across different technological devices and national markets.[114] As I have argued elsewhere, an experimentalist-minded agency might be open to allowing Google to adopt different measures across different devices or even national markets as a way of testing both the underlying theories of harm and different remedial mechanisms.[115]

The other seemingly legalist element of the remedy was the unprecedented fine that the Commission levied on Google. On one view, the fine was inappropriate both because Google may not have had notice that it committed a violation, given the novelty of the conduct in light of existing doctrines, and because the Commission had earlier contemplated the acceptance of commitments. More

[111] B Vesterdorf and K Fountoukakos, 'An Appraisal of the Remedy in the Commission's Google Search (Shopping) Decision and a Guide to its Interpretation in Light of an Analytical Reading of the Case Law' (2018) 9 *Journal of European Competition Law and Practice* 3.
[112] *Google Search (Shopping)* (n 99) [698].
[113] ibid [699].
[114] ibid [700].
[115] Svetiev, 'Settling or Learning (2014) 497.

fundamentally, given that the Commission saw the *Google Shopping* case as a first foray in regulating digital platforms via competition law, it is also important to consider whether the decision to levy a fine undermines an experimentalist approach to that task.

Yet from the experimentalist perspective, the fine may also be viewed as a penalty default for Google's failure to approach its strategy formulation consistently with the (meta-regulatory) platform stewardship principles that emerged from the EU *Microsoft* litigation. That litigation impugned unilateral decisions by a platform owner that devalued its collaborators' investments and took advantage of the lack of sophistication of final users. Furthermore, Google's approach to the resolution of the case in the face of the Commission's initial concerns may be regarded as inconsistent with the experimentalist objective of collaborative problem-solving.

The first justification for levying a fine, consistent with an experimentalist account, is that the fine responds to Google's failure to adopt a meta-regulatory approach so as to incorporate competition law objectives into its business strategy formulation.[116] The Commission's decision faulted Google for the failure of the process of self-assessment of its conduct in light of existing competition law principles, despite the fact that similar conduct had not been examined in existing precedents.[117] While it may be argued that Google used existing precedents to formulate strategy in a way that seeks to skirt around those precedents,[118] a meta-regulatory approach would entail Google testing the extent of its own dominance, including its ability to act independently of any constraint by competitors, collaborators or users. Instead of acting as the steward of a platform that derives value by bringing together applications and users,[119] its internal documents revealed that Google made its decisions unilaterally, aware that it would negatively affect existing collaborators to favour its own offering, without evaluating multiple strategies and their effect on collaborators' (as well as its own) interests. Moreover, its internal documents also revealed that Google's strategy formulation was not subject to competitive constraint from final users because of users' lack of knowledge or cognitive biases in consulting and interpreting search results.[120] As a platform steward, rather than seeking to better inform users about interpreting the results display in ways that might even have attenuated the impact on other comparison shopping websites, Google apparently sought to exploit users' lack of knowledge and biases.

[116] For a generalisation of the argument for formulating corporate strategy, while integrating public regulatory objectives, see British Academy, *The Principles of Purposeful Business* (2019), https://www.thebritishacademy.ac.uk/publications/future-of-the-corporation-principles-for-purposeful-business.

[117] *Google Search (Shopping)* (n 99) [724], [729].

[118] See M Ahmed and T Bradshaw, 'Parallels, and Differences between EU's Google and Microsoft Cases', *Financial Times*, 20 April 2016, https://www.ft.com/content/f1d7b3fc-06dd-11e6-a70d-4e39ac32c284.

[119] *Google Search (Shopping)* (n 99) [381]–[390] and [343]: 'Google did not invent comparison shopping. Google's first comparison shopping service, Froogle, was not gaining traffic as it did not appear visibly in Google's general search results pages'.

[120] ibid [437], [443]; *cf* ME Stucke, 'Behavioral Antitrust and Monopolization' (2012) 8 *Journal of Competition Law and Economics* 545.

A second justification for imposing a fine was Google's minimalist approach to remedial negotiations under Article 9, which was inconsistent with the experimentalist principles of joint design. Where a competition agency adopts an experimentalist enforcement approach that openly acknowledges it is acting under uncertainty and enforcement constraints, a cooperative stance to case resolution may weaken its credibility in negotiations and make it vulnerable to minimalist remedial proposals by undertakings.[121] The Commission underscored that it had 'set out its competition concerns regarding the Conduct in the Preliminary Assessment adopted on 13 March 2013'. As pointed out, Google submitted three sets of commitments, all of which were rejected following market participants' input through the market testing procedure. As such, Google's minimalist approach in the remedial negotiations further extended the duration of the impugned conduct and its ongoing effects on its counterparties in a highly dynamic market.

Having undertakings adopt a meta-regulatory approach in formulating business strategy (which, consistent with the analysis by Farrell and Weiser, may also involve a more deliberate evaluation of their own self-interest) as well as a collaborative stance in joint remedial formulation are essential for an evolution towards experimentalist competition regulation of platforms. As such, the violation route – including a fine – can act as a credible penalty default for failures to establish both management-based and collaborative mechanisms that aid experimentalist regulation. Consistent with the principles discussed in Chapter 1, the violation remedy in *Google Shopping* satisfies the requirements of a penalty default because it is undesirable for Google, but also for the Commission, since it affords much less flexibility in remedial monitoring and adjustment, a point to which we will return below.

While the Commission's decision in the *Google Shopping* case was formulated in the generic antitrust language about foreclosure and anti-competitive effects, as discussed above, it also acknowledges – albeit implicitly – uncertainties in the demonstration of such effects. What we aimed to show is that the Commission's approach may be viewed as an instance of experimentalist regulation of Google's search platform, whereby the competition intervention is used in a diagnostic way to identify weaknesses of the competitive constraints on the platform owner, either due to insufficient rivalry or because Google's counterparties (both 'down stream' collaborators and final users) cannot effectively exercise their contractual autonomy.[122] Such root-cause analysis may diagnose traditional market failures, network failures, regulatory failures or even fundamental values that require protection, notwithstanding sacrifices in market efficiency. It may either identify fairly minor modifications in market conduct that can effectively address the

[121] This problem may be particularly acute in the process of transition towards a fully experimentalist regime from a classic violation regime.

[122] See J Basedow, 'Freedom of Contract in the European Union' (2008) 16 *European Review of Private Law* 901.

concerns or the need for engaging a more elaborate regulatory apparatus through the legislative process.[123] A key question that remains unresolved is whether *explicitly* adopting an experimentalist stance to implementation would enhance an authority's regulatory capability.

ii. Social Networks: Competition Law and Data Protection

In the run-up to the Commission's competition enforcement foray against Google, numerous complainants, which included many prominent and successful providers of e-commerce services on both sides of the Atlantic, sought to impugn different species of conduct through which Google was said to devalue their investments and services to favour its own offerings. Since some of these forms of conduct are subject to specialised regulatory regimes, observers pointed out that part of what was at stake in the Commission's effort to discipline digital platforms was the purity of competition law as a market discipline:

> In the upcoming European reflection on competition policy, e-commerce and online intermediaries, EU policymakers should try to focus on sound economics and resist a number of temptations, which come from the overall debate taking place in Brussels but have generally very little to do with antitrust. First, EU institutions should resist the temptation to use antitrust to solve problems that are not strictly related to competition. Just as competition policy was used for a period of time to regulate the banking sector during the recent financial crisis, a similar tendency seems to be emerging in the public debate on 'Internet giants'. Privacy concerns, tax concerns, regulatory and consumer protection stances, and copyright concerns are being translated into antitrust issues, to be solved through ad-hoc investigations or sectoral inquiries. But antitrust is a very technical field, governed by the rules of industrial economics: it cannot be used to solve non-antitrust matters.[124]

As discussed in Chapter 1, similar criticism was levelled at the German BKA's holding that Facebook committed an abuse of dominance given its contractual terms governing the way in which it collects and deals with users' data. The case forms part of a broader debate about the digital and multi-sided platform nature of markets that puts into sharp relief the interaction of competition law enforcement and data protection law.[125] The provision of free services by online providers

[123] The experimentalist approach may be contrasted to the precautionary approach, which would constrain conduct wherever there is uncertainty about harmful effects, as well as a stricter effects approach, which would allow conduct whenever effects cannot be established to some level of probability.

[124] Renda (n 101) 45.

[125] See generally F Pasquale, 'Privacy, Antitrust and Power' (2013) 20 *George Mason Law Review* 1009; M Kuschewsky and D Geradin, 'Data Protection in the Context of Competition Law Investigations: An Overview of the Challenges' (2014) 37 *World Competition* 69; F Costa-Cabral and O Lynskey, 'Family Ties: The Intersection between Data Protection and Competition in EU Law' (2017) 54 *Common Market Law Review* 11.

(including search, social networking and others), where such provision is monetised through the collection, use and marketisation of personal data[126] brings the two apparently distinct market regulatory regimes into close interaction. Many have questioned whether competition enforcement should – in light of such proximity – take into account a firm's compliance with data protection principles in assessing anti-competitive conduct or whether the two regimes should be kept distinct.

On the one hand, interaction across regulatory regimes may be seen as offering a possibility to disrupt existing knowledge about how markets operate, as well as the stabilised framing of antitrust problems that limits attention to certain forms of harm.[127] On the other hand, at least at the EU level, there has been a reluctance to explicitly incorporate data protection concerns into competition law analysis. Both the EU Commission and the CJEU have insisted on keeping the two separate regulatory silos distinct, both institutionally and analytically. Already back in 2006, the CJEU in *Asnef-Equifax* observed that 'possible issues relating to … personal data are not … a matter for competition law' and should be resolved by applying 'governing data protection' provisions.[128] Similarly, in clearing the Facebook/WhatsApp merger, the EU Commission explained that 'privacy related concerns', even if attributable to the increase in the concentration of data, are not 'within the scope' of EU competition law, but rather of EU data protection law.[129] As the Competition Commissioner has surmised, 'privacy and competition concerns should be considered separately'.[130]

Notwithstanding the above views, as we pointed out in Chapter 1, the strict separation of competition enforcement and data protection has been contested at the policy, legislative and decisional levels in the Member States. The joint report of the French and German NCAs pointed out that data protection can be relevant from a competition enforcement point of view. While acknowledging that data protection and competition law have different goals, the authorities argued that there can be a 'close link between the dominance of the company, its data collection processes and competition on the relevant markets'.[131] This argument also reflects

[126] User profile data can be repackaged and sold by the entity collecting it, but it can also be used by the entity to sell targeted advertising or facilitate personalised pricing. The fact or extent of such commercial transformation may or may not be appreciated by the user who takes advantage of the 'free service'. See MS Gal and DL Rubinfeld, 'The Hidden Costs of Free Goods: Implications for Antitrust Enforcement' (2016) 80 *Antitrust Law Journal* 521.

[127] R Baldwin and J Black, 'Driving Priorities in Risk-Based Regulation: What is the Problem?' (2016) 43 *Journal of Law and Society* 564; *cf* A Ezrachi, 'Sponge' (2017) 5 *Journal of Antitrust Enforcement* 49.

[128] Case C-238/05 *Asnef-Equifax v Ausbanc* [2006] ECR I-11145 [63].

[129] See Case Comp/M.7217 – *Facebook/WhatsApp*, 3 October 2014, C(2014) 7239 final [164]. *cf* G Schneider, 'Testing Art 102 TFEU in the Digital Marketplace: Insights from the Bundeskartellamt's Investigation against Facebook' (2018) 9 *Journal of European Competition Law & Practice* 213, surveying the separate regulatory silos view in merger decisions of the Commission.

[130] M Vestager, 'Competition in a Big Data World' (DLD 16 Conference, Munich, 17 January 2016), http://web.archive.org/web/20171203023359/https://ec.europa.eu/commission/commissioners/2014-2019/vestager/announcements/competition-big-data-world_en.

[131] Autoritè de la Concurrence and Bundeskartellamt, 'Competition Law and Data', 10 May 2016.

the EU Data Protection Supervisor's call for a holistic approach to data governance, including coordination between data protection, consumer protection and competition agencies, notwithstanding their distinctness and independence.[132]

In its investigation against Facebook, the BKA ultimately found that the social networking company abused its dominant position,[133] given its data collection and privacy practices, which were said to be contrary to applicable data protection rules. While the case appears to diverge from the strict separation view, the Commission did not seek to decide the case itself, despite the fact that Facebook operates in all EU Member States.[134] Thus, as in the hotel booking cases discussed in Chapter 1, allowing NCAs to decide a case and develop an analytical and remedial framework for addressing the problem can be a route to experimentalism in EU competition policy.

The BKA adopted the view that Facebook's dominance in the market of social networking enabled it to impose unclear and misleading terms and conditions regarding its data collection policies. Such misleading terms, infringing data protection law, were held to amount to 'unfair trading conditions' under §19 GWB, the equivalent of Article 102 TFEU. The abuse was said to arise because Facebook requires users to give consent to limitless collection of their personal data by forcing them to choose between accepting the entire Facebook package, including extensive personal data collection, or not using Facebook's service at all. The impugned practices included Facebook's collection, use and merging of users' personal data, including from third-party sources, such as secondary websites and applications with embedded Facebook application programming interfaces (APIs).[135] Moreover, the German NCA cooperated with data protection authorities to analyse the significance of the data protection issues involved.[136]

Much of the debate surrounding the German authority's decision focused on the question of whether the imposition of Facebook's terms and conditions,

[132] European Data Protection Supervisor, 'Privacy and Competitiveness in the Age of Big Data: The Interplay between Data Protection, Competition Law and Consumer Protection in the Digital Economy', March 2014, https://edps.europa.eu/sites/edp/files/publication/14-03-26_competitition_law_big_data_en.pdf.

[133] Bundeskartellamt, 'Bundeskartellamt Initiates Proceeding against Facebook on Suspicion of Having Abused its Market Power by Infringing Data Protection Rules', 2 March 2016, http://www.bundeskartellamt.de/SharedDocs/Meldung/EN/Pressemitteilungen/2016/02_03_2016_Facebook.html?nn=3599398.

[134] See Commission Notice on cooperation within the Network of Competition Authorities [2004] OJ C101/03, https://eur-lex.europa.eu/LexUriServ/LexUriServ.do?uri=OJ:C:2004:101:0043:0053:EN:PDF.

[135] Bundeskartellamt, 'Preliminary Assessment in Facebook Proceeding: Facebook's Collection and Use of Data from Third-Party Sources is Abusive', 19 December 2017, http://www.bundeskartellamt.de/SharedDocs/Publikation/EN/Pressemitteilungen/2017/19_12_2017_Facebook.pdf?__blob=publicationFile&v=3.

[136] Bundeskartellamt, 'Bundeskartellamt Prohibits Facebook from Combining User Data from Different Sources', https://www.bundeskartellamt.de/SharedDocs/Meldung/EN/Pressemitteilungen/2019/07_02_2019_Facebook.html.

to the extent it amounted to an exploitative abuse, could be made referable to Facebook's dominant position.[137] However, consistent with the Commission's approach in *Google Shopping*, the BKA's approach appeared to use the competition investigation in a diagnostic manner – identifying the reasons why rivalry and user choice do not impose a constraint on Facebook's contracting and data use practices. Such reasons include: (i) documented user inattentiveness to the details of extensive terms and conditions disclosures (both in analogue and in digital settings); and (ii) the way in which such user inattentiveness (whether because of convenience or lack of understanding) interacts with Facebook's contractual terms for collecting and combining user data (which even a fully rational consumer may have difficulty comprehending). Adopting a data protection perspective on the problem reveals a possible regulatory failure: a data protection regime based on a formalist approach to obtaining user consent fails to achieve data protection objectives.[138] Diagnostically, failures in both competitive disciplines and the data protection regime in this case entrench the position of a dominant player.[139]

Finally, despite the formal violation finding, the BKA's remedy adopted a problem-solving approach by aiming to enhance the user discipline on Facebook's data collection and usage practices. While not preventing Facebook-related entities such as Instagram and WhatsApp from collecting data, the combination of such data onto a user's Facebook account would only be possible if Facebook implemented *appropriate protocols* to obtain users' voluntary consent. Such a remedy is a relatively minimalist approach to coping with the data concentration problem that has been said to arise from Facebook's prior acquisitions of digital services providers.[140] Preventing Facebook from obtaining bundled consent for merging data may re-engage users' autonomy in evaluating how they manage the collection and use of their data,[141] though it is by no means clear that such a measure would in itself be sufficient to protect either consumer rights or competition.[142]

[137] See generally, Schneider (n 129).

[138] The BKA drew explicit attention to the interaction of civil law principles about protecting a contracting party in a position of unequal bargaining power and data protection rules aiming to ensure that users can decide freely and without coercion how their personal data are used: Bundeskartellamt (n 135) 4.

[139] C Biancotti and P Ciocca, 'Opening Internet Monopolies to Competition with Data Sharing Mandates', *Peterson Institute for International Economics Policy Brief* 19-3, April 2019, https://www.piie.com/system/files/documents/pb19-3.pdf, highlight both the benefits and risks of data concentration by dominant companies and the extent to which such companies have incentives to act consistently with public interest objectives. In their view, a key risk of data concentration is limiting competition.

[140] At least compared to more radical proposals such as break-ups or data sharing mandates. See ibid; Wu, *The Curse of Bigness* (2018).

[141] Regulatory interventions can aim to make corporate actions more transparent and induce users to change their actions and decisions as a means to improving policy or market outcomes; see A Fung, M Graham and D Weil, *Full Disclosure: The Perils and Promise of Transparency* (Cambridge, Cambridge University Press, 2007).

[142] Biancotti and Ciocca, 'Opening Internet Monopolies' (2019) 4 highlight the difficulty for users to effectively exercise consumer and privacy rights through informed consent in the digital environment.

An experimentalist implementation of the remedy could evolve into more intrusive obligations, though the BKA also reserved its right to revoke its decision in full or in part, presumably in the light of observation of remedial effects.

B. Traditional Industries and Non-competition Objectives

The digital platforms from the above examples are integrated systems offering 'variety of information services under one brand' and, as such, they link separate markets using technical protocols to control participation and access.[143] Given such links between different activities and the relatively fast pace of technological evolution, digital platforms generate fluidity in market boundaries and bring into sharp relief the interaction between different regulatory mandates and their respective policy goals.

However, competition authorities have also been called upon to consider the social value of innovation in production and distribution in more traditional industries and markets, where such innovations may carry risks to competition. In the remainder of this chapter, I wish to focus on the role of competition authorities in assessing coordination agreements among producers that are said to provide novel solutions that advance non-economic objectives in exercise of their mandate to evaluate anti-competitive agreements pursuant to Article 101 (or its national equivalents).

As some authors have noted, NCAs are now responsible for the overwhelming majority of infringement investigations in the multi-level framework introduced by the modernisation reforms. Moreover, given the fact-intensive nature of such investigations and the margin of discretion available both in assessing the anti-competitive effects of coordination agreements and in weighing them vis-a-vis any claimed benefits, the application of Article 101 by NCAs can lead to substantial fragmentation.[144] In highlighting the divergences observed in NCA enforcement practices, Brook notes that while the Commission's guidance documents have sought to limit the social benefits that an NCA can consider pursuant to Article 101 to narrow economic efficiencies, NCAs have not consistently adhered to such an approach.[145] This finding may seem surprising, given the mechanisms that have been introduced to ensure coherence and convergence in the networked enforcement regime, as well as in the light of Commission reports on the functioning of

[143] JE Cohen, 'The Regulatory State in the Information Age' (2016) 17 *Theoretical Inquiries in Law* 369.
[144] O Brook 'Struggling with Article 101(3) TFEU: Diverging Approaches of the Commission, EU Courts, and Five Competition Authorities' (2019) 56 *Common Market Law Review* 121, 123.
[145] ibid 125.

the decentralised system (discussed in Chapter 1) identifying substantial levels of convergence in the application of the rules by the NCAs.[146]

And yet, rather than being a source of concern, if guided by the disciplines of experimentalist governance, such fragmentation and diversity could also be a source of learning through monitoring concrete implementation initiatives.

i. Competition and Sustainability

To assess the extent to which the strictures of EU competition law provide a constraint on the experimentalist evolution of national competition enforcement to cope with local market specificities and social policy preferences, we may note a set of decisions by the Dutch competition authority (ACM) assessing coordination efforts among rivals that were said to produce broader societal and sustainability benefits. As Voss and Kemp have argued, because sustainability is concerned with the long-term and systemic nature of processes, it brings to the fore the problems of complexity, uncertainty and regime interaction. As a mode of problem-framing, sustainability emphasises the 'interconnectedness of different problems and scales' and the 'long-term and indirect effects of actions', including regulatory actions themselves. As such, sustainability-oriented solutions are not amenable to the sort of decision-making blueprints used for 'delimitable, decomposable problems',[147] though, as we will see, such solutions can by disciplined by experimentalist governance infrastructures.

As discussed in Chapter 1, the Dutch ACM was itself created to interlink market regulation mandates by combining different authorities so as to produce cross-pollination and innovation in market regulation. Moreover, the ACM (like other Dutch market regulatory authorities)[148] openly acknowledges adopting a problem-solving approach in pursuing its mandate as opposed to a rule-oriented approach, which may be understood as a preference for avoiding formal enforcement proceedings that lead to violation findings. And yet, despite such an interlinked mandate and problem-solving orientation, the ACM has also been criticised for a narrow technocratic focus in assessing sustainability coordination agreements.

In a widely debated decision shortly after its establishment, the ACM assessed an agreement to close down five coal-fired power stations (as part of the so-called Energieakkoord), for its compatibility with competition law rules. The Energieakkoord was a broad-based societal agreement aiming to govern the

[146] ibid 124. See also G Monti, 'Independence, Interdependence and Legitimacy: The EU Commission, National Competition Authorities, and the European Competition Network' (2014) EUI Working Paper, Law 2014/01, https://cadmus.eui.eu/handle/1814/29218.

[147] JP Voss and R Kemp, 'Sustainability and Reflexive Governance: Introduction' in JP Voss and R Kemp (eds), *Reflexive Governance for Sustainable Development* (Cheltenham, Edward Elgar, 2006) 3–4.

[148] eg, the Dutch Authority for the Financial Markets (AFM), discussed in Y Svetiev and A Ottow, 'Financial Supervision in the Interstices between Private and Public Law' (2014) 10 *European Review of Contract Law* 496.

Netherlands' transition towards cleaner sources of energy and the achievement of climate change objectives. The accord was negotiated under the auspices of the responsible ministry, and those negotiations included many relevant stakeholders, such as energy supply companies, unions and environmental organisations. Given that the accord involved an agreement among competitor energy suppliers to close down coal-fired plants, it also had to be analysed by the ACM as a potentially anti-competitive arrangement.

The ACM's conclusion that the proposed agreement would violate competition law, as it would reduce consumer welfare by raising electricity prices, generated considerable debate in the Netherlands. In a joint press release, five Dutch environmental groups accused the authority of 'tunnelvision', assailing the ACM's reasoning and its method of comparing social benefits and costs.[149] This triggered reflection about the appropriate competition law approach for deciding cases involving interacting public interest objectives.[150] On one view, the ACM's decision amounted to privileging the allocative efficiency variant of competition policy,[151] emphasising the short-term quantifiable costs of the accord (such as electricity price increases) at the expense of the longer-term, more diffuse and less easily quantifiable benefits (including reducing pollution or addressing climate change).[152] Alternatively, an ACM official sought to explain that the authority did not assume it had the competence to make the final determination on the net public benefits of the Energieakkoord purely on the basis of price effects. Instead, the decision was said to reflect the ACM's evaluation that the consumer interest had not been adequately represented in the accord.[153]

Notwithstanding such reluctance on the ACM's part to be the arbiter of net public benefits, the Dutch Ministry of Economic Affairs issued a policy rule instructing the agency to consider the positive longer-term effects of coordination initiatives to promote sustainability in applying Article 101(3) and its local equivalent. However, the policy instruction provided little in the way of guidance about the methodologies for the competition authority to follow in assessing and balancing sustainability/long-term and competition/short-term objectives.[154]

[149] See, eg, Greenpeace, 'Tunnelvisie ACM maakt kolendeal in SER-Energieakkoord onmogelijk', 26 September 2013, http://www.greenpeace.nl/2013/Persberichten/Tunnelvisie-ACM-maakt-kolendeal-in-SER-Energieakkoord-onmogelijk.

[150] E Kloosterhuis and M Mulder, 'Competition Law and Environmental Protection: the Dutch Agreement on Coal-Fired Power Plants' (2015) 11 *Journal of Competition Law & Economics* 855; C Fonteijn and J Sinderen, 'Economic Analysis as a Tool to Improve Decision-Making' (2015) 11 *Competition Law International* 77.

[151] Y Svetiev, 'European Regulatory Private Law: From Conflicts to Platforms' in KP Purnhagen and P Rott (eds), *Varieties of European Economic Law and Regulation* (Cham, Springer International, 2014).

[152] Cohen (n 143).

[153] Interview with ACM officials, The Hague, November 2015.

[154] As Monti and Mulder point out, the instruction only identified the obvious free-rider and first-mover problems that might be an obstacle to sustainability initiatives: G Monti and J Mulder, 'Escaping the Clutches of EU Competition Law: Pathways to Assess Private Sustainability Initiatives' (2017) 42 *European Law Review* 635, 637.

Notwithstanding the challenges posed by such a policy rule, the ACM issued a 'vision document' on the relationship between competition and sustainability which recognised that sustainability-related characteristics may be valued by consumers and therefore taken into account in competition law decision-making. Moreover, in reports about its enforcement initiatives, the ACM has canvassed cases in which longer-term more diffuse benefits have been considered in its competition interventions.[155] The authority's officials have emphasised the 'multi-dimensional nature' of the analysis needed in such cases and three preconditions for its intervention, including the harm that the conduct inflicts on consumers, the public interests at stake and, importantly, the ability of the ACM to effectively take action and monitor coordination activities.

We could envisage at least three different approaches that a competition authority could follow in performing the foregoing task: proceduralist, technocratic or experimentalist. Following the proceduralist approach, the market authority would simply ensure that all affected interests were adequately represented in the negotiation of a sustainability accord, without entering into an evaluation of the substance of the agreement.[156] Pursuant to the technocratic approach, the competition authority evaluates the substance of the agreement by using available methodologies to weigh short-run consumer price increases against quantifiable benefits so as to assess whether the accord on balance improves social welfare.

It is worth noting that neither of the above approaches adequately deals with the problem of uncertainty. The procedural approach may seem less onerous for a market regulatory authority, but it raises the question of who needs to be at the negotiation table for a sustainability accord, including the selection of the entities that can adequately represent diffuse interests, such as the consumer interest (remembering that different classes of consumers may also have different interests).[157] Moreover, some groups may not be able to foresee the effects of a sustainability accord until it is implemented, and once they observe its actual effects. As such, certain 'interests' may only crystallise following the implementation of the accord, whereby social actors decide to challenge or seek to improve accord in view of its actual observed effects.[158]

In contrast to the procedural approach, the technocratic approach requires the competition authority to both have sufficient foresight about the likely effects that should be considered in the balancing exercise and to identify a methodology through which the effects (including longer-term ones) can be assessed, quantified and balanced, which is itself quite a tall order. Schinkel and Spiegel argue, for

[155] See C Fonteijn, 'Netherlands: ACM' in *The European, Middle Eastern and African Antitrust Review 2017* (London, Global Competition Review, 2016).

[156] *cf* H Schepel, 'Delegation of Regulatory Powers to Private Parties under EC Competition Law: Towards a Procedural Public Interest Test' (2002) 39 *Common Market Law Review* 31.

[157] See generally NK Komesar, *Imperfect Alternatives: Choosing Institutions in Law, Economics, and Public Policy* (Chicago, University of Chicago Press, 1994).

[158] Svetiev (n 70).

example, that 'sustainability coordination is generally a poor idea', since it is difficult for a competition authority to ensure that consumers are at least as well-off in the case of sustainability coordination as in the case of no coordination among undertakings.[159]

A third, experimentalist, approach to assessing sustainability coordination initiatives is neither purely procedural nor technocratic, but dialogic. Ensuring broad interest representation in the negotiation of an accord is an important necessary step, but it is not sufficient. As such, the competition authority might conditionally approve such an accord, subject to creating an adequate monitoring mechanism to evaluate its effects, which provides affected parties a venue through which they can represent their interests following implementation. Further, such an accord could benefit from peer review, for example, by comparison to no action taken or comparable measures adopted in other jurisdictions or industries. Moreover, to the extent that sustainability coordination raises multidimensional regulatory issues, the implementation of an accord would also be subject to peer review in other salient regulatory regimes (such as environmental, health or food safety regulation).[160] Finally, implementation evidence and peer review of such evidence can be used to recursively adjust the sustainability accord itself.

In evaluating its enforcement activities, including with respect to Article 101 and its national equivalent, the ACM has demonstrated an awareness of the need to combine competition enforcement action with post-enforcement monitoring and dialogue with affected actors. Such ongoing market monitoring – even in the aftermath of formal findings of violation through coordination – are said to build joint responsibility with market actors about what competition law requires. It has also made the ACM more attuned to the effects – including unintended effects – of its interventions, which may diminish product quality and innovation, and require corrective action. For example, following a formal enforcement action against coordinating practices among medical practitioners, ongoing monitoring and communication with the sector revealed that concerns about competition law violations led doctors to become exceedingly cautious about entering into collaborations that could promote patient welfare.[161] As a result of such normative uncertainty, the ACM sought to institute a dialogue with representatives of both doctor and patient organisations. The aim of such dialogue was to ensure that concerns about competition law violation would not diminish useful forms of collaboration among medical service providers and harm patient welfare:

> [The] ACM wishes to make healthcare providers aware of the room that exists for collaboration that offers benefits to consumers, such as collaboration that improves healthcare affordability or the quality of treatment.[162]

[159] MP Schinkel and Y Spiegel, 'Can Collusion Promote Sustainable Consumption and Production?' (2017) 53 *International Journal of Industrial Organization* 371, 394–95.
[160] See ch 3.
[161] Interview with ACM officials, The Hague, November 2015.
[162] Fonteijn (n 155).

Such post-enforcement monitoring also revealed cross-sectoral problems in the interaction between medical services providers and insurers. Uncertainty about the cost and quality of care was heightened by the fact that higher concentration in insurance markets gave insurers much greater bargaining power. Such root-cause analysis led the ACM to conduct market studies of the various market segments so as to clarify modalities of 'healthy cooperation' safeguarding the interests of patients.[163] As part of its 'norm-transmitting dialogue with market participants', the ACM issued an opinion on cooperation agreements relating to cancer treatment (following the assessment of proposed collaborations involving joint purchase of therapy and joint negotiation of purchase conditions with insurers), as well as 'a guide for primary healthcare providers who had questions concerning the application of [competition law] to possibilities for cooperation among care providers'.[164] In the light of such experiences, the ACM highlighted its aim to use a broader set of strategies – beyond violation findings – to develop 'customized solutions based on sound problem analyses'.[165]

The ACM's approach to assessing sustainability coordination was further tested in the 'Chicken of Tomorrow' case involving an agreement among the principal supermarket chains in the Netherlands to raise sustainability standards in chicken meat production. In the light of animal welfare campaigns with respect to chicken farming conditions in the country, the sustainability accord to replace regularly produced chicken meat was based on private standards, agreed between representatives of key players in the agro-food sector (farmers, processors and supermarkets).[166] It included standards about the use of a slower-growing chicken breed, the density of chickens in broiler barns, the use of litter material and antibiotics, as well as other animal welfare standards (relating to injuries or hours of darkness in barns). Other environmental standards related to ammonia and particulate emissions, manure processing, reduction of the carbon footprint and usage of sustainable energy sources. The agreed standards went beyond the statutory production rules, yet were intended as a minimum standard for chicken sold by supermarkets in the Netherlands from 2020, without covering butchers, small retail stores or exported chicken.

In analysing the above arrangement as a potentially anti-competitive restriction, the ACM expressed the view that under both EU and Dutch law, sustainability benefits could be taken into consideration in granting an exemption under

[163] ibid. Similarly in the port industry, the ACM investigated the existence of 'illegal agreements', while aiming to advise companies about legal forms of collaboration.

[164] Fonteijn (n 155) 2–3. See Netherlands Authority for Consumers and Market, 'Competition in the Dutch Health Insurance Market Interim Report', February 2016, https://www.acm.nl/sites/default/files/old_publication/publicaties/16129_competition-in-the-dutch-health-insurance-market.pdf.

[165] Netherlands Authority for Consumers and Market, 'Strategy Document', https://www.acm.nl/sites/default/files/old_publication/publicaties/11993_strategy-document-20140801.pdf.

[166] JM Bos, H Belt and PH Feindt, 'Animal Welfare, Consumer Welfare, and Competition Law: The Dutch Debate on the Chicken of Tomorrow' (2018) 8 *Animal Frontiers* 20, 25.

Article 101(3) (consistently also with the ministerial policy instruction on competition and sustainability). The availability of the exception was conditional on the following set of criteria:

- the arrangement contributes to improving production or distribution, or promoting technical or economic progress;
- consumers are allowed a 'fair share' of the benefits of the arrangement;
- the arrangement is necessary and proportionate to the objectives pursued;
- sufficient residual competition continues to exist in the market.

The most controversial and criticised aspect of the ACM's provisional finding that the accord was anti-competitive was the methodology used to weigh the restriction of competition inherent in the agreed standards against their social benefits. In particular, the ACM's assessment was based on a cost-benefit analysis, comparing the increased estimated cost of the chicken employing the agreed production standards to the potential benefits of such standards. The ACM collected data to estimate consumers' 'willingness-to-pay' (WTP) for the proposed chicken attributes, showing the consumers' WTP considerably below the estimated increase in the price of chicken meat. Such analysis suggested an absence of a measurable consumer benefit from the sustainable chicken standards.[167]

As a number of commentators observed, the ACM's analysis seemed to privilege a fairly narrow and technocratic view of competition policy: giving more weight to short-term price effects as opposed to longer-term and more diffuse social benefits that are not as easy to quantify.[168] Such a narrowly technocratic approach, apparently supported by the EU Commission, may be seen to discourage experimentation with novel production methods that have ethical, societal or aesthetic salience.[169] However, I would argue that the ACM's approach is largely consistent with the premises of experimentalist governance. Moreover, explicitly adopting an experimentalist stance would further improve sustainability regulation in a dialogic and recursive fashion.

First, it is worth underscoring that under the applicable CJEU caselaw,[170] the ACM did not have the power to issue a decision declaring the agreement compatible with Article 101. In fact, the CJEU's approach on this point is consistent with the movement away from the *ex ante* clearance regime[171] and with the experimentalist disfavour of safe harbours based on purely *ex ante* assessment. Second,

[167] ibid 22.

[168] ibid; Monti and Mulder (n 154). See also Cohen (n 143) 23.

[169] Bos, Belt and Feindt (n 166) 23; Monti and Mulder (n 154).

[170] Case C-375/09 *Prezes Urzędu Ochrony Konkurencji i Konsumentów v Tele2 Polska sp z oo, now Netia SA* [2011] 5 CMLR 2.

[171] As Monti and Mulder (n 154) point out (at 648) the Commission itself has not used its power to issue such a compatibility declaration under art 10 of Regulation 1/2003.

from a procedural perspective, the participants in the Chicken of Tomorrow accord represented producer interests, without the participation of civil society organisations or consumer associations. This raises significant concerns about the development of the standard and its possible anti-competitive effects.[172] Third, the ACM acknowledged the predictive uncertainty of its technocratic cost-benefit evaluation, reaching only a provisional conclusion that the 'sustainability arrangements *do not seem* to meet the first exemption criterion'.[173] While the WTP study was crude, it did reveal heterogeneity and uncertainty in consumer understanding and valuation of sustainable chicken attributes.[174] Such uncertainty about valuations (and arguably also *values*) would suggest caution about committing the market to a single (potentially sticky) production standard, particularly in the light of the available alternatives canvassed by the authority.[175] Finally, the ACM's decision acknowledged that consumer preferences (or values for that matter) are not fixed and may evolve, including through actions that would increase consumer awareness and confidence in specific production standards.[176]

An explicitly experimentalist stance by the authority might approve a standard developed through a more participative process, with stronger evidence of broader societal support and benefit, while subjecting it to monitoring and peer review. For example, the Dutch financial authority (AFM) triggered a fully experimentalist dialogue in efforts to regulate the marketing of leveraged financial products (turbos) to retail investors.[177] Consumer studies conducted by the AFM indicated poor understanding of the products by retail investors, and preliminary modelling by the AFM suggested that high-leverage turbos had a high probability of loss. Acknowledging the limits of its modelling and consumer studies, the AFM invited further evidence from financial institutions about investor behaviour.

[172] Bos, Belt and Feindt (n 166) 25. See Sabel and Simon, 'Contextualising Regimes' (2011) 38 (emphasising the importance of balanced and inclusive representation in setting up an experimentalist regime).

[173] Netherlands Authority for Consumers and Market, 'ACM's Analysis of the Sustainability Arrangements Concerning the Chicken of Tomorrow', 26 January 2015, https://www.acm.nl/sites/default/files/old_publication/publicaties/13789_analysis-chicken-of-tomorrow-acm-2015-01-26.pdf.pdf.

[174] While the WTP for the attributes of the 'Chicken of Tomorrow' standard was relatively low, considerably higher WTP was detected for the attributes of the 'Better Life' chicken label of the Dutch Society for the Protection of Animals, which was not reflected in the latter's market share; Bos, Belt and Feindt (n 166). See also RA Pielke, *The Honest Broker: Making Sense of Science in Policy and Politics* (Cambridge, Cambridge University Press, 2007) 2 (clarifying the scope of choice for decision-making).

[175] ACM (n 173) 6: 'the market share of … 'Better Life' label is not large … which seems to indicate that the market is unable to communicate the benefits of this chicken to consumers effectively … the ACM does see room for improvement, and opportunities for businesses'.

[176] ibid 7.

[177] Netherlands Authority for the Financial Markets (AFM), 'Report on Leveraged Products: Review Results', July 2013, https://www.afm.nl/~/profmedia/files/rapporten/engels/leveraged-products.ash. See also DA Zetzsche, RP Buckley, JN Barberis and DW Arner, 'Regulating a Revolution: From Regulatory Sandboxes to Smart Regulation' (2017) 23 *Fordham Journal of Corporate and Financial Law* 31; HJ Allen, 'Regulatory Sandboxes' (2019) 87 *George Washington Law Review* 579.

The suppliers' input challenged the assumptions of the AFM's model, suggesting that the products were beneficial for certain classes of investors. In the face of uncertainty about the benefits of the product, not least due to the heterogeneity of investor needs, the AFM and the suppliers set up an experimentalist framework for monitoring and recursive learning, beginning with a relatively minimal remedy of coordinated disclosure efforts by the suppliers:

> [T]he turbo providers on the market offered a number of voluntary remedial commitments to the AFM designed to (1) improve customers' understanding of the products and the expectations with which they purchase such products and (2) provide a mechanism for modifying the offerings in light of further experience with these products. Specifically, the providers agreed to improve the explanations and warnings about turbos on their own websites, and to create a common website with further non-sales oriented information about how these products work. The providers also agreed to formulate guidelines for the issuance of turbos and form a structured products association to provide a forum for developing market standards for such products. The providers envisaged that product guidelines may need to be amended in light of market developments and in consultation with the AFM … [T]he AFM stressed that [the measures] would have to be periodically evaluated, partly on the basis of further evidence about … effects, including whether investors avoid products that offer little or no prospect of return and the issue of whether other similar types of investment products should be subject to regulatory scrutiny as well.[178]

ii. Private or Public Regulation?

It may be argued that sustainability initiatives, involving trade-offs between different policy objectives and value choices, should be pursued through traditional public regulation rather than evaluated in competition proceedings.[179] However, as some authors have recognised, 'designing effective regulation is a complex task and the government may lack the needed information to do so'.[180] Perhaps unsurprisingly, rather than assuming this task by drafting public regulation, the Dutch government repeatedly attempted to delegate it to the ACM even proposing to revise the policy rule and give the ACM the power to consider both the longer-term effects of sustainability initiatives and the benefits accruing to society as a whole.[181] In the face of opposition to such a proposal from the EU Commission, the Dutch government finally proposed incorporating private sustainability initiatives into public legislation, if the design of such initiatives

[178] See Svetiev and Ottow (n 148) 517.

[179] This was the apparent view of the EU Commission in the wake of the sustainability debates in the Netherlands. See Monti and Mulder (n 154) 642.

[180] Schinkel and Spigel (n 159).

[181] Monti and Mulder (n 154) 642 (citing Policy Instruction of 5 October 2016 (Official documents Stcrt 2016, 52945)).

involves broad-based consultation of interested stakeholders and a demonstration of the expected positive effects of the accord.[182]

However, as the previous discussion illustrates, there is continuity between private initiatives (steered by regulatory agencies) and the crystallisation of the need and appropriate form of public regulation.[183] The regulatory knowledge gap identified by Schinkel and Spigel can be supplied by an experimentalist framework, acknowledging that both public and private actors operate subject to the scope condition of uncertainty, as well as the fact that a private regulatory scheme may be subverted to private interests.[184] In fact, in the light of the above challenges, as an alternative to assigning the task to the ACM or to state regulation, the Dutch Social and Economic Council suggested clarifying the relevant 'public interest' involved in sustainability initiatives and pursuing them via 'conditioned self-regulation'.[185] The relevant public interests could include the protection of a competitive and open market infrastructure which delivers benefits for consumers and is not a guise for protectionism,[186] as well as the promotion of sustainability improvements (clarifying the sustainability interests involved, such as continuity of supply, health or environmental benefits).[187] In an experimentalist framework, such self-regulation is conditioned not only on the definition of the framework objectives and inclusive participation in the design of an accord, but also on the formalisation of monitoring and peer review mechanisms, through which affected parties – consumers, civil society or producers with alternative production techniques – can both signal the effects of the accord and propose modifications.

VI. Conclusion

In this chapter we have examined the choice of competition enforcement technique from the perspective of experimentalist governance, given that the scope conditions of uncertainty and the limits of hierarchical enforcement are relevant to the relationship between a competition (or regulatory) authority and its target undertakings. One aim was to show that experimentalist governance can

[182] ibid 643.

[183] See G Berk, 'From Collective Action to Collaborative Learning: Developmental Association in Commercial Printing' in *Louis D Brandeis and the Making of Regulated Competition* (Cambridge, Cambridge University Press, 2009) (on the role of competition authorities in establishing and diffusing collaborative learning among competitive producers).

[184] Sabel and Simon (n 64).

[185] Bos, Belt and Feindt (n 166) 24.

[186] See Monti and Mulder (n 154) 651–55.

[187] See M Vestager, 'Competition and Sustainability' (GCLC Conference on Sustainability and Competition Policy, Brussels, 24 October 2019), http://web.archive.org/web/20191129200523/https://ec.europa.eu/commission/commissioners/2014-2019/vestager/announcements/competition-and-sustainability_en.

rationalise and incorporate various flexible approaches for regulating markets that rely on collaboration, self-regulation and dynamic adjustment. The common thread running through the cases discussed is that they involve competition authorities assessing the consumer as well as wider social benefits of innovations, which either due to network effects or the need for coordination may attenuate competitive rivalry. As Ford has argued, assessing whether market-based innovations create any benefits can be difficult,[188] which in turn means that any technocratic effort to assess net social welfare effects of such innovations would be largely indeterminate, particularly if such evaluation considers multiple public policy objectives.[189]

Neither regulating through litigation nor through technocratic tools solves that problem. Faced with the need to oversee such innovations, competition authorities could become the arbiters of the public interest or even ethics through technocratic means, however limited and crude such means are.[190] Alternatively, competition authorities can act to diagnose problems in the operation of markets, including insufficient discipline by rivals, collaborators and users, the salience of non-economic objectives (or values), as well as the operation and limits of specialised regulatory frameworks. In the face of such diagnosis, competition authorities can also open the regulatory dialogue with undertakings and other stakeholders to identify provisional solutions, including relatively less intrusive ones (such as those that re-activate market discipline by consumers, by enhancing their knowledge and engagement either as market actors or as citizens), as well as solutions that allow a plurality of market institutions to subsist. Experimentalist monitoring and peer review of the implementation of adopted solutions can also identify the need for more intrusive (as opposed to more punitive) measures through either remedial modifications or the creation of new regulatory frameworks.

[188] Ford, *Innovation and the State* (2017).

[189] Sabel and Simon (n 64) 27.

[190] This concern was expressed by the Dutch Bar Association in response to the Dutch Ministry's proposed rule to delegate to the ACM the oversight of sustainability initiatives. See Bos, Belt and Feindt (n 166) 24.

3

Peer Review in Experimentalist Market Regulation

As we observed in the previous chapters, experimentalist governance involves a move away from legal enforcement techniques and allows a considerable degree of discretion for lower-level units – including both authorities and target undertakings – to fashion problem-solving remedies. As a result, in the absence of relatively clear stable legal rules that provide guidance to undertakings, while simultaneously ensuring the accountability of enforcement authorities (following the transmission-belt model of public regulation), experimentalist governance relies on other mechanisms to ensure that regulatory action is both effective and accountable. In particular, peer review is typically regarded as a key element of experimentalist governance. In this chapter, we will explore how experimentalist peer review can be used both as an input into regulatory decision-making and as a form of oversight and monitoring, thus contributing to both the efficacy and accountability of regulatory authorities. However, the mere presence of some form of peer review in the regulatory architecture does not necessarily make the regime experimentalist. As such, one of the aims of this chapter is to distinguish different forms and functions of peer review drawing both on the existing scholarly literature on global governance and the practice of using peer-review mechanisms in competition law and market regulation in the EU. Picking up on a persistent theme, a key distinction we will draw is between the use of peer review as a tool of experimentalist learning through regulatory innovation and its use as a mechanism of informal convergence or technocratic governance. At the same time, we will also observe that in the face of uncertainty and the limits of hierarchical enforcement, peer-review mechanisms that were not necessarily designed as experimentalist may be transformed or combined to assemble an experimentalist governance regime.

The different functionalities of peer review of agency decisions that we will outline have different efficacy and legitimacy implications, not least because they afford different opportunities for input by affected stakeholders and modalities of interaction with legal and political forms of decision-making that frame and constrain regulatory action. The more traditional understanding of peer review is as a governance mechanism used by closed communities as guardians of their specialist disciplinary knowledge, such as scientific and scholarly communities.[1] When this governance mechanism is incorporated into regulatory decision-making, a crucial question to consider is whether it provides a form of agency escape[2] from oversight (through epistemic closure) or whether it can either substitute or even complement legislative, executive and judicial control of the market-regulatory apparatus.

To answer the above questions, this chapter begins by developing a typology of the functions of transnational peer review in regulatory governance by drawing on the global and EU governance literature. The typology developed will be based on how peer review influences the choice of enforcement technique, the making of normative or policy trade-offs, as well as the kind of oversight it provides over agency decisions, so as to conceptually distinguish the experimentalist from other possible peer review functionalities. In section II, we will examine the ways in which peer-review mechanisms have been formalised in EU competition law and market regulation architectures. In section III, we demonstrate how different peer-review mechanisms may be transformed and assembled into a form of experimentalist review. We will revisit the question of the interaction of peer review and other forms of agency oversight in Chapter 4, while we will also examine the use of peer review in transnational regulatory networks beyond the EU in Chapter 5.

I. The Forms and Functions of Peer Review

Scholarly interest in regulatory peer review has followed the insertion of such review mechanisms in different regulatory settings, particularly where regulation is highly specialised and dependent on scientific or other specialist knowledge.[3] In such settings, scholars have both observed the incorporation of peer review[4] and made proposals for borrowing this governance tool – used by communities of specialised knowledge – into regulation.[5] Apart from the use of regulatory peer

[1] *cf* T Gundersen, 'Scientists as Experts: A Distinct Role?' (2018) 69 *Studies in History and Philosophy of Science* 52.

[2] S Wilks, 'Agency Escape: Decentralization or Dominance of the European Commission in the Modernization of Competition Policy?' (2005) 18 *Governance* 431.

[3] G Dimitropoulous, 'Compliance through Collegiality: Peer Review in International Law' (2015) 37 *Loyola Los Angeles International and Comparative Law Review* 275; T Conzelmann, 'Beyond the Carrot and the Stick: State Reporting Procedures in the WTO and the OECD' in J Joachim et al (eds), *International Organizations and Policy Implementation* (New York, Routledge, 2008).

[4] See, eg, T Conzelmann, 'The Politics of Peer Reviewing: Comparing the OECD and the EU' in T Bloom and S Vanhoonacker (eds), *The Politics of Information: The Case of the European Union* (London, Palgrave Macmillan, 2014); C de la Porte, 'Is the Open Method of Coordination Appropriate for Organising Activities at European Level in Sensitive Policy Areas?' (2002) 8 *European Law Journal* 38.

[5] See, eg, JB Ruhl and J Salzman, 'In Defense of Regulatory Peer Review' (2006) 84 *Washington University Law Review* 1.

review in the EU discussed later in this chapter, this mechanism has also been widely adopted in transnational regulatory networks (TRNs) after having been apparently pioneered by the OECD.[6] Thus, recent efforts to cope with important shared global challenges, including that of strengthening the global financial architecture in the face of crisis[7] or climate change,[8] as well as money laundering and terrorism,[9] have used variants of transnational peer review of both general policy-making and administrative decision-making at the national level.

A. Peer Review as a Tool of Informal Transnational Convergence

According to scholars of TRNs, a key advantage of such networks for international cooperation is their relative informality, affording them the flexibility to respond to emergent regulatory challenges, while allowing regulatory officials to learn from each other through more direct channels of communication. In particular, Slaughter argued that TRNs can be more effective at establishing cross-border regulatory cooperation precisely because they do not rely on formal enforcement.[10] On this view, informal mechanisms – such as peer pressure, reputation and socialisation – are more effective at promoting cooperation among regulators by contrast to the glacial, state-based and typically voluntary formal enforcement mechanisms under international law.[11]

To the extent that TRNs are seen as a vehicle for soft convergence, incorporating peer review in network deliberations can reinforce the informal mechanisms identified above. Transnational peer reviews could lead to more direct horizontal diffusion of best practices, including both rules and enforcement methods, among like-minded regulatory peers. In order for peer pressure, reputation and socialisation to be effective in ensuring compliance with common norms, regulatory networks require a mechanism through which the actions and decisions

[6] F Pagani, 'Peer Review as a Tool for Co-operation and Change: An Analysis of an OECD Working Method' (2002) 11 *African Security Review* 15. While the OECD is an international organisation, it imposes few formal obligations on Member States and emphasises mutual learning and voluntary convergence.

[7] See, eg, Financial Stability Board, *Charter of the Financial Stability Board* (2012), art 6.1; Financial Stability Board, *FSB Framework for Strengthening Adherence to International Standards* (2010).

[8] See, eg, UNFCCC, 'The Multilateral Assessment Process under the International Assessment and Review Process', COP Decision 1/CP.16; AR Douvan and G Castaldi, 'The G20 Peer Review of Fossil Fuel Subsidies' in MV Ezcurra et al (eds), *Environmental Fiscal Challenges for Cities and Transport* (Cheltenham, Edward Elgar).

[9] R Bossong, 'Peer Reviews in the Fight against Terrorism: A Hidden Dimension of European Security Governance' (2012) 47 *Cooperation and Conflict* 519.

[10] AM Slaughter, *A New World Order* (Princeton, Princeton University Press, 2004).

[11] ibid; D Zaring (2005) 'Informal Procedure, Hard and Soft, in International Administration' (2005) 5 *Chicago Journal of International Law* 547.

of participating authorities can be made observable to their peer agencies, and characterised as compliant or not with commonly identified best practices.[12] Thus, even without having any legally binding effects, peer review can provide a mechanism of mutual observability and collegial pressure that enhances soft convergence to best practice within regulatory networks.

For reasons that were discussed in Chapter 1, the use of peer review in aid of informal governance in regulatory networks ought not to be regarded as a form of experimentalist governance for a number of reasons. The focus of peer review in many TRNs (as we will see in Chapter 5) may be on the harmonisation or convergence of rules and regulatory practices, which may have precisely the opposite effect to the experimentalist objective of tailoring and innovation as a response to heterogeneous local conditions and a dynamic enforcement environment.[13] Network deliberations about harmonisation or convergence are typically focused on the norms or analytical tools applied by agencies rather than on follow-up of the design and actual effects of specific interventions. As such, peer review focused on convergence may rely on achieving consensus, which is more likely if the participants to a group deliberation are like-minded.[14] Contrary to some interpretations, experimentalism does not require regulatory consensus.

Finally, the use of peer review as a mechanism of informal regulatory convergence raises significant legitimacy and accountability problems. To the extent that cooperation or convergence deliberations in TRNs typically mix normative questions with those of enforcement technique, they provide an opaque channel through which transnational norms can affect local decision-making. Sceptics about TRNs have observed that the efficacy of transnational regulatory cooperation can be impeded by national actors – legislators, the executive or judges – that define, oversee and supervise the activities of regulatory agencies and do not participate in TRNs. But if transnational peer review directly influences the way in which national agencies exercise regulatory discretion, this may be regarded as a form of agency escape from domestic oversight. The latter is an important concern where the open texture of applicable domestic rules and the fact-intensive nature of decision-making, as in competition law, leave considerable scope for agency discretion when deciding individual cases.

Thus, as in other settings, informal cooperation mechanisms are faced with an apparent efficacy-legitimacy trade-off: if regulatory network efficacy – in terms of achieving convergent decision-making by agency officials – depends

[12] Y Svetiev, 'The Limits of Informal International Law: Enforcement, Norm-Generation, and Learning in the ICN' in J Pauwelyn, R Wessel and J Wouters (eds), *Informal International Lawmaking* (Oxford, Oxford University Press, 2012); see also GK Hadfield and BR Weingast, 'What is Law? A Coordination Account of the Characteristics of Legal Order' (2010) 4 *Journal of Legal Analysis* 471.

[13] *cf* WE Kovacic, 'Achieving Better Practices in the Design of Competition Policy Institutions' (2005) 50 *Antitrust Law Journal* 511.

[14] J Elster, 'Norms' in P Hedström and P Bearman (eds), *Oxford Handbook of Analytical Sociology* (Oxford, Oxford University Press, 2009).

on informality and flexibility and bypassing of national oversight, this raises legitimacy problems.[15] Such legitimacy problems are compounded by the fact that some local stakeholders, such as diffuse interest groups and civil society actors, might find it more difficult to access and influence transnational regulatory forums compared to domestic rule-making or the political or judicial process. As a result, transnational (including EU) peer deliberations may be disproportionately influenced by representatives of industry and other concentrated interests, which appreciate the salience of regulatory networks and therefore direct resources to influence their deliberations.[16]

B. Peer Review as Technocratic Trustee Governance

In the EU, the use of regulatory networks and peer review has often been characterised as a tool of informal or soft convergence,[17] particularly given its earlier incorporation into policy areas where the EU had no formal competences.[18] However, still within the broad paradigm of informal convergence, networked governance has come to have a more specific interpretation in the context of EU market regulation as a form of trustee governance.

A number of authors have noted that the regulation of the EU internal market has proceeded through 'agencification'[19] at both the Member State and EU levels. At the Member State level, the creation of regulatory authorities separate and independent from political decision-makers and industry is now often mandated by EU law. In seeking to fulfil their new mandates and implement EU law obligations domestically, such national authorities began to form informal groups 'to share experiences and points of view', as well as 'cooperate and exchange best practice', such as the Independent Regulators Group in electronic communications[20] or the Council of European Energy Regulators in energy. Groupings of national regulators were also encouraged or sponsored by the Commission, such as the Committee

[15] See generally PH Verdier, 'Transnational Regulatory Networks and Their Limits' (2009) 31 *Yale Journal of International Law* 113.

[16] S Picciotto, 'Networks in International Economic Integration: Fragmented States and the Dilemmas of Neo-liberalism' (1996) 17 *Northwestern Journal of International Law and Business* 1014.

[17] D Hodson and I Maher, 'The Open Method as a New Mode of Governance: The Case of Soft Economic Policy Co-ordination' (2001) 39 *Journal of Common Market Studies* 719.

[18] For example, peer review was used as part of the Open Method of Coordination in the approximation of social and employment policy. See J Zeitlin and P Pochet (eds), *The Open Method of Co-ordination in Action: The European Employment and Social Inclusion Strategies* (Brussels, Peter Lang AG, 2012).

[19] E Chiti, 'Decentralisation and Integration into the Community Administrations: A New Perspective on European Agencies' (2004) 10 *European Law Journal* 402; M Everson, 'Independent Agencies: Hierarchy Beaters?' (1995) 1 *European Law Journal* 180.

[20] N Boeger and J Corkin, 'How Regulatory Networks Shaped Institutional Reform under the EU Telecoms Framework' (2012) 14 *Cambridge Yearbook of European Legal Studies* 49.

of European Securities Regulators (CESR) in finance.[21] Over time, such groupings of regulators have become formalised or even formally incorporated into the EU regulatory architecture as networks (the ECN), 'bodies' of sectoral regulators (the Body of European Regulators for Electronic Communications (BEREC)) or EU-level agencies (the Agency for the Cooperation of Energy Regulators (ACER) or the European Securities and Markets Authority (ESMA)). This process has been accompanied by formalisation in EU law of peer review for the practices, decisions and even remedies adopted by both EU and national regulators, which we will discuss in more detail below.

Agencification at the national level and the networking of agencies at the EU level could be understood as a vehicle for improving compliance with EU law and administrative efficiency.[22] At the same time, agencification, agency networking and peer review also enhance the role of non-majoritarian institutions in market regulation.[23] To the extent that transnational peer input is consequential in the work of national authorities, it further isolates them from influence and control by national actors, including governments, legislatures or courts, which are seen to supply them with democratic legitimacy or to ensure the accountable exercise of their powers and discretion.[24]

To legitimate this process of regulatory autonomisation or self-sufficiency, Majone[25] has argued that specialised non-majoritarian regulators of the EU internal market cannot be understood based on standard theories of delegation, but as 'trustees' for a defined aspect of the public interest: the efficient operation of the internal market. Such authorities are deliberately isolated from direct political control as a way of ensuring that they build expertise necessary for their regulatory tasks, while stabilising policy commitments to alleviate time-inconsistency problems in market regulation. On this view, transnational networking of like-minded regulatory officials enhances the trustee role of market regulatory agencies by expanding the pool of expertise, while building professionalism and a common set of norms, which facilitates the adoption of best regulatory practice and acts as a further buffer against political interference.[26]

Conceiving the role of competition and market agencies as technocratic trustees is intended to attenuate legitimacy concerns about any convergence effects of peer review discussed above. Maggetti explains that the 'normative justification for

[21] A Ottow, 'Europeanization of the Supervision of Competitive Markets' (2012) 18 *European Public Law* 191.

[22] Chiti (n 19).

[23] M Egeberg and J Trondal, 'National Agencies in the European Administrative Space: Government Driven, Commission Driven or Networked?' (2009) 87 *Public Administration* 779.

[24] *cf* Everson (n 19).

[25] G Majone, 'Two Logics of Delegation: Agency and Fiduciary Relations in EU Governance' (2001) 2 *European Union Politics* 103.

[26] This apparently mimics the 'new approach' for the integration of the goods market via technical standardisation, also based on the premise of separability of technical issues (such as inter-operability or safety) from political ones.

legitimizing regulatory governance by independent agencies is, first and foremost, supposed to derive directly from [their] separateness from politics and organised interests'.[27] However, as Majone has acknowledged, with reference to the example of EU competition law, the trustee account of market agencies assumes that there is a workable separation between ordinary cases appropriate for technocratic decision-making (on the basis of economic or enforcement efficiency criteria) and cases unsuitable for technocrats (such as those involving distributive effects and policy goal trade-offs). When this boundary is traversed – which according to Majone occurs in exceptional cases that raise broader economic and social implications and that cannot (or should not) be made by specialist experts – such cases ought to be rerouted through transparent and costly procedures to political or even judicial actors.[28]

On the trustee account, ensuring an independent agency's compliance with best practices in market regulation through peer review can be both effective and legitimate. However, such a conclusion only follows so long as: (i) the distinction between technical questions of efficiency and political questions involving normative choices is operable in a significant set of cases; (ii) there is a mechanism to bring the exceptional cases to the attention of non-technocratic bodies; and (iii) such non-technocratic bodies are capable *and* willing to deal with such cases.[29]

Considerable doubts have been expressed about the separability of technical and political questions that underlies the technocratic trustee as an effective and legitimate governance model.[30] As we have already seen in earlier chapters, even issues of efficient enforcement technique, such as the use of leniency to detect cartels, may not be amenable to technocratic convergence. Agencies can face uncertainty about which leniency techniques lead to cartel detection (particularly if we consider novel forms of price coordination), while also respecting normative commitments to the rule of law, including national rules of public law or evidence that guard against arbitrariness or safeguard the rights of defence. As we will see below, the formal instruments setting up EU (networked) agencies and peer-review mechanisms often seek to operationalise the policy-technique distinction as a way of bootstrapping the legitimacy of non-majoritarian decision-making to the goal of an open, competitive and efficient internal market.[31] However, if the

[27] M Maggetti, 'Legitimacy and Accountability of Independent Regulatory Agencies: A Critical Review' (2010) 2 *Living Reviews in Democracy* 1, 2.

[28] G Majone, 'State, Market, and Regulatory Competition in the European Union: Lessons for the Integrating World Economy' in A Moravcsik (ed), *Centralization or Fragmentation? Europe Facing the Challenges of Deepening, Diversity, and Democracy* (New York, Council on Foreign Relations, 1998).

[29] *cf* PH Shuck, *Why Government Fails So Often* (Princeton, Princeton University Press, 2014); M Thatcher, 'The Third Force? Independent Regulatory Agencies and Elected Politicians in Europe' (2005) 18 *Governance* 347.

[30] See generally A Eriksen, 'Political Values in Independent Agencies' *Regulation and Governance* (forthcoming).

[31] In fact, it has been argued that being trustees of the competitive market is the only constitutionally permissible function of the Commission and NCAs in enforcing EU competition law. See E Loozen, 'Strict Competition Enforcement and Welfare: A Constitutional Perspective Based on Article 101 TFEU and Sustainability' (2019) 56 *Common Market Law Review* 1265.

scope conditions of uncertainty and the limits of hierarchy make it difficult to identify any technocratic consensus about best practices applicable across different contexts, peer exchange about current enforcement practices can provide a stepping stone to experimentalist governance. Such peer review can reveal a menu of available regulatory techniques, without necessarily leading to convergence across different jurisdictions or market contexts.

C. Peer Review as Scientific Input

Peer review can also be used as a mechanism for scientific input into regulatory decision-making. As Ruhl and Salzman explain:

> Just as scientific peer review involves independent evaluation of scientific research, regulatory peer review refers to the outside evaluation of an administrative agency's compilation, selection, or use of scientific data to support a proposed regulatory decision.[32]

The argument is that if peer review is fundamental in scientific practice, such peer review should be used in regulatory decision-making that is based at least in part on scientific expertise, such as food safety, pharmaceuticals and medical devices.[33] In those settings, peer review can be used to strengthen or test the scientific basis of agency decision-making. Just as in the technocratic function above, the legitimacy of this form of peer review would hinge on a robust distinction between facts and norms: scientific peer review input is aimed at distilling the state of scientific knowledge on a specific issue, which then forms part of the factual basis for an agency's decision (consistent with policy choices presumably made beforehand by political actors).[34] While clearly not a substitute for judicial or political oversight, incorporating scientific peer review could aid the oversight of agency decision-making to the extent that it distinguishes the (factual) scientific basis from the choices made by agencies in reaching decisions, thus also identifying areas for appropriate deference to administrators.

Scientific peer review can also be transnational so as to broaden access to scientific expertise not only outside the deciding agency itself, but also outside its own jurisdiction. The expansion of available scientific expertise through transnational peer review can be particularly important for under-resourced agencies from smaller jurisdictions. Agencies sometimes resort to external scientific expertise informally, and transnational peer review can be a way to both broaden and formalise such input and make it more transparent. The scientific committees and

[32] See, eg, Ruhl and Salzman (n 5) 6.
[33] ibid 6–7.
[34] *cf* Gundersen (n 1).

panels of the European Food Safety Authority (EFSA)[35] as well as the European Chemicals Agency (ECHA)[36] are charged with providing scientific advice to regulatory authorities by drawing on transnational scientific expertise as a prelude to decision-making. Some authors have suggested that even in EU networks tasked with competition regulation, such as the ECN, social scientific expertise – and in particular economics – provides the main basis of deliberations.[37]

To the extent that scientific peer review and input is 'conducted prior to the agency's final decision by qualified, independent experts',[38] such review is not in itself experimentalist. However, there is no reason in principle why scientific peer review input should lead to normative or even enforcement convergence: it may clarify the scientific basis for decision-making, but leave enforcement and normative choices to the deciding agency subject to the ordinary channels of review. Concerns over the legitimacy of transnational scientific peer review arise when the scope of the scientific input is expanded so as to conceal normative choices and/or where uncertainty in the scientific field itself goes unacknowledged.[39] This is not least because the scope condition of uncertainty affects scientific just as much as regulatory knowledge. Thus, while the use of scientific peer review and input does not in itself amount to experimentalist governance, it can be consistent with experimentalism: by identifying the state of scientific knowledge – including scientific uncertainty – relevant to regulatory decision-making, it can provide a reason for formalising experimentalist mechanisms.[40]

D. Peer Review as Transnational Administrative Law

Transnational peer review could also have an administrative law function by focusing on the decision-making procedures of the reviewed authority. In their seminal contribution on the emergence of global administrative law (GAL), Kingsbury, Krisch and Stewart[41] identified at least five areas of regulatory decision-making in

[35] A Alemanno, 'The European Food Safety Authority at Five' (2008) *European Food and Feed Law Review* 2, 9–10; A Szajkowska and BMJ van der Meulen, 'Science-Based Governance? EU Food Regulation Submitted to Risk Analysis' in M Fenwick, SV Uytsel and S Wrbka (eds), *Networked Governance, Transnational Business and the Law* (Berlin, Springer, 2014).

[36] E Korkea-Aho, *Adjudicating New Governance: Deliberative Democracy in the European Union* (Abingdon, Routledge, 2015) 114–15.

[37] DJ Gerber, 'Two Forms of Modernization in European Competition Law' (2007) 31 *Fordham International Law Journal* 1235, for instance, has argued that economics provides the common language for the operation of the ECN.

[38] Ruhl and Salzman (n 5).

[39] *cf* C Ossege, 'Driven by Expertise and Insulation? The Autonomy of European Regulatory Agencies' (2015) 3 *Politics and Governance* 101.

[40] See, eg, K Biedenkopf, 'EU Chemicals Regulation: Extending its Experimentalist Reach' in J Zeitlin (ed), *Extending Experimentalist Governance? The European Union and Transnational Regulation* (Oxford, Oxford University Press, 2015).

[41] B Kingsbury, N Krisch and RB Stewart, 'The Emergence of Global Administrative Law' (2005) 68 *Law and Contemporary Problems* 15.

transnational administrative space, including: (i) administration by supranational organisations; (ii) administration through transnational networks of regulatory officials; (iii) distributed transnational administration by national agencies; (iv) administration by hybrid public-private arrangements; and (v) administration outsourced to private institutions. As they argue, such regulatory activity may often fall outside established national oversight mechanisms, in turn producing an accountability deficit. The need for legitimation of such decision-making can lead to the emergence of GAL mechanisms, including rules and procedures that enhances the accountability of transnational administration through ensuring compliance with administrative law principles and values, such as transparency, participation, rationality and legality. These administrative law criteria traditionally limit administrative overreach and protect both the rule of law and individual rights.

The literature on GAL was sometimes implicitly based on the transposition of national – or even US models – of administrative control to transnational regulatory spaces.[42] Review by regulatory peers from other jurisdictions can, by contrast, provide a uniquely transnational oversight mechanism on the basis of administrative law principles. As Kingsbury and colleagues acknowledged, transposition of national models to transnational administration is constrained by the fact that national administrative laws are built around a core of command-and-control administration, which does not exist in a world of transnational governance. Moreover, if it is true (as was argued in Chapter 2) that even *domestic* regulatory governance is increasingly not well captured by command-and-control and strict delegation principles either, then national administrative oversight of regulators may be aided by transnational peer review that not only shines a light on agency decision-making procedures, but also compares them to those of peer agencies from other jurisdictions.[43]

Administrative decision-making by transnational actors, such as the Commission or other EU agencies, as well as distributed administration of EU law by national regulators or private bodies (such as standard-setting organisations) are quite common in EU market regulation. As we have foreshadowed in Chapter 2 and will elaborate further in the next chapter, public law oversight by EU and national courts can itself be constrained where agencies engage in novel enforcement mechanisms focused on problem-solving rather than rule violations. Moreover, regulatory action of a mixed or multi-level nature, such as through EU networks and networked agencies, may fall within the interstices of oversight and control between the national and EU levels. In such circumstances, transnational peer review can provide either a substitute or a complement to

[42] DC Esty, 'Good Governance at the Supranational Scale: Globalizing Administrative Law' (2006) 115 *Yale Law Journal* 1490; RB Stewart, 'US Administrative Law: A Model for Global Administrative Law?' (2005) 68 *Law and Contemporary Problems* 63. See also A von Bogdandy et al (eds), *The Exercise of Public Authority by International Institutions* (Berlin, Springer, 2010).

[43] Maggetti (n 27) 4. See also ch 4.

traditional forms of administrative oversight. For example, writing on the basis of the experiences of market regulatory agencies and EU regulatory networks, Ottow has argued that legality, independence, transparency, effectiveness and responsibility can be identified as key principles for 'good agency behaviour'.[44] These – or similar – criteria about the organisation and decision-making procedures of agencies could themselves be used as part of EU peer evaluations.[45]

If transnational peer review is based on administrative law criteria, it would raise different questions about efficacy and legitimacy compared to the other peer review functions described. On the one hand, it could be argued that since public law review criteria are chiefly procedural, they raise fewer legitimacy concerns since they leave the substantive decisions and choices in the hands of locally embedded authorities.[46] Further, given that peer review is usually conducted by other authority officials, the adaptation of administrative law criteria through peer review need not lead to the ossification of regulatory practice as judicial review is sometimes said to do.[47] At the same time, however, if peer review based on administrative law criteria is conducted by officials from agencies with similar mandates, it may be viewed as inadequate discipline on regulatory discretion. After all, peer agency officials at both the national and EU levels may be more focused on preserving a broader scope for regulatory discretion, as opposed to safeguarding the rule of law and individual rights.[48]

Peer review focused purely on agency compliance with administrative law procedural criteria would not be characterised as experimentalist in itself. However, transnational peer review based on administrative law criteria to ensure transparency, participation and reason-giving can support experimentalist frameworks, since such review can shine a light on both the kind of input received by the deciding agency as well as the methodologies and reasons underlying their decisions. Justification obligations about how stakeholder or expert input has been taken into account can also reveal the significance of the scope conditions of uncertainty and enforcement constraints in agency decision-making, thus leading to the formalisation of mechanisms for broad consultation not only in decision-making, but also in implementation monitoring.

[44] A Ottow, *Market and Competition Authorities: Good Agency Principles* (Oxford, Oxford University Press, 2015).

[45] See, eg, ECN+ Directive (Directive (EU) 2019/1), arts 3 (fundamental rights safeguards) and 11(3) (legality and proportionality of interim measures). Also, a number of the recommendations developed by the ECN for its member authorities focus on procedural good administration requirements.

[46] Observance with procedural criteria can, of course, have a significant impact on substantive decisions, including in particular on the way in which different interests are considered and weighed in regulatory enforcement decisions. See ch 2.

[47] See, eg, RB Stewart, 'Administrative Law in the Twenty-First Century' (2013) 78 *New York University Law Review* 437.

[48] See also M Busuioc, *European Agencies: Law and Practices of Accountability* (Oxford, Oxford University Press, 2013).

E. Peer Review in Experimentalist Governance

The above discussion underscores the point that review of agency decision-making by regulatory peers from other jurisdictions can serve different functions, and as such the mere presence of a peer-review mechanism does not in itself identify an experimentalist governance architecture. In experimentalist governance, peer review is a mechanism for promoting disciplined policy innovation through tailoring rather than one that ensures convergence in substantive decision-making towards technocratic best practice through informal peer pressure. Experimentalist recursive governance can arise where decision-makers acknowledge uncertainty about the means through which to achieve the desired policy outcomes and their limited capability to enforce through hierarchical means. Such uncertainty – even in highly technical fields of market regulation – can result from an absence of scientific or expert consensus, or due to decision-makers' doubts about how certain implementation techniques can be transplanted into settings with different local circumstances or about how to cope with unpredictable market dynamics (such as technological developments).

Treating lower-level discretion as both inevitable and desirable in such cases, experimentalist peer review is a mechanism of holding implementing agents (whether authorities or firms) accountable. In return for the autonomy afforded to innovate in developing regulatory solutions and remedies, implementing agents are required to justify such solutions to their regulatory peers by reference to the state of scientific knowledge, existing regulatory best practices and the local circumstances or market dynamics they are faced with. Notwithstanding a tendency in the literature to assimilate the different functionalities of transnational peer review outlined here, the present discussion suggests a number of key distinctions. First, experimentalist peer review is focused on both the *design* and the *effects* of concrete problem-solving interventions. This requires transnational or EU networks as well as national authorities to develop mechanisms for monitoring and evaluating the effects of interventions, which is a challenging discipline. Second, to stimulate policy innovation and contextualisation, the deliberative discourse in experimentalist peer review ought not to be fixed on normative convergence, whether through the adoption of certain legislative texts or the verification of the use of certain analytical or enforcement practices by a regulatory authority.[49] Third, to perform an experimentalist function, peer review should not be closed to participation for the regulatory (epistemic) community only, but creates openings for participation by stakeholders or parties affected by regulatory interventions.

[49] Y Svetiev, 'Scaling Experimentalism: From Convergence to Informed Divergence in Transnational Competition Policy' in J Zeitlin (ed), *Extending Experimentalist Governance? The European Union and Transnational Regulation* (Oxford, Oxford University Press, 2015).

In other words, the requirements of participation and consultation in experimentalist governance extend all the way through the problem-solving and remedial monitoring stages, rather than being limited to interest representation in *ex ante* rule-making or expert input prior to taking a decision. This underscores the point that experimentalist peer review is not a self-governance mechanism for a closed epistemic community. As such, while collegiality, professionalism, reputation and other informal bonds of trust may facilitate inter-agency cooperation and convergence, they can also be an impediment to experimentalist peer governance to the extent that such collegiality favours consensus and blunts searching review and constructive input.[50] In fact, stakeholder participation in review frameworks can be one way to disrupt a tendency towards consensus and convergence.

As will be shown below, peer-review mechanisms have now been incorporated into many governance frameworks for EU market regulation, though such reviews follow apparently heterogeneous operational forms. As a result, any particular peer review framework may pursue a mixture of the functionalities and techniques identified above depending on the conduct and criteria for review and the level of stakeholder participation. Importantly, however, unlike more traditional forms of judicial review or ministerial oversight of regulatory agencies at the national or EU level, given that the peer review formats discussed below are relatively new, they are also less rigid. As such, there is greater freedom for participants to transform the peer review formats in response to identified problems and limitations of their operation. To the extent that we argued that some of the peer review functionalities identified above are generally consistent with experimentalist market regulation, different review mechanisms may also be combined to assemble an experimentalist regime.[51]

II. Formalising Peer Review in EU Market Regulation

As already mentioned, peer review as a structured form of mutual exchange and learning across jurisdictions was incorporated into EU governance as part of the Open Method of Coordination (OMC) in areas where the EU had no formal competences such as social[52] or research policy.[53] In competition law and market

[50] N Stame, 'The European Project, Federalism and Evaluation' (2008) 14 *Evaluation* 117, 130; *cf* Dimitropolous (n 3).

[51] See C Overdevest and J Zeitlin, 'Assembling an Experimentalist Regime: Transnational Governance Interactions in the Forest Sector' (2014) 8 *Regulation & Governance* 22.

[52] BH Casey and M Gold, 'Peer Review of Labour Market Programmes in the European Union: What Can Countries Really Learn from One Another?' (2005) 12 *Journal of European Public Policy* 23.

[53] N McGuinness and C O'Carroll, 'Benchmarking Europe's Lab Benches: How Successful Has the OMC Been in Research Policy?' (2010) 48 *Journal of Common Market Studies* 293.

regulation, by contrast, the (often newly established) national agencies tasked with implementing EU mandates started creating informal fora for peer exchange, either with or without the Commission's participation. These informal regulatory clubs provided a stepping stone for the creation of EU networks and networked agencies as part of the EU regulatory architecture and the formalisation of peer-review mechanisms.

The informal 'epistemic' network for communication and exchange involving the Commission's Competition Directorate and the NCAs was formalised and 'juridified' as the ECN in Regulation 1/2003.[54] Quite apart from establishing the ECN, the Modernisation Regulation also incorporated the NCAs into the decision-making procedure for cases decided under EU law through the Advisory Committee on Restrictive Practices and Dominant Positions mentioned in Chapter 1. Article 14 of the Modernisation Regulation grants the Advisory Committee a number of peer review functions. First, as a matter of course, the Commission must obtain the opinion of the Advisory Committee 'prior to the taking of any decision' under a number of provisions in the Regulation, including both violation (Article 7) and commitment (Article 9) decisions. Second, either at 'the request of a competition authority of a Member State' or 'on its own initiative', the Commission can 'include on the agenda of the Advisory Committee cases that are being dealt with by a competition authority of a Member State'.[55] Finally, an NCA can also request a referral to the Advisory Committee of cases where the Commission intends to initiate proceedings to relieve a specific NCA of its competences under Article 11(6).

The Regulation does provide limited guidance on the procedure to be followed in obtaining the Advisory Committee's opinion in the foregoing cases, though not on the scope of the Committee's review function. In performing its review of individual decisions, the Advisory Committee is 'composed of representatives of the competition authorities of the Member States'.[56] The default procedure is that the Committee is to meet and consider 'a summary of the case, an indication of the most important documents and a preliminary draft decision', having been given at least 14 days' notice.[57] In the case of Commission decisions, the Committee delivers a written opinion on the preliminary draft decision, although it does not issue formal opinions on decisions dealt with by the NCAs. No guidance is provided on who may be consulted before the Committee finalises its opinion, suggesting that it follows a relatively closed deliberation format. Some insight into the deliberations can be gauged from the final opinion, as the Committee can

[54] F Cengiz, 'Multi-level Governance in Competition Policy: The European Competition Network' (2010) 35 *European Law Review* 660.

[55] Regulation 1/2003, art 14(7).

[56] ibid art 14(2).

[57] ibid art 14(3). The procedure can also be written, although any Member State can request that a meeting be convened under art 14(4).

request the publication of its opinion on the draft decision, subject to revisions to protect legitimate business secrets.[58] The opinion of the Committee is not binding on the Commission, although the latter is obliged to take 'utmost account of the [Committee's] opinion' and to 'inform the Committee of the manner in which its opinion has been taken into account'.[59]

In the regulation of electronic communications, EU legislation has also incorporated review of decisions of regulatory agencies by peer authorities before such decisions are implemented. In particular, the electronic communications body, BEREC,[60] can review both the analytical methodologies used in decision-making and the remedies proposed by a national regulator.[61] Article 7 of the Framework Directive[62] requires NRAs to 'contribute to the development of the internal market by working with each other and with the Commission and BEREC in a transparent manner … to ensure the consistent application, in all Member States, of the [relevant legislation]' and to 'work with the Commission and BEREC to identify the types of instruments and remedies best suited to address particular types of situations'.[63] Where an NRA intends to take specified measures pursuant to the legislative package, it must notify the draft measure and the reasoning upon which it is based to other NRAs, BEREC and the Commission, which in turn have a one-month period to provide comments on the draft measure. The deciding NRA must take utmost account of any comments provided.[64]

In relation to two types of decisions taken by NRAs, the Framework Directive effectively granted the Commission a veto power if it 'considers that the draft measure would create a barrier to the single market or if it has serious doubts as to its compatibility with Community law'. These include a measure that defines a relevant market *diverging* from the definitions provided in a Recommendation adopted by the Commission[65] on defining product and service markets, as well as

[58] ibid art 14(6).

[59] ibid art 14(5).

[60] Regulation (EU) 2018/1971 of the European Parliament and of the Council of 11 December 2018 establishing the Body of European Regulators for Electronic Communications (BEREC) and the Agency for Support for BEREC (BEREC Office) (hereinafter 'BEREC Regulation'), art 3 (BEREC is tasked with ensuring the 'consistent implementation of the regulatory framework' and 'draw[s] upon the expertise' of the NRAs).

[61] Article 4(1)(c) of the BEREC Regulation lists the different types of opinions BEREC can issue. See also art 35 of the Recast Directive allowing NRAs to (voluntarily) request a peer review to examine a proposed selection procedure for radio spectrum through the Radio Spectrum Policy Group.

[62] Council Directive (EC) 2002/21 of the European Parliament and of the Council of 7 March 2002 on a common regulatory framework for electronic communications networks and services (Framework Directive) [2002] OJ L108/33; see also Council Directive (EU) 2018/1972 of the European Parliament and of the Council of 11 December 2018 establishing the European Electronic Communications Code (Recast) [2018] OJ L321/36, art 32 (hereinafter 'the Telecoms Recast Directive').

[63] Telecoms Recast Directive, art 32(2).

[64] ibid art 32(8).

[65] ibid art 64(1). To issue such a Recommendation itself requires the Commission to conduct a public consultation, including with NRAs, and to take utmost account of BEREC's opinion.

a decision whether to designate an undertaking as having market power. However, the Commission's use of the veto is conditional upon it taking 'utmost account' of an opinion issued by BEREC on the proposed measure, as well as providing a detailed and objective analysis of why it considers that the draft measure should not be adopted together with 'specific proposals for amending the draft measure'.[66] Despite such veto power, the Commission is not – as such – given the final word, as the deciding NRA has to revise its proposed measure in light of the comments and objections it has received, and the revised measure is then subjected to the same peer review procedure.

Finally, Article 7a of the Framework Directive[67] imposed peer review disciplines on any NRA decision to impose one of the regulatory remedies envisaged under the telecoms regulatory package upon a communications operator. Here too, the Commission can provide the NRA with a reasoned notification if it considers that the proposed remedy would create a barrier to the single market or otherwise has serious doubts as to the remedy's compatibility with EU law. The Article 7a procedure for reconciling differences between the NRA proposing the regulatory remedies, on the one hand, and the Commission, on the other, again gives a key role to BEREC. First, BEREC, the Commission and the proposing NRA are required to 'cooperate closely to identify the most appropriate and effective measure' consistent with the objectives of the Framework Directive, while also being obliged to 'tak[e] due account of the views of market participants and the need to ensure the development of consistent regulatory practice'.[68] Second, BEREC must issue a reasoned opinion assessing the Commission's challenge of the NRA's proposed remedy, which has to be made public and of which the Commission must take utmost account. Again, the input and review by regulatory peers provided through BEREC is not binding. The NRA need not ultimately follow the Commission's recommendation, or BEREC's opinion for that matter, though in such a case it must provide a reasoned justification for its divergence.[69]

In the field of energy, the Regulation establishing ACER tasks this agency with assisting the NRAs in performing their regulatory tasks and contributing 'to the establishment of high-quality common regulatory and supervisory practices' and 'the consistent, efficient and effective application of Union law in order to achieve the Union's climate and energy goals'. ACER is charged with a number of different functions that can be assimilated into peer review, given that the Board of Regulators, which is responsible for providing the Agency's opinions, is composed of senior representatives of all NRAs and a non-voting member of

[66] ibid art 32(5). While the Directive does not set out criteria upon which BEREC is to base its opinion, presumably the opinion evaluates the substance of the Commission's claims that the proposed measure creates an internal market barrier or is inconsistent with EU law.

[67] ibid art 33.

[68] ibid art 33(2).

[69] ibid art 33(7). See Case C-28/15 *Koninklijke KPN NV v Autoriteit Consument en Markt (ACM)* discussed in ch 4.

the Commission.[70] Such tasks include the delivery of non-binding opinions and guidelines to the EU institutions (the Parliament, Council or the Commission), as well as NRAs, transmission system operators (TSOs) and distribution system operators (DSOs).[71]

Specifically with respect to the activities of NRAs, ACER can issue decisions on 'technical issues' provided for in the energy legislative package[72] and, at the request of the Commission, it can 'make recommendations to assist regulatory authorities and market participants in sharing good practices'.[73] ACER is also provided with the power – at the request of either NRAs or the Commission – to issue non-binding opinions on matters of fact, which assess whether a decision taken by a specific NRA complies with 'the network codes and Guidelines referred to in [the directives and regulations of the energy package] *or with other relevant provisions of those directives or regulations*' (emphasis added).[74] Such opinions – characterised as a form of peer review by ACER itself[75] – can be requested by an NRA to review its own decisions and practices,[76] as well as to review those of other authorities.[77] By contrast, ACER is also given powers to make binding decisions on 'regulatory issues having effects on cross-border trade or cross-border system security which require a joint decision by at least two regulatory authorities', though only by way of default where competent NRAs have not been able to reach an agreement or make a joint request to ACER to do so.[78]

Finally, peer review has also been given a prominent role in the EU financial supervision infrastructure, particularly as EU-level supervision was enhanced following the financial crises. For instance, Article 8 of the ESMA Regulation[79]

[70] Regulation (EU) 2019/942 of the European Parliament and of the Council of 5 June 2019 establishing a European Union Agency for the Cooperation of Energy Regulators (hereinafter 'ACER Recast Regulation'), art 21.

[71] ibid arts 3–5.

[72] ibid art 6(1).

[73] ibid art 6(2).

[74] ibid art 6(5).

[75] See ACER, Agency's Opinion No 09/2015 of 23 September 2015 on the compliance of national regulatory authorities' decisions approving the methods of allocation of cross-border transmission capacity in the Central-East Region with Regulation (EC) No 714/2009 and the Guidelines on the management and allocation of available transfer capacity of interconnections between National Systems contained in Annex I thereto, https://www.acer.europa.eu/Official_documents/Acts_of_the_Agency/Pages/ANNEXES_CCR_DECISION.aspx.

[76] See, eg, ACER, Agency's Opinion No 03/2015 of 13 July 2015 on the Compliance Decision of NCC (Lithuania), https://www.acer.europa.eu/Official_documents/Acts_of_the_Agency/Opinions/Opinions/ACER%20Opinion%2003-2015.pdf.

[77] See, eg, ACER, Agency's Opinion No 09-2015 of 23 September 2015 on the compliance of NRAs' decisions approving methods of cross-border capacity allocation in the CEE region, https://www.acer.europa.eu/Official_documents/Acts_of_the_Agency/Opinions/Opinions/ACER%20Opinion%2009-2015.pdf.

[78] ACER Recast Regulation, art 6(10).

[79] Council Regulation (EU) 1095/2010 of the European Parliament and of the Council of 24 November 2010 establishing a European Supervisory Authority (European Securities and Markets Authority), amending Decision No 716/2009/EC and repealing Commission Decision 2009/77/EC [2010] OJ L331/84. Recital 22 of the Regulation emphasises that ESMA is to rely on 'highly specialised expertise'.

defines its tasks and powers includes the task 'to organise and conduct peer review analyses of competent authorities, including issuing guidelines and recommendations and identifying best practices, in order to strengthen consistency in supervisory outcomes'.[80] Article 30 sets out the objectives and mechanisms for conducting such peer reviews, mandating ESMA to develop methods that 'allow for objective assessment and comparison between the authorities reviewed'. On the basis of such reviews, ESMA can issue specific guidelines and recommendations, which the reviewed national authority 'shall endeavour to follow'. It can also identify 'best practices' for the benefit of other national authorities that may decide to adopt them. Furthermore, ESMA is to 'take into account the outcome of the peer review when developing draft regulatory technical or implementing technical standards' under the ESMA Regulation. Notably, the founding Regulation emphasises that regulatory[81] and implementing[82] technical standards 'shall be technical' and 'shall not imply strategic decisions or policy choices'.[83]

As we can see from the above survey, peer review formats have been incorporated into a number of EU market regulatory framework, either as a precondition of taking a decision or as a form of review of divergent approaches by national authorities. At the same time, however, the peer-review frameworks established in the different legislative instruments are heterogeneous in form and mandate, and do not appear to follow a common template with respect to the object, scope or criteria of review. In fact, in most instances the legislative instruments do not necessarily specify the review criteria suggesting that reviewing bodies can examine both procedural and substantive aspects of the measure or decision under consideration.

In order to understand the scope for experimentalist use of the above market regulatory peer-review mechanisms, it is worth highlighting a few of their common features. First, most if not all of the above frameworks envisage the review by regulatory peers of concrete measures or decisions proposed to be implemented by a particular agency (either at the EU or the national level), as opposed to more general informal and unstructured and abstract exchanges about norms and enforcement practices. Such review may extend to the underlying fact-finding, the analytical methodologies used to assess the problem at hand, as well as the design of a remedy to be implemented. Second, many of the legislative frameworks also impose procedural administrative law-type obligations in regulatory decision-making, such as transparency, reason-giving and consultation of affected stakeholders for national authorities, the Commission and, in some cases, the peer review bodies themselves.[84]

[80] ibid art 8(1)(e).

[81] ibid art 10.

[82] ibid art 15.

[83] See M Busuioc, 'Rule-Making by the European Financial Supervisory Authorities: Walking a Tight Rope' (2013) 19 *European Law Journal* 111; M Everson, 'A Technology of Expertise: EU Financial Services Agencies' (2012) LEQS Paper No 49, https://ssrn.com/abstract=2085233.

[84] See, eg, Telecoms Recast Directive, arts 23 and 24; ACER Recast Regulation, art 6(11).

Third, the fact that the above frameworks focus on providing *ex ante* input and review on draft decisions (ie, before their implementation) as well as the emphasis on ensuring consistent decision-making may suggest that peer review is used as a mechanism of trustee governance in order to ensure convergence to regulatory best practice. The legislative frameworks emphasise that the peer review bodies operate autonomously and on the basis of expertise, and the policy-technique distinction is specifically invoked at least in the case of ESMA peer review. In a similar vein, the EU Commission has suggested that the 'main advantage of using [EU-level] agencies is that their decisions are based on purely technical evaluations of very high quality and are not influenced by political or contingent considerations'.[85] Importantly, however, it is worth noting that the peer oversight mechanisms do not preclude and some, such as the telecoms framework, explicitly envisage divergent approaches being followed by national agencies subject to the deliberative disciplines of transparency, consultation and justification.

Finally, an experimentalist evolution of these formal peer review frameworks is made possible by the fact that most incorporate the 'no final decider' feature discussed in earlier chapters.[86] In other words, peer review opinions in the above frameworks are not binding on the reviewed agency, in the sense of directing it to a particular outcome or decision. Instead, the general obligation imposed is to take 'utmost account' of peer review opinions, which allows the reviewed authority to explain divergence from a peer recommendation or a departure from common practice – by reference, for example, to the need for tailoring to specific local conditions. As we will see below, by imposing justificatory discipline on such divergence, *ex ante* peer review can spill over into *ex post* monitoring of the effects of the intervention implemented, so as to compare outcomes across different authorities. As such, whatever the intended purpose or design of the above peer-review mechanisms when originally formalised in legislation, they may also be transformed or assembled into an experimentalist governance architecture.

III. Transformation and Assemblage: Experimentalist Peer Review in Competition Law?

In light of the typologies of form and function described at the beginning of this chapter, experimentalist peer review could be viewed as normatively desirable for a number of reasons. In particular, experimentalist peer review: (i) does not require (or assume) the separation of technical/scientific and political elements from

[85] EU Commission, 'The operating framework for the European Regulatory Agencies' COM (2002) 718 final.

[86] CF Sabel and J Zeitlin, 'Experimentalism in the EU: Common Ground and Persistent Differences' (2012) 6 *Regulation and Governance* 413, 420.

the scope of review, the separation of which in many areas of market regulation may be tenuous;[87] (ii) does not aim for strong-form harmonisation of decision-making practices, let alone identical decisions in different Member States; (iii) is permissive to innovation and tailoring to the local context and could allow the incorporation – or hybridisation – of local policy preferences as expressed by political actors; (iv) may attenuate the legitimacy concerns raised about distant transnational expertocracies because it obliges consultation of affected stakeholders both in the design of interventions and in the *ex post* monitoring of their effects.

However, experimentalist peer review is also quite demanding both for the EU-level review infrastructure and for the authorities that are subject to and that must participate in such reviews. As outlined above, an experimentalist review infrastructure requires *ex post* monitoring of the outcomes of specific interventions, including through monitoring mechanisms relatively open to input from affected stakeholders. Moreover, experimentalist governance also incorporates a mechanism of recursivity, whereby peer review of implementation experience can lead to revisions of the identified best practices of enforcement and even of the overall definition of the goals of the regulatory regime. Finally, the different authorities participating in a network must dedicate resources not only to their enforcement activities, but also to reviewing their regulatory peers' interventions both at the time of taking a decision and also following implementation.

The remainder of this chapter will focus on the mechanisms of peer review in competition law enforcement. The key object is to examine how we may trace the evolution of peer review frameworks towards experimentalist governance. Particularly as regulatory actors attempt to cope with enforcement problems in the face of the scope conditions of uncertainty and the limitations of coercive enforcement, we may observe an assemblage of review mechanisms – individually performing different functions – that together result in an experimentalist regime.[88]

A. *Ad Hoc* Peer Review: The Limits of Static and Indirect Deliberation

As competition law in the EU, and elsewhere, moved away from being a purely rule-based discipline to rely instead on modelling the effects of business conduct – including through expert input – both scholars and practitioners recognised the desirability of some form of peer review on expert input into decision-making by agencies and courts.[89] For example, informal review, such

[87] See, eg, Everson (n 83).
[88] Overdevest and Zeitlin (n 51).
[89] cf P Areeda, 'Always a Borrower: Law and Other Disciplines' (1988) *Duke Law Journal* 1029, 1036 (publishing antitrust economic expert reports in peer-reviewed journals).

as through devil's advocate input, has been used in competition decision-making by agencies on an *ad hoc* basis.[90] Apart from seeking expert review on an informal basis, agencies have also incorporated it into their internal structures. After all, the Chief Economist Unit in the Commission's Competition Directorate was itself formed after the (then) Court of First Instance assailed the Commission's economic reasoning in consecutive merger decisions. The Chief Economist Unit originally performed a variant of the scientific peer review function, essentially overseeing whether the analysis and theories of harm developed by the case team is sound from an economic point of view.[91] Subsequently, however, both lawyers and economists have been integrated into the Commission's case teams from the very outset so that the case legal analysis and the economic theories of harm essentially co-evolve as part of the investigation.

In light of the growing reliance on economic expertise, private parties in proceedings before the Commission have also sought to rely on *ad hoc* peer review to challenge the Commission's economic modelling of competitive interactions and market dynamics in establishing likely anti-competitive effects.[92] In the Outokumpu-Inoxum proposed acquisition, for example, the Commission's economic modelling endorsed by the Chief Economist Unit suggested the existence of competition concerns. As a result, the Commission requested significant divestments of assets by Outokumpu, which were said to considerably undermine the business case for the acquisition. While the legal team shepherding the merger believed that the Commission's economic modelling did not adequately capture the competitive dynamics of the market, it was apparently not willing to have an argument about the appropriateness of alternative economic models in a judicial review proceeding by challenging the decision before the EU courts. As a result, Outokumpu's legal team proposed an *ad hoc* peer review of the Commission's economic modelling by three respected and independent academic economists. The panel was to produce a peer review report on the Commission's modelling without direction or input from Outokumpu's legal team; this report was to be delivered simultaneously to both parties.

The somewhat unorthodox procedure proposed by Outokumpu's legal team sought to provide a form of scientific peer oversight on the Commission's analysis, while controlling for the hired gun (or lack of independence) problem of an expert paid by a party to the proceeding.[93] While the Commission's decision

[90] EM Fox, 'Antitrust and Institutions: Design and Change' (2010) 41 *Loyola University Chicago Law Journal* 473, 486; Y Svetiev, 'Partial Formalization of the Regulatory Network' (2010), http://ssrn.com/abstract=1564890 (with reference to an interview with an official of the South African Competition Authority, Zurich, June 2009).

[91] DJ Neven, 'Competition Economics and Antitrust in Europe' (2006) 21 *Economic Policy* 742.

[92] An attorney regularly involved in proceedings before the Commission pointed to at least two examples: *Procter & Gamble/VP Schickedanz (II)* (Case IV/M.430) Commission Decision 94/893/EC [1994] OJ L354; *Outokumpu/INOXUM* (Case COMP/M.6471) Commission Decision 2013/C312.06, paras 95–131.

[93] Areeda (n 89).

did refer to the economist experts' report, a legal representative of Outokumpu suggested that the static nature of the questions posed to the expert panel, and the absence of subsequent testing through direct deliberation, left the panel's conclusions open to misinterpretation or even misrepresentation. At best, this type of static peer review can attenuate the possible ignorance or bias in the economic assessment of the decision-maker, as well as groupthink bias in favour of the internal consensus by the case team. However, such a format of peer review by independent experts cannot eliminate the more radical forms of uncertainty where expertise itself is at its limits. In fact, the absence of the opportunity for deliberation involving not only the experts, but also the affected stakeholders, may limit the usefulness of such peer review even in terms of correcting the problems of erroneous methodology or bias.[94]

B. An Experimentalist Assemblage?

As discussed earlier, experimentalist peer review does not rely merely on scientific or regulatory experts and does not take place on an *ad hoc* basis. Instead, experimentalism relies on continuous and systematised revision, based on learning from open scrutiny of actual implementation.[95] In competition law, a few different peer-review mechanisms – some formalised in Regulation 1/2003 and others emerging spontaneously – combine to produce such an assemblage.

i. Regulatory Peer Input

The Advisory Committee on Restrictive Practices and Dominant Positions discussed earlier provides a form of systematic review of the Commission's competition decision-making by its regulatory peers.[96] However, based on our description of the formal role and institutional design of the Committee as a peer-review mechanism, it is clear that it cannot, by itself, perform the function of experimentalist peer review for a few reasons. First, as we observed, Article 14 provides for *ex ante* review of a proposed draft decision by the Commission, though its formal oversight role does not extend to reviewing the effects of the decision's

[94] For an experimentalist take on coping with uncertainty in merger decision-making, particularly in highly dynamic technology markets, see M Jennejohn, 'Innovation and the Institutional Design of Merger Control' (2015) 41 *Journal of Corporation Law* 167.

[95] CF Sabel, 'Beyond Principal-Agent Governance: Experimentalist Organizations, Learning and Accountability' in ER Engelen and SD Ho (eds), *De staat van de democratie. Democratie voorbij de staat* (Amsterdam, Amsterdam University Press, 2004).

[96] The Advisory Committee in fact existed even under the earlier Regulation 17/62, though its functions and proceedings were even more opaque. See P Larouche, *Competition Law and Regulation in European Telecommunications* (Oxford, Hart Publishing, 2000) 350.

implementation.[97] Second, as a matter of course, the Advisory Committee reviews only the Commission's decisions. While decisions by the NCAs may be placed on its agenda, the Committee does not issue a formal opinion on such decisions and in any event, discussion of NCA decisions by the Committee does not appear to be common practice.[98]

Going beyond the formal definition of its role, the actual operation of the Advisory Committee and its effect on individual decisions of the Commission, as well as on the evolution of EU competition law more generally, is not well understood. One reason for this is the relative obscurity in which the Committee operates in its review of proposed decisions, typically behind closed doors and with its members bound by obligations of professional secrecy.[99] In addition, the Committee's published opinions usually indicate general agreement with the Commission's approach and may be relatively uninformative about the nature and content of deliberations within the Committee on specific cases.[100] Thus, a study of the publicly available materials might lend support for the view that the Advisory Committee is a weak source of oversight – acting as a technocratic consensus-oriented rubber stamp – even within its limited mandate.[101]

The ability of many NCAs to effectively participate in the review process is apparently constrained by the human resources and time available to devote to reviewing the cases placed on the Committee's agenda, including the supporting documents.[102] For complex cases, this constraint may be significant even for more well-established and resourced, but particularly for smaller NCAs.[103] As a result, one national official observed that such constraints might often lead to

[97] In Case AT.39740 – *Google Search (Shopping)*, 27 June 2017, C(2017) 4444 final [105], the Commission described the Advisory Committee's opinion as 'the final stage of the procedure before the adoption of the decision', even if new market information had already been available after the Committee's deliberation in that case.

[98] B Bender, 'Experimentalist Governance in the European Competition Network' in J Bailleux and A Vauchez (eds), *Exploring the Transnational Circulation of Policy Paradigms: Law Firms, Legal Networks and the Production of Expertise in the Field of Competition Policies* (Fiesole, EUI Robert Schuman Centre, 2014). In fact, in interviews with NCA officials, some were not even aware of the possibility of discussion of a national decision by the Advisory Committee, notwithstanding art 14(7).

[99] Regulation 1/2003, art 28(2). The Committee meetings are not open to the public and this seems to be the case more generally for the peer-review mechanisms described earlier in the chapter, the proceedings of which are difficult even for academic researchers to access. See, eg, M Cantero-Gamito, 'The Private Law Dimension of the EU Regulatory Framework for Electronic Communications: Evidence of the Self-Sufficiency of European Regulatory Private Law', DPhil thesis, EUI, 2015, https://cadmus.eui.eu/bitstream/handle/1814/37647/2015_CanteroGamito.pdf.

[100] Bender, (n 98) 18 argues that the Committee's review appears to rarely result in a negative opinion or fundamental changes to the draft decision, though there are cases where the Committee's members have decided by majority, rather than consensus.

[101] ibid: 'The committee meeting itself therefore seems more of a formality.'

[102] *cf* M Busuioc, 'European Agencies and Their Boards: Promises and Pitfalls of Accountability Beyond Design' (2012) 19 *Journal of European Public Policy* 719.

[103] Quite apart from the question of staff and resources, some authorities have problems in accessing relevant expertise. A Czech official reported that the authority had difficulty finding an industrial organisation economist to work on its own case analysis.

a 'silent majority' of NCA representatives supporting the Commission's approach by default, leaving the more significant probing to be done by larger or better-resourced NCAs that can study the materials and develop an alternative view.[104] But even the interviewed official suggested that in the typical case, if it wished to influence the Commission's approach in a case, the NCA would seek to do so at an earlier stage of the proceedings and before the draft decision is considered by the Committee.[105] The conduct of deliberations thus appears to favour consensus and coherence in EU competition enforcement rather than open disagreement. Purely informal patching-up of differences behind closed doors would suggest coordination and accommodation through informal peer pressure.[106] By contrast, seeking to resolve divergences in approach to individual cases through open acknowledgement of uncertainty, broadening participation and ongoing monitoring of interventions as a way of contesting or re-examining current best practice in enforcement would tend to evidence experimentalism.

ii. Stakeholder Participation and Monitoring Implementation

Unlike the more familiar understanding of peer review as the guardian of disciplinary knowledge (whether scientific or regulatory), experimentalist peer review is not limited to oversight by closed knowledge communities.[107] Given that the Advisory Committee does not hold open hearings, in which affected stakeholders may provide input about a draft decision, nor does it continue its monitoring over the implementation and effects of reviewed decisions, a key question is whether those experimentalist functionalities exist elsewhere in the governance architecture for EU competition enforcement. In other words, in order to assemble an experimentalist regime, the Advisory Committee would need to be supplemented by a mechanism for stakeholder participation, a mechanism for monitoring implementation and a mechanism linking the experience from implementing specific decisions and remedies with the revision of enforcement rules and practices or even framework policy goals.

As discussed in the previous chapter, the commitments procedure under Article 9 of the Modernisation Regulation (and for NCAs, Article 12 of the ECN+ Directive) for directly negotiated remedies with affected undertakings is suitable

[104] *cf* N Font, 'Informal Rules and Institutional Balances on the Boards of EU Agencies' (2018) 50 *Administration & Society* 269. In fact, procedural mechanisms have been introduced in the operation of the Committee to enhance the quality and breadth of deliberation, such as assigning lead NCAs responsible for presenting each case to the Committee. This procedure could to some extent encourage participation and enhance deliberation.

[105] Bender (n 98) 17–18 (Committee meetings occur in a late stage of the proceedings).

[106] cf M Kekelekis, 'The European Competition Network (ECN): It Does Actually Work Well' (2009) *EIPA Scope* 35, http://aei.pitt.edu/12378 (suggesting the ECN working groups are a medium for informal coordination through peer pressure).

[107] S Quack, 'Expertise and Authority in Transnational Governance' in R Cotterrell and MD Mar (eds), *Authority in Transnational Legal Theory: Theorising across Disciplines* (Cheltenham, Edward Elgar, 2016).

for the experimentalist implementation of remedies under conditions of uncertainty. Much attention has been devoted to the procedural advantages and cost savings of finalising cases through this procedure, as well as the risks of capture of the authority, given the light form of judicial review for this procedure discussed in Chapter 4. However, it is worth noting that Article 9 commitment decisions are procedurally more burdensome at least at the remedial formulation stage compared to violation decisions. Specifically, the Regulation imposes a procedural requirement for 'market testing' of the proposed remedy through consultation and input from market stakeholders.

Market testing may be regarded as another form of *ex ante* peer review on the design of proposed remedies, which relies on input from the 'peers' of the target undertaking(s), including competitors, customers and consumers, given that Article 27(4) extends the right of consultation broadly to all 'interested third parties'. Like the Committee review, market testing occurs before the decision is finalised and adopted, though input is provided by parties relatively more knowledgeable about the market involved. As such, market testing has frequently led to the revision or abandonment of proposed negotiated remedies.[108]

Apart from *ex ante* review of the design of remedies, experimentalist governance also requires ongoing review of their implementation. With respect to commitment decisions again, recall our earlier mention of the Commission's practice of using monitoring trustees for the implementation of commitment-based remedies. A remedial monitor may be conceived as a compliance-verification mechanism, whereby it ensures that the monitored undertaking is respecting the obligations formalised in the decision. However, the monitoring trustee being tasked with overseeing implementation also generates a record about the effects of the remedy in the market, which might reveal either that the remedy adopted was ineffective or that it has been superseded by changed market conditions. As such, the monitoring trustee also provides a forum for channelling stakeholder input about the effects of the remedy and the Commission has explicitly envisaged that such input can lead to a re-examination of the adopted commitment remedies.[109] In such cases, the monitoring trustee acts as the implementation oversight mechanism of the experimentalist assemblage. Notably, while the Modernisation

[108] See, eg, Case C-441/07 *Commission v Alrosa Company Ltd* [2010] ECR I-5949; COMP/39230 – *Rio Tinto Alcan* AT39.230 (20 December 2012); European Commission, 'Antitrust: Commission Fines Google €2.42 billion for Abusing Dominance as Search Engine by Giving Illegal Advantage to Own Comparison Shopping Service – Factsheet', 27 June 2017, https://ec.europa.eu/commission/presscorner/detail/en/MEMO_17_1785: 'the feedback the Commission received from third parties showed that [the proposed commitments] were not effective to address the Commission's competition concerns in full'.

[109] COMP/B-1/37.966 – *Distrigaz*; COMP/39.386 – *Contrats Long Terme France (EDF)* (11 August 2010). By contrast, in the absence of a monitoring trustee in a violation decision, the infringement apparatus must be re-engaged if the remedial effects are judged unsatisfactory. See FY Chee, 'Axel Springer Unit, Others Say Google Still Playing Unfairly, Want EU to Act', *Reuters*, 28 November 2019, https://www.reuters.com/article/us-eu-alphabet-antitrust/axel-springer-unit-others-say-google-still-playing-unfairly-want-eu-to-act-idUSKBN1Y20W4.

Regulation does not mention the monitoring aspect of commitment decisions, the use of monitoring trustees is a regular feature of the Commission's practice and the ECN+ Directive requires the use of monitoring mechanisms for commitment decisions at the national level.[110]

iii. Recursivity

Finally, in an experimentalist regime, review of implementation experience for specific cases decided and remedied by different regulatory actors leads to a re-examination and reformulation of existing enforcement rules and best practice techniques, as well as the revision of the overall framework goals of the regime. Again, observing the network infrastructure for competition enforcement in the EU, we have pointed to a number of venues that allow for this type of recursivity by creating a feedback loop from monitoring actual implementation practice to the overall enforcement or normative parameters of the competition framework.

Consider first the role of the Advisory Committee, whereby Article 14 specifies that for 'discussion of individual cases', the Committee is to be composed of representatives of the NCAs, while for 'meetings in which issues other than individual cases are being discussed, an additional Member State representative competent in competition matters may be appointed'. On the one hand, this may suggest that the evaluation of decisions in individual cases is a technocratic task, which requires input from expert officials of the independent NCAs *prior* to the taking of a decision. On the other hand, given that the Regulation envisages that the Advisory Committee can discuss 'issues other than individual cases' related to policy formulation, the Committee provides a mechanism of recursivity between individual case decisions, assessment of their effects and the formulation of policy, thus supplying the link between implementation (execution) and rule-making or policy-formulation that is at the heart of experimentalist governance. Importantly, the Committee as a peer review body does not seem to fit into traditional models of separating the rule enforcement and rule-making or policy-making functions.

Apart from the Advisory Committee, as we discussed in Chapter 1, the ECN as a forum works through thematic working groups, where the participant authorities discuss implementation challenges and experiences faced transversally or in specific sectors.[111] Dekeyser and Jaspers have suggested that the working groups play an important role in handling uncertainty, allowing participants 'to develop

[110] ECN+ Directive, art 12(2). Paragraph 21 of the ECN Recommendation on Commitment Procedures lists a number of different monitoring mechanisms that have been used by authorities in such decisions; see https://ec.europa.eu/competition/ecn/ecn_recommendation_commitments_09122013_en.pdf.

[111] The working groups are not static and are formed based on identified needs. Horizontal working groups have included the cartels, advocacy, due process and chief economists' working group, while sectoral groups and sub-groups have focused on food, energy, payment systems, taxi services etc: European Competition Network, 'ECN BRIEF – A Look Inside the ECN: Its Members and its Works' (2010), https://ec.europa.eu/competition/ecn/brief/05_2010/brief_special.pdf.

common economic and legal principles for the assessment of complicated business practices, which are taking place in quickly developing markets and which are subject to evolving economic thinking'.[112] While there is no formal peer review framework for NCA decisions, national competition officials have indicated that they frequently report on specific case decisions and remedies in the ECN's thematic working groups.[113] As such, the working groups provide another mechanism of recursivity – linking review of implementation of decisions with the formulation of best practices and policy – since they have been used to contribute to the preparation of new guidance documents and legislation, including, for example, the 2009 guidelines on enforcement priorities of abuse of dominance or the 2011 guidelines on horizontal cooperation, as well as the technology transfer block exemption regulation.[114] Similarly, as we observed in the hotel booking platforms case in Chapter 1, following the adoption of a set of remedial mechanisms by different NCAs, a working group was created and specifically tasked with monitoring the implementation of remedies so as to 're-assess the competitive situation in due course' and act as an early warning system for novel issues.[115]

C. Regime Interactions

Finally, an important element of assembling an experimentalist architecture is the interaction between market regulatory regimes tasked with delivering different – and possibly conflicting – public policy objectives. Recall that under a technocratic conception of competition law and market regulation, cases that involve the trading off of different policy objectives are not appropriate for technocratic resolution and ought to be escalated for decision by a politically legitimate actor. As we observed in the sustainability cases in the Netherlands discussed in Chapter 2, competition officials deciding cases using the competition law toolkit may either ignore or be unable to assess the consequences of impugned business conduct on non-competition or non-economic policy objectives. At the same time, we also observed that political actors (including both the executive and the legislature) may be either unable or unwilling to provide solutions to such policy goal trade-offs, preferring instead to delegate the task to regulators or to private self-regulation.

Consistent with the aim of opening up the deliberations of communities of expertise to external input and contestation, experimentalist governance can be both triggered and supported by building bridges across different regulatory

[112] K Dekeyser and M Jaspers, 'A New Era of ECN Cooperation: Achievements and Challenges with Special Focus on the Leniency Field' (2007) 30 *World Competition* 3, 11.

[113] ibid; interview with officials of the Dutch ACM, The Hague, November 2015.

[114] Bender (n 98) 18. Bender also notes interview evidence of uneven participation and contribution to the working groups, based on the lack of salient experiences or resources by NCAs, even if the Commission apparently defrays travel costs.

[115] ECN, 'Outcome of the Meeting of ECN DGs on 17-02-2017', https://ec.europa.eu/competition/antitrust/ECN_meeting_outcome_17022017.pdf.

regimes or specialist silos. Interacting different frameworks of peer review has two beneficial consequences. One is that such interaction can disrupt regulatory habits and reveal novel implementation possibilities, which can simultaneously pursue different public policy objectives, particularly if subject to ongoing monitoring for the purposes of learning and dynamic adjustment. Apart from identifying a richer set of policy options, such interaction can also make explicit the relative costs and trade-offs in pursuing different policy options, so as to allow more informed action even by political actors.

For example, the Dutch ACM's interventions in the sustainability accords, such as the 'Chicken of Tomorrow' decision discussed in Chapter 2, involved the balancing of different and potentially conflicting policy objectives. Such national cases would not, as a matter of course, be subjected to review by the competition Advisory Committee. However, Dutch officials have reported making presentations about specific interventions in various settings, including the agri-food markets sectoral working group of the ECN,[116] and the ACM's approach has apparently been endorsed by the Commission.[117] Notwithstanding the Commission's endorsement, sustainability advocates and scholars assailed the Dutch ACM's methodology in analysing this case, including the reliance on a Wageningen University study assessing the additional cost of chicken using the new production standards and – more controversially – a survey of willingness to pay for sustainability attributes of chicken by consumers.

Quite apart from the discussion of the ACM's approach in these cases within the competition epistemic community, the chairman of LTO Netherlands (the Dutch Federation of Agriculture and Horticulture, representing almost 50,000 agricultural entrepreneurs) brought the ACM's *competition* decision to the attention of the Agricultural Markets Taskforce.[118] The EU-level taskforce was established as a group of 12 experts drawn from across the food supply chain with the objective 'to discuss a wide range of issues affecting agricultural markets and in particular the role of farmers'.[119] The LTO's submission to the Taskforce levelled two criticisms of the ACM's methodology in the sustainable chicken case. The LTO questioned both

[116] Bundeskartellamt, 'European Competition Network', https://www.bundeskartellamt.de/EN/Internationalwork/ECN/ECN_node.html;jsessionid=BBA338C7C684317A965E665101CE39E8.1_cid378#doc4219540bodyText1 (listing a number of ECN reports related to enforcement in the food and agriculture sector).

[117] See ch 2.

[118] E Hubers, 'Competition Law & Sustainable Production' (LTO Nederland, June 2016).

[119] The Taskforce met between January and November 2016 and produced a report on enhancing the position of farmers in the food supply chain. See Agricultural Markets Task Force, Improving Market Outcomes – Enhancing the Position of Farmers in the Supply Chain' (2016), https://ec.europa.eu/info/sites/info/files/food-farming-fisheries/farming/documents/amtf-report-improving-markets-outcomes_en.pdf: 'The TF was tasked with providing the European Commission with advice and expertise regarding the functioning of agricultural markets and farmers' position in the supply chain, as well as with making recommendations and proposing policy initiatives in this field – taking into account global challenges for sustainable agriculture.' One chapter of the report is entitled 'The CAP and Competition Law' and is devoted to the interaction of these EU policy areas at both the policy

whether the ACM accurately estimated customers' willingness to pay and whether consumers are able to estimate the 'true price' of the new standards, favouring instead a different method for assessing 'the benefit of more sustainable production to users and the society as a whole, short-term and long-term'. Moreover, the LTO's submission explicitly highlighted the issue of institutional choice about the appropriate forum for deciding such questions, proposing alternatives such as: (i) the producer and interbranch organisations in the Single Common Market Organisation (sCMO) of the Common Agricultural Policy; and (ii) the EU High Level Forum for a Better Functioning Food Chain. The latter High Level Forum was itself to operate as a broad-based peer network comprising political decision-makers (national authorities responsible for the food sector at the ministerial level), market operators and stakeholders and their organisations, as well as non-governmental entities and experts.[120]

The formalisation of monitoring and reporting obligations combined with peer review frameworks in many different fields of EU regulation provide ample opportunities for this kind of cross-sectoral consideration of decisions that touch upon multiple public policy objectives. In fact, even in the Commission's competition enforcement practice, the interaction between competition decisions and developments in other regulatory regimes, such as sectoral market regulation, has been explicitly considered.[121] Quite apart from incidental or *ad hoc* review, systematically subjecting both the design and implementation of interventions to cross-sectoral peer review allows for 'diverging understandings of value' to 'emerge through specific interaction between forums'.[122] Such interaction enhances the use of competition law as a diagnostic tool, whereby attention to a specific problem by the competition authority highlights problems in the operation of markets as well as public (or even private) regulatory failures, helping to identify root-cause misconnections – and opportunities for improvement – in the achievement of a broader set of public policy objectives.

objective and operational rule levels. The ECN itself had published a Resolution on the Reform of the CAP in December 2012 (available at https://ec.europa.eu/competition/sectors/agriculture/resolution_nca_en.pdf), referencing an earlier Report on competition law enforcement and market monitoring activities by European competition authorities in the food sector (24 May 2012), developed by the ECN food sub-group (available at https://ec.europa.eu/competition/ecn/food_report_en.pdf).

[120] European Commission, 'Decision Establishing a New High Level Forum for a Better functioning Food Supply Chain' (2015), https://ec.europa.eu/growth/content/decision-establishing-new-high-level-forum-better-functioning-food-supply-chain-0_en; European Commission, 'Forum for a Better Functioning Food Supply Chain', https://ec.europa.eu/growth/sectors/food/competitiveness/supply-chain-forum_en.

[121] COMP/39.386 – *Contrats Long Terme France (EDF)* (re-examination clause for commitment remedies in light of market or national regulatory developments). In fact, the French national energy regulatory authority was appointed as the implementation monitor of the commitments decision.

[122] Eriksen (n 30) 9.

IV. Conclusion

This chapter has examined the role of peer review in competition law and market regulation in the EU. It has highlighted the proliferation of formal peer-review mechanisms in various fields of EU market regulation, even if such mechanisms do not follow a common operational form. We have also shown that at the conceptual level, transnational peer review of regulatory action can be used for different purposes, which may or may not be consistent with the experimentalist goals of learning through implementation, as the basis for recursive remedial adjustment and rule-making. Given that experimentalist peer review is quite a demanding form of accountability, we also showed how a set of emergent monitoring and review mechanisms in the EU architectures for competition law and sectoral regulation can be transformed and assembled to provide a fully recursive experimentalist regime. This suggests that evolution towards experimentalism is possible, as actors acknowledge the constraints of uncertainty and the limits of hierarchical enforcement. However, this chapter also identifies areas for fruitful further research in better understanding the role and effects of these relatively opaque and understudied frameworks of EU regulatory governance. In the next chapter, we will also consider the interaction of peer review with a more traditional form of regulatory oversight, namely judicial review.

4

Courts and Experimentalist Competition Governance

The EU courts have played an important role in giving effect to and consolidating the status of EU competition law as a supranational policy. The CJEU buttressed the Commission's use of competition law as a tool for building the internal market from its early competition case law. As we discussed earlier, EU competition law used as an instrument for building the internal market could be based on relatively simple rules focused on non-discrimination in cross-border transactions. However, as the role of EU competition law shifted and the Commission sought to make it more economically informed, this enlarged the scope for decision-making based on expert evaluation of harmful effects of market conduct. On such evaluative questions, including complex facts and even economic modelling, the CJEU has allowed considerable deference to the Commission. At the same time, the EU courts have robustly exercised the power to fully review fines for competition law violations.

Growing use of novel governance techniques in EU competition enforcement – such as networked enforcement[1] and non-adversarial case resolution[2] – has led to concerns about the continued robustness of judicial review in controlling the exercise of discretion, ensuring coherence in the law, protecting fundamental rights and maintaining the rule of law. At the same time, the Modernisation Regulation envisaged a broader role not only for NCAs, but also for national courts in the enforcement of competition law. In addition, the Commission has long sought to stimulate private litigation in antitrust[3] and after protracted controversy, legislation

[1] O Brook, 'Struggling with Article 101(3) TFEU: Diverging Approaches of the Commission, EU Courts, and Five Competition Authorities' (2019) 56 *Common Market Law Review* 121; C Harding, 'Enforcement Inconsistency in EU Competition Cases as a Rule of Law Problem' (2019) 46 *Legal Issues of Economic Integration* 363; GD Federico, 'EU Competition Law and the Principle of *Ne Bis in Idem*' (2011) 17 *European Public Law* 241.

[2] FW von Papp, 'Best and Even Better Practices in Commitment Procedures after *Alrosa*: The Dangers of Abandoning the "Struggle for Competition Law"' (2012) 49 *Common Market Law Review* 929; *cf* K Yeung, 'Better Regulation, Administrative Sanctions and Constitutional Values' (2013) 33 *Legal Studies* 312.

[3] A Wigger and A Nölke, 'Enhanced Roles of Private Actors in EU Business Regulation and the Erosion of Rhenish Capitalism: The Case of Antitrust Enforcement' (2007) 45 *Journal of Common Market Studies* 495.

was introduced at the EU level to provide a framework for such actions, despite earlier strong opposition at the national level.

As argued in earlier chapters, from an experimentalist governance perspective, the formalisation of networked enforcement and non-adversarial mechanisms can be understood as a response to the scope conditions of radical uncertainty and the limitations of hierarchical coercive enforcement in competition law and market regulation. One key implication of the scope conditions is an inability to effectively implement competition policy through a combination of relatively clear violation rules elaborated through doctrinal precedents. Moreover, technocratic mechanisms, based on modelling of likely effects, are also constrained under conditions of radical uncertainty in volatile markets. The technocratic approach is also strained if competition policy comes to take into account a broader range of policy-relevant effects beyond short-term price effects (such as data protection or sustainability). Finally, both traditional enforcement techniques and judicial institutions are ill-equipped to monitor effects – whether narrowly or broadly defined – through stakeholder input, so as to engender recursive learning through assessing the efficacy of adopted solutions as the basis for revision of adopted remedies or existing rules. As a result, the preceding chapters have outlined how transformations in enforcement technique and the forms of input into regulatory decision-making, either by design or through workarounds, point to an experimentalist evolution in EU market regulation.

This chapter focuses on the role of courts at the EU and national levels, in light of the fact that experimentalist implementation of competition policy is not an EU variant of regulation through litigation. Experimentalist governance relies on non-adversarial enforcement, focused on problem-solving, monitoring, stakeholder input and different forms of accountability, such as peer review. As a result we may well ask whether courts, as the traditional legal guardians of the rule of law, become redundant or can still play a useful role in building or sustaining an experimentalist framework for market regulation. This chapter will focus on the public law role of courts as an oversight mechanism of regulatory decision-making through judicial review, as well as their private law role in private antitrust litigation. The aim of the chapter is twofold: first, to identify how courts performing their traditional functions can undermine experimentalist mechanisms; and, second, to explore to what extent courts can support experimentalism. It will be argued that courts can support experimentalist mechanisms if judicial review standards encourage authorities and undertakings to openly acknowledge – rather than conceal – sources of uncertainty, as well as enhancing problem-solving deliberation and stimulating regulatory innovation. The chapter will highlight existing practices to suggest that at the very least, courts do not ignore the scope conditions for experimentalist governance in fashioning their review standards. It will also develop a normative framework about transforming the courts' function to actively promote experimentalist solutions through the use of techniques already familiar to them.

I. Judicial Review of Competition Decision-Making

Judicial review is a key traditional mechanism that ensures the accountable exercise of regulatory discretion, respecting the constitutional and legislative mandate of the authority, protecting rule of law principles (such as non-arbitrary decision-making and the principle of legality) and fundamental rights (including the right of defence). In EU competition law, through providing authoritative interpretations of the legislative or Treaty texts and guidance through precedents, judicial review can also promote legal certainty for target undertakings by defining the boundaries of legal business conduct.

In Chapter 1, we discussed a German competition official's endorsement for an experimentalist evolution of competition law enforcement in the EU, though the same official also noted that the idea of experimentalism may not 'sound so good when you are before a judge'. This observation is unsurprising, given that a number of features of experimentalist competition enforcement present a challenge for traditional judicial review. Rather than focusing on the retrospective characterisation of conduct, experimentalist enforcement is forward-looking. It seeks to alleviate harmful effects of conduct, without being focused only on known risks, but also emergent forms of harm, the significance and severity of which may be difficult to gauge at the time the authority has to take a decision. Experimentalist enforcement relies on the broad participation of affected parties both in design and ongoing monitoring of regulatory interventions. This means that experimentalist interventions are typically not one-off interventions, whereby a formal violation finding is combined with a one-off remedy that aims to reverse the impugned conduct and neutralise its effects. Instead, experimentalist remedies are characterised as dynamic 'regimes'[4] because they seek to use information in the course of implementation to recursively adjust adopted solutions to achieve the stated regulatory objectives, which themselves are open to revision in the light of experience. Moreover, under conditions of uncertainty, experimentalism would necessarily allow different remedial approaches to address apparently similar cases.

One possible judicial response given the above features of experimentalist governance is to allow the enforcement authority considerable discretion, while limiting judicial review to procedural aspects of the decision-making process. However, as we will demonstrate below, judicial review can also be more ambitious in supporting – without disrupting – experimentalist problem-solving. First, judicial review can delimit areas where rule-based violation enforcement is appropriate. Second, with respect to effects-based enforcement, courts can condition deference on open acknowledgement of uncertainty by the enforcement authority

[4] CF Sabel and WH Simon, 'Contextualising Regimes: Institutionalization as a Response to the Limits of Interpretation and Policy Engineering' (2011) 110 *Michigan Law Review* 1265; O Gerstenberg, 'Constitutional Reasoning in Private Law: The Role of the CJEU in Adjudicating Unfair Terms in Consumer Contracts' (2015) 21 *European Law Journal* 599.

and the engagement of peer review and *ex post* remedial monitoring as alternative accountability checks on discretion. As will be argued, the current practice of judicial review appears sensitive to the constraints of the scope conditions of uncertainty and the limits of hierarchy, though it could benefit from an explicit re-orientation towards experimentalism.

A. Violation Decisions

Traditionally, competition enforcement under the Treaty competition articles involves the Commission as the primary decision-maker, with its decisions being subject to review by the EU courts pursuant to Article 263 TFEU. It relies on the Commission finding a violation of the applicable Treaty articles, as those articles have been interpreted by the Commission and EU courts. According to CJEU jurisprudence, 'legality review' of competition violation decisions extends 'to all the elements of the Commission's decisions in the light of the elements raised by the parties irrespective of whether or not these elements have been submitted in the administrative procedure'.[5] With respect to the degree of discretion afforded to the Commission in competition decision-making generally, in *Chalkor* the CJEU explained that 'in areas giving rise to complex economic assessments, the Commission has a margin of discretion with regard to economic matters'. But such a margin of discretion:

> [D]oes not mean that the Courts of the [EU] must refrain from reviewing the Commission's interpretation of information of an economic nature. Not only must those Courts establish, among other things, whether the evidence relied on is factually accurate, reliable and consistent but also whether that evidence contains all the information which must be taken into account in order to assess a complex situation and whether it is capable of substantiating the conclusions drawn from it.[6]

Further, in *Kone*, the CJEU clarified that:

> [W]hen it falls to the [EU] judicature to review the legality of Commission decisions imposing fines for infringements of the EU competition rules, it cannot encroach upon the discretion available to the Commission in the administrative proceedings by substituting its own assessment of complex economic circumstances for that of the Commission, but, where relevant, must demonstrate that the way in which the Commission reached its conclusions was justified in law.[7]

The foregoing statements reflect a relatively traditional division of labour between the administrative decision-maker who enjoys substantial discretion on the

[5] Case C-603/13 *Galp Energia España and Others v European Commission*, Judgment of the Court (Fifth Chamber) of 21 January 2016 ECLI:EU:C:2016:38.

[6] Case C-386/10 P *Chalkor AE Epexergasias Metallon v European Commission* [2011] ECR I-13085, para [54].

[7] Case C-510/11 P *Kone Oyj v European Commission* [2014] 4 CMLR 10 para [27].

substantive assessment (including on the basis of expertise), while judicial review focuses on errors of law, as well as procedural aspects of decision-making.

At the same time, according to knowledgeable observers, in distinct areas of competition enforcement, there can be a perception that the depth of judicial review of the Commission's decisions can be uneven and 'vary from case to case'.[8] Such a conclusion may not come as a surprise, particularly in an evolution towards an effects-oriented policy where there is considerable uncertainty about the effects of conduct. However, a high degree of substantive deference by the courts might lead the enforcement authority to seek to impose its own preferred solution even under conditions of uncertainty and to choose a blunt remedy that seems easier to enforce (such as a fine). Further, judicial emphasis on procedural controls on decision-making encourages strategic presentation of information by the defendant undertaking(s) so as to be able to use the review process to overturn the resulting decision. Both of the foregoing effects suggest that traditional judicial review may undermine the crafting of experimentalist solutions.

i. *Infringements by Object and Experimentalist Enforcement*

Under the existing doctrinal framework, apart from effects-based analysis, competition violations may be established by the retrospective characterisation of conduct. The reliance on interfirm restraints or dominant firm conduct characterised as an infringement by object is supposed to ease the burden on the enforcement authority in identifying competition violations, while also providing a guide to undertakings as to conduct that triggers antitrust liability. For present purposes, it is worth noting that the evolution of this jurisprudence suggests that the definition of infringements by object is not based on some deontic notion that certain species of business conduct are pernicious in and of themselves. Instead, this category of infringements is based on a pragmatic logic that – based on experience – certain species of conduct have anti-competitive effects with few offsetting benefits.[9] As such, they are subject to outright condemnation, thereby conserving enforcement resources from having to prove anti-competitive effects.

Though they involve form-based categories of prohibited conduct, infringements by object are not inherently inconsistent with experimentalist enforcement, so long as such categories can accommodate the scope condition of uncertainty about effects of similar conduct in different market contexts. Recall that under conditions of radical uncertainty, it may be difficult to predict effects of conduct by extrapolation either from past experience or from one industry to another. As a result, the availability of the infringements by object category may undermine experimentalist solutions through three effects: (i) placing excessive attention

[8] G Monti, 'EU Competition Law in a Global Context' in D Patterson and A Soderberg (eds), *A Companion to European Union Law and International Law* (Chichester, John Wiley & Sons, 2016) 321.

[9] *cf* N Petit, 'The Judgment of the EU Court of Justice in *Intel* and the Rule of Reason in Abuse of Dominance Cases' (2018) 43 *European Law Review* 728.

on characterising conduct on the basis of pre-defined categories (whether price-setting across firm boundaries or territorial restrictions) instead of gauging the dynamics of the industry or technology, as well as other contextually relevant considerations about the impugned conduct; (ii) providing an incentive for the enforcement authority to squeeze conduct within an established category to avoid the greater evidentiary burden of analysing effects; and (iii) diverting attention from the need to craft and monitor competition remedies that track effects, instead encouraging the resort to fines (a remedy which is easier to impose and to communicate to the public as a mark of successful enforcement activity).

The question of establishing infringements by object (as opposed to effects) was aired before both the General Court and the CJEU in the *Intel* litigation. A central question in *Intel* was whether exclusive dealing and loyalty rebates should be treated as an infringement by object, which would mean that they are 'prima facie prohibited irrespective of their effects on competition'.[10] The General Court characterised the rebates as an object infringement, based on prior case law distinguishing between loyalty rebates (that constitute a violation by object), quantity rebates (that are deemed legal) and other rebates evaluated on a case-by-case basis by demonstration of anti-competitive effects.[11] Notwithstanding such precedents, scholars had observed that this distinction was not particularly informative about the competitive significance of rebates in different market and industry contexts.[12] AG Wahl's opinion for the CJEU, as underscored by Ibáñez-Colomo,[13] highlighted that such formal characterisation of dominant firm rebate practices did not adequately account for the existing case law under Article 102, was inconsistent with the treatment of similar practices under Article 101 and had been subject to voluminous scholarly criticism.[14]

In its decision, the CJEU[15] apparently abandoned any purely formalistic characterisation of conduct in establishing an infringement by object and instead proposed a more deliberative framework that *could* be oriented at gauging *not only* likely effects, *but also* the level of uncertainty about the anti-competitive effects of impugned practices. In particular, the CJEU's approach recognises that infringements by object provide the enforcer with an evidentiary advantage, though such an advantage appears to be no more than a presumption as to effects. In other words, form-based characterisation would not be able to carry the entire weight in establishing a violation totally avoiding consideration of the economic and legal context in which the practice was implemented. Instead, the impugned undertaking

[10] P Ibáñez Colomo, 'AG Wahl in *Intel*, or the Value of Realism and Consistency in the Context of Article 102 TFEU', 5 January 2017, https://ssrn.com/abstract=2894343; see also P Ibáñez Colomo, 'The Future of Article 102 TFEU after *Intel*' (2018) 9 *Journal of European Competition Law & Practice* 293.

[11] Case T-286/09 RENV *Intel Corporation v European Commission* ECLI:EU:T:2014:547.

[12] Ibáñez Colomo, 'AG Wahl' (2017); Petit (n 9).

[13] Ibáñez Colomo, 'AG Wahl' (2017).

[14] See, eg, A Eilat, D Gilo and G Sagi, 'Loyalty Discounts, Exclusive Dealing and Bundling: Rule of Reason, Quasi-per-se, Price-Cost Test, or Something in between?' 4 *Journal of Antitrust Enforcement* 345.

[15] Case C-413/14 P *Intel Corp v European Commission* ECLI:EU:C:2017:632

should be allowed to rely on contextual evidence to demonstrate why the conduct is either incapable of having anti-competitive effects or may otherwise be justified. Upon such a showing by the impugned undertaking, as Ibáñez-Colomo explains, the enforcement authority is obliged to engage with the contextual evidence before reaching a decision.[16]

Experimentalist enforcement can accommodate form-based prohibitions if pre-existing experience suggests that certain conduct has anti-competitive effects. However, two points should be underscored. First, a question arises as to what constitutes prior *experience* that justifies a form-based prohibition.[17] For an experimentalist, there is a difference between the mere existence of a prior court precedent finding certain conduct to be an infringement and evidence based on observed experience about the effects of such conduct. Second, in an experimentalist framework, a form-based (object) prohibition may be justified by *prior* experience, but such a rule must still be open to revision in the light of *new* experience, particularly in novel and dynamic settings.

Based on Ibáñez-Colomo's analysis, the CJEU's reasoning in *Intel* leaves scope for a zone of relative certainty about the existence of a violation where conduct falls in a pre-established violation category,[18] but refocuses the analysis away from mere characterisation of the conduct. Identifying that conduct bears a resemblance to a recognised infringement by object is only a first step in the analysis, which remains open to evidence as to whether the conduct was capable of having anti-competitive effects.[19] For example, if the conduct was clandestine, this may confirm that the undertaking was aware of an existence of a prohibition, as well as the existence of an anti-competitive strategy. Alternatively, the impugned undertaking may show that any exclusionary effects are wholly implausible,[20] or the enforcer may show that any proffered efficiency or other justifications are themselves wholly implausible. Arguably, conduct is unlikely to fall within a zone of certainty about effects where the underlying industry context is subject to unpredictable dynamics. The greater the novelty or volatility of the market under consideration, the more likely it is that relying on prior experience would be insufficient, requiring the authority to engage in the messier business of assessing the potential harmful effects of the impugned conduct, as well as proffered justifications.[21]

[16] Ibáñez Colomo, 'AG Wahl' (2017).

[17] KH Ladeur, 'The Introduction of the Precautionary Principle into EU Law: A Pyrrhic Victory for Environmental and Public Health Law? Decision-Making under Conditions of Complexity in Multi-level Political Systems' (2003) 40 *Common Market Law Review* 1455.

[18] Ibáñez Colomo, 'The Future of Article 102' (2018).

[19] *Intel* (n 15) paras 138–40.

[20] In the art 101 context, Ibanez Colomo identifies cases such as *E.ON Ruhrgas* (Case T-360/09 *E.ON Ruhrgas AG and E.ON AG v Commission* EU:T:2012:332) and *Micro Leader* (Case T-198/98 *Micro Leader Business v Commission* EU:T:1999:341) as ones demonstrating wholly implausible anti-competitive effects, where the legal restrictions on entry to the markets were such that no exclusionary effect of the conduct was possible, irrespective of the formal characterisation of the impugned conduct. Ibáñez Colomo, 'The Future of Article 102' (2018) 297.

[21] Ladeur (n 17).

ii. Infringements by Effect and the Problem of Uncertainty

Once we move to conduct which requires evaluation of anti-competitive effects on the basis of the specific case, the CJEU has not made an unequivocal pronouncement about how such effects are to be gauged based on evidence available at the time of decision. AG Kokott in *Post Danmark II*[22] observed that in order to prevail, the enforcement authority must demonstrate on the available evidence that 'a practice is more likely than not to have anticompetitive effects'. Endorsing this view, Ibanez-Colomo suggests that an 'intervention would be justified where it can be shown that the probability of an anticompetitive effect is above 50%'.[23] However, both the Commission's analysis in cases such as *Microsoft* and *Google Shopping*, as well as interviews with Commission officials,[24] suggest that a probabilistic framework linking the available evidence with anti-competitive effects is problematic in highly dynamic environments, given that the methodologies for evaluating effects are often static and backward-looking.[25] Experience of the application of effects analysis in US antitrust suggests that effects are difficult to establish for the agencies on the balance of probabilities, particularly where the presently observable effects of conduct are ambiguous, in light of the complex analysis of factual evidence and the need for economic interpretation.[26]

It may be that there is a set of cases of intermediate uncertainty, where anti-competitive effects can be established probabilistically and where the violation route may still be feasible.[27] However, from an experimentalist perspective, the most significant enforcement constraint arises in situations of radical (or Knightian) uncertainty, in which it would not be possible to even enumerate the future states of the world, let alone assign probabilities.[28] As such, using a probabilistic framework incentivises the enforcement authority to disguise rather than openly acknowledge sources of uncertainty and the constraints on its own capacity to gauge the effects of conduct. In such cases, neither a rule-based nor a probabilistic framework is an adequate discipline on enforcement discretion. But this does not mean that enforcement discretion should be left unconstrained. Instead, in cases of uncertainty, the judicial review framework may seek to steer the parties towards problem-solving

[22] Case C-23/14 *Post Danmark A/S v Konkurrencerådet* EU:C:2015:651.

[23] Ibáñez-Colomo, 'The Future of Article 102' (n 10) 300.

[24] Interview with Chief Economist Unit official, Washington DC, April 2009.

[25] D Coyle, 'Discussion on "Competition Economics and Antitrust in Europe"' (2006) 21 *Economic Policy* 786, 787.

[26] Y Svetiev, 'Antitrust Governance: The New Wave of Antitrust' (2007) 38 *Loyola University Chicago Law Journal* 593.

[27] Ibáñez-Colomo suggests that *Post-Danmark II* was such a case: Ibáñez Colomo, 'The Future of Article 102' (2018) 300. Notably in that case, AG Kokott observed that 'the added value of expensive economic analyses is not always apparent and can lead to the disproportionate use of resources': *Post Danmark A/S* (n 22), Opinion of AG Kokott delivered on 21 May 2015 para [66].

[28] C Ford, *Innovation and the State: Finance, Regulation and Justice* (Cambridge, Cambridge University Press, 2017); FH Knight, *Risk, Uncertainty and Profit* (Boston, Houghton Mifflin Company, 1921) (distinguishing probabilistic risk from uncertainty).

solutions, such as commitment decisions, and to lean on experimentalist frameworks for accountability through peer review and implementation monitoring. In other words, in cases where there is uncertainty about the effects of conduct, an experimentalist court would seek to regulate the resort to violation vis-a-vis commitment decisions given that commitment decisions provide a greater scope for innovating solutions and creating a participative infrastructure of monitoring and adjustment in the face of observed remedial and market effects.

B. Commitment Decisions and Experimentalist Judicial Review

In the absence of much legislative guidance, the question of the appropriate review of commitment decisions by the courts has been contested. One way in which the EU courts have incentivised the use of commitment decisions generally is by adopting a very light-touch review standard for such decisions. The highly deferential review standard announced by the CJEU in *Alrosa*,[29] and subsequently followed by the General Court in *Morningstar*,[30] appears principally based on a contractarian (or settlement) view of commitments as a form of resolution through voluntary concessions by the impugned undertaking.[31] Such an approach leaves the Commission's discretion in pursuing commitments largely unchecked, which has been roundly criticised by commentators principally because it reduces the accountability of the Commission. Some authors have expressed concern that the Commission may be captured and accede to minimalist commitments by the impugned undertaking, while others suggest that the Commission is likely to over-reach as it has the upper hand in negotiations with an undertaking seeking to avoid a violation decision.[32] Commitments are also said to deprive undertakings of the guidance provided by precedent violation decisions by the Commission and the courts.[33] In light of calls for rebalancing discussed in earlier chapters, one possibility is to strengthen the standard of review of commitment decisions, possibly aligning it to that of violation decisions, while another is to reduce the Commission's resort to commitment decisions.

[29] Case C-441/07 P *European Commission v Alrosa Company Ltd* [2010] ECR I-05949.

[30] Case T-76/14 *Morningstar v European Commission*, Judgment of the General Court (Eighth Chamber) of 15 September 2016 ECLI:EU:T:2016:481 (where the Court held that the Commission has 'a wide discretion' in accepting commitments and that courts exercise only a 'restricted review').

[31] von Papp (n 2).

[32] ibid; Y Svetiev, 'Settling or Learning: Commitment Decisions as a Competition Enforcement Paradigm' (2014) 33 *Yearbook of European Law* 466. See also C Parker, 'Restorative Justice in Business Regulation? The Australian Competition and Consumer Commission's Use of Enforceable Undertakings' (2004) 67 *Modern Law Review* 209.

[33] Notably, precisely the fact that commitment decisions have a limited precedential effect enhances their problem-solving efficacy in individual cases. See F Schauer, 'The Failure of the Common Law' (2004) 36 *Arizona State Law Journal* 765 (the formulation of precedent applicable in heterogeneous and dynamic settings hampers context-sensitive decision-making).

From the experimentalist point of view, limiting the precedential effects of decisions need not be seen as a loss, but precisely as one of the advantages of the commitments mechanism in situations where there is heightened uncertainty due to the heterogeneous or dynamic market contexts and where a problem-solving orientation should not be constrained by precedent.[34] The loss of accountability problem is indeed a concern, particularly if we take the limits of hierarchical enforcement seriously. And yet, because a generalist court has relatively less expertise or access to contextual knowledge than either the Commission or the impugned undertaking, we may have doubts as to whether strengthening the standard of judicial review either of the required evidence of anti-competitive harm or of the appropriateness of the proposed remedy can overcome such concerns. In light of our discussion above, it would seem unwise to rely on a probabilistic framework linking current evidence to the likelihood of anti-competitive effects, or on a proportionality framework for the substantive remedy proposed. This is particularly so because the evidentiary record in an Article 9 setting is considerably lighter[35] and because the court review of the decision typically occurs *ex ante*, prior to the full implementation of the negotiated remedy.

In fact, it is not just the EU courts that have adopted a hands-off approach to negotiated resolutions. Consider by way of comparison the US statute promulgated specifically to oversee negotiated 'consent judgments', the Tunney Act,[36] requiring judicial approval for such judgments based on the broad standard that 'entry of such judgment is in the public interest'. Recognising the limits on the court's ability to make an assessment where both parties have consented to a remedy, this statute imposes procedural and participation requirements as a precursor to curial review, including an obligation for the agency to publish the proposed judgment and a competitive impact statement of the settlement (including the alternative remedial approaches considered), as well as a right for interested third parties to comment on the proposed settlement. Notwithstanding the broad public interest standard of review and avenues for consultation, if the courts are incapable to process such stakeholder input so as to assess the substance of the proposed remedy vis-a-vis other alternatives, they will adopt a deferential approach, approving the settlement if it was negotiated *bona fide* (in the absence of improper influences on the enforcement agency) and is 'within the realm of the public interest'.[37]

As for disciplines on the *use* – rather than *content* – of commitments by the Commission, Regulation 1/2003 does provide some (cryptic) guidance. In defining

[34] ibid; *cf* P Lugard and M Mollman, 'The European Commission's Practice under Article 9 Regulation 1/2003: A Commitment-a-Day Keeps the Court away?' (2013) 3 *CPI Antitrust Chronicle* 1, 11.

[35] Case C-547/16 *Gasorba SL v Repsol Comercial de Productos Petrolíferos SA* ECLI:EU:C:2017:891.

[36] Antitrust Procedures and Penalties Act (15 USC § 16).

[37] Svetiev, 'Antitrust Governance' (2007) 672 (referring to *Microsoft Corp v US*, 56 F 3d 1448, 1460 (DC Cir. 1995) (where the court largely ignored the voluminous third-party input on the Microsoft antitrust settlement); *US v Gillette Co*, 406 F Supp 713, 715–16 (D Mass 1975) (the Tunney Act is a check on the government's good faith in settling the case as the court is not in a position to determine if the settlement is the best one that could be obtained).

the division of labour as between violation and commitment decisions, Recital 13 provides that 'commitment decisions are not appropriate where the Commission intends to impose a fine'. As discussed earlier, from an experimentalist perspective, Recital 13 may be interpreted to mean that the use of the commitments is appropriate in cases where there is uncertainty about the anti-competitive effects of conduct (also in light of its possible economic or even non-economic justifications) at the time the Commission takes a decision. The uncertainty about effects makes the violation route inappropriate – from both an efficacy and legality perspective – and the fine an inapposite remedy. Instead, it becomes necessary to engage in behaviour modification so as to attenuate concerns about harm, as well as in monitoring and remedial adjustment. Such an interpretation is bolstered by the language of Recital 13, which provides that commitment decisions amount to a finding 'that there are no longer grounds for action by the Commission without concluding whether or not there has been or still is an infringement'.

In disciplining the use of commitments, a court can give bite to the experimentalist interpretation of Recital 13 by requiring the Commission to disclose the reasons for choosing Article 9. Consistent with the earlier analysis on the use of commitments, Recital 13 could be interpreted to mean that a commitment can be used by the enforcement authority in cases where: (i) there is evidence of a competition violation, but the violation was either insufficiently serious to warrant a fine or was somehow novel;[38] or (ii) there is uncertainty about the effects of the impugned conduct at the time that the Commission takes a decision and the remedy is implemented to attenuate concerns about anti-competitive harm. In *Gasorba*,[39] AG Kokott emphasised the first justification by observing that Article 9 protects the 'principle of discretionary prosecution' allowing the Commission to proceed 'as efficiently and economically as possible'. But in deciding on the legal effect of an Article 9 decision, the Court did not follow AG Kokott's opinion that a 'commitment decision provides a *strong* indication'[40] of the anti-competitive nature of the conduct, holding instead that such a decision is only an 'indication' of anti-competitive conduct,[41] which lends some support to the second experimentalist justification for using commitments.

Adopting such a discipline on the use of Article 9 immediately confronts the problem of whether it would be possible for a court to assess and control assertions of uncertainty by the enforcer. Otherwise, the second justification for using commitments seems unambiguously preferable for the enforcer. One way to address that problem is to impose what I have called a 'variable geometry' of *ex ante* and *ex post* review mechanisms. If commitments are used to conserve enforcement resources in easy cases that are not serious, this means that the

[38] See, eg, Case AT.39985 – Motorola – Enforcement of GPRS Standard Essential Patents, Comm'n Decision (Motorola) (summary at [2014] OJ C344, 6, at para 561, ec.europa.eu/competition/antitrust/cases/dec_docs/39985/39985_928_16.pdf

[39] *Gasorba SL* (n 35), Opinion of AG Kokott at para [40].

[40] ibid [35].

[41] ibid, Opinion of the Court at para [29].

Commission is invoking 'existing precedents or well-tested theories of harm and remedial forms' and the resolution is a settlement of a violation without a fine. As such, the Commission would bear a 'heavier burden of establishing its case on the evidence available at the time of decision', should 'be required to explain why a fine is inappropriate in the case' and should use a remedy proportionate to the claimed violation.[42]

If, by contrast, the Commission uses Article 9 because the conduct is novel or otherwise there is uncertainty in assessing anti-competitive effects, 'the *ex ante* burden of justification' at the time of decision would be lighter. The Commission could, for example, point to disagreements among experts or peer authorities about the risk or seriousness of an anti-competitive scenario. Instead, 'the Commission would bear a heavier burden of *ex post* disclosure and justification, including obligations to engage in implementation monitoring, disclose monitoring reports and compare the evolution of the market with the preliminary concerns' that led to the decision.[43] Disciplining the Commission's use of Article 9 in this way can incorporate both the peer accountability framework (including the Advisory Committee and the market testing procedure) and the *ex post* monitoring framework, a point to which we will return in the next section.

One final implication of the foregoing approach to disciplining the use of commitment decisions is that the Commission should not be foreclosed from using the violation route if, during the investigation, it considers accepting commitments.[44] The discussion of the *Google Shopping* case in Chapter 2, suggests two reasons against closing the violation route if commitments are considered: first, in the course of commitment negotiations, evidence could come to light suggesting the existence of a violation;[45] and, second, and perhaps more importantly, the violation alternative can act as the penalty default ensuring that both parties adopt a problem-solving orientation in the remedial negotiations. As we elaborated in Chapter 1, an effective experimentalist penalty default is a hierarchical alternative that is unambiguously disfavoured by all parties involved in a problem-solving exercise. As some authors have pointed out, the threat of a blunt or formalistic decision can act as a penalty default stimulating collaborative problem-solving.[46] The violation route would appear less desirable for the defendant and also for the Commission as the enforcer. Apart from the cost and uncertainty of follow-on

[42] Svetiev, 'Settling or Learning' (2014) 496.
[43] ibid.
[44] B Vesterdorf and K Fountoukakos, 'An Appraisal of the Remedy in the Commission's *Google Search (Shopping)* Decision and a Guide to its Interpretation in Light of an Analytical Reading of the Case Law' (2018) 9 *Journal of European Competition Law and Practice* 3.
[45] Article 9(3)(b) of Regulation 1/2003 suggests that this may occur even after a commitment decision is adopted.
[46] RE Scott, 'The Case for Formalism in Relational Contract' (2000) 94 *Northwestern University Law Review* 847; BC Karkkainen, 'Information-Forcing Environmental Regulation' (2006) 33 *Florida State University Law Review* 861.

judicial proceedings, the violation route offers much less flexibility for adopting problem-solving remedies.[47]

II. Dialogic Review: Judicial Review and Peer Accountability

As the above discussion suggests, experimentalist governance in cases of uncertainty may be hampered by traditional judicial review of enforcement. However, it also suggests that judicial review can steer parties towards more open acknowledgement of uncertainty and use of problem-solving remedies. Moreover, judicial review can also lean on experimentalist forms of accountability, such as peer review of the design and implementation of remedies.

As we showed in Chapter 3, Regulation 1/2003 imposes at least two forms of peer oversight on the use of commitment decisions, including review by the Advisory Committee and market testing through third-party input. As with other EU market regulatory frameworks, the Regulation imposes a legal duty for the Commission to take utmost account of the opinion of the Advisory Committee. Notably, the peer-review frameworks discussed in Chapter 3 do not provide guidance on the meaning of the utmost account obligation or on the question of whether and how courts should give any cognisance to peer-review opinions in performing their function of judicial oversight. This section will provide an experimentalist dialogic account of the interaction between judicial review and peer review. Such an account gives meaning to the utmost account obligation; it allows peer and judicial review to be mutually supportive and maintains the no-final decider feature of experimentalist governance under conditions of uncertainty.

By way of background, authors have long recognised the benefits and drawbacks of incorporating judicial review into governance frameworks that rely on specialist expert decision-makers. On the one hand, as Jaffe pointed out long ago, if isolated from oversight by generalist courts, specialist decision-making bodies are likely to develop 'distorted positions'.[48] Distortions can result from a tendency for overreach, including due to specialists' lack of attention to systemic values related to the rule of law and fundamental rights protection.[49] They can also result from industry capture[50] as well as from the tendency for specialist decision-makers

[47] Article 7 requires the remedy to be tailored to the violation and limits the scope for both monitoring and adjusting remedies. See Case T-201/04 *Microsoft v Commission* [2007] ECR II-3601 [1268] (striking down the appointment of an independent monitoring trustee – to be paid by Microsoft – as an impermissible delegation of the Commission's functions to a third party).

[48] LL Jaffe, 'Judicial Review: Constitutional and Jurisdictional Fact' (1957) 70 *Harvard Law Review* 953, 963.

[49] LL Jaffe, 'Primary Jurisdiction Reconsidered: The Anti-trust Laws' (1954) 102 *University of Pennsylvania Law Review* 577, 590: 'The jurisdiction and experience of the judge embraces all of the social conflicts regulated by law [and] a canon of legal objectives … correspondingly broader or … less likely than the administrator's to be distorted by specialized interest and responsibility.'

[50] ibid 596. While competition enforcement is transversal rather than industry-specific, competition officials do in fact act at least to some extent as monitors regularly overseeing and negotiating solutions

to narrowly frame problems through the prism of the goals and means of their regulatory discipline, thereby ignoring other policy objectives and unintended consequences of decisions.[51]

However, others have pointed out that judicial oversight of specialist regulatory regimes also risks hampering their problem-solving efficacy. Teubner's 'regulatory trilemma' identifies three problematic forms of interaction between courts and specialised governance regimes. These include: (i) 'mutual indifference', whereby law is irrelevant to and takes no cognisance of a specialist governance regime; (ii) 'creeping juridification', whereby judicial review damages the problem-solving capabilities of the governance regime by imposing legal or procedural constraints; and (iii) 'over-socialisation of law', whereby judicial attempts to incorporate the concerns of the specialised governance regime may be inconsistent with the values of the legal system and the coherence of the law.[52]

At least formally, the legislative instruments creating the peer-review frameworks in EU market regulation do not explicitly envisage if and how peer review should interact with judicial review. Courts also do not appear to take much cognisance of peer review, notwithstanding the formalisation of this mechanism. Peer review may be seen to have a different purpose and operate in a different jurisdictional plane from either EU or national judicial review, even if the two review mechanisms have overlapping scope and may complement each other. Moreover, such relative indifference may have deleterious consequences. For example, the tendency to demonstrate outward consensus and iron out divergences behind closed doors, as is apparently the case in the Advisory Committee on Restrictive Practices and Dominant Positions discussed in Chapter 3, may arise precisely out of concerns that an open acknowledgement of disagreement among competition agency peers may be exploited in subsequent judicial review proceedings by undertakings seeking to overturn an enforcement decision.

However, a scenario in which courts unlock the availability of commitment decisions and their remedial flexibility upon a showing that the enforcement authority is acting under uncertainty may stimulate more open deliberation about different implementation instruments within the Advisory Committee's peer review. Similarly, stakeholder input in market testing can reveal uncertainty about the competitive significance and effects of conduct or proposed remedies.[53] Such scenarios illustrate the benefit of courts using peer-review input from both regulatory peers and market stakeholders through dialogic review architectures, whereby judicial review facilitates deliberation and acknowledgement of

with the same undertakings, whereby such solutions come to shape the industry. *cf* RV Loo, 'Regulatory Monitors: Policing Firms in the Compliance Era' (2019) 119 *Columbia Law Review* 369. In addition, competition enforcers can also be captured by the complainants who bring problems to their attention.

[51] Jaffe, 'Judicial Review' (1957) 963: 'road-maintenance authorities sorely pressed to find gravel within the parish will not place a high value on the amenities of the gentry's parks'.

[52] G Teubner, 'Juridification Concepts, Aspects, Limits, Solutions' in G Teubner (ed), *Juridification of Social Spheres: A Comparative Analysis in the Areas of Labor, Corporate, Antitrust and Social Welfare Law* (Berlin, De Gruyter, 1987).

[53] Commission Decision of 11 October 2007, Case COMP/B-1/37.966 – *Distrigaz*.

uncertainty by effectively imposing a cost on consensus. Dialogic judicial review can also support experimentalist competition law by mandating monitoring and sunset mechanisms as a way of coping with enforcement uncertainty. In fact, these dialogic techniques are familiar to EU courts.

A. The Techniques of Dialogic Judicial Review: Between Procedural and Substantive Control

The analysis thus far seeks to sketch out a form of judicial review that can enhance experimentalist governance in competition law and market regulation more broadly. While it has not been argued that courts have framed judicial review standards with experimentalism in mind, I have sought to show that evolving judicial approaches are not inconsistent with an experimentalist judicial review framework (including the open justificatory framework for infringements by object, the lack of precision about the method of evaluating effects for a violation decision and the relatively deferential review standard for commitment decisions). As such, it may be that courts are themselves attuned to the constraints of uncertainty and the limits of coercive enforcement, even if we may expect them to be more cautious about experimentalist solutions in light of the key functions of judicial review to protect rule of law principles (including legality, limits on discretion or arbitrary differential treatment) as well as fundamental rights.

In what follows, three examples will be examined in which courts have reviewed public regulatory decisions under conditions of uncertainty and where such decisions have also been subject to some variant of peer review or input. The aim here is twofold. First, we will demonstrate that dialogic – as opposed to hierarchical – forms of judicial review that can support experimentalist market regulation are not entirely unfamiliar in the practice of the EU courts. Second, the examples may show how judicial and peer review can be complementary and mutually reinforcing forms of accountability on regulators through dialogic frameworks thereby avoiding Teubner's concerns about mutual indifference or the superposition of one form of oversight over another. In the first example, we will observe how a court can review decision-making uncertainty and operationalise the obligation to take utmost account of peer input. The second example demonstrates how EU peer review can inform a national court's review of regulatory decision. In the third example, we will observe how the CJEU's review of Commission decisions provides an occasion for interacting two peer-review frameworks that can assist both the EU court's oversight of the Commission and national oversight of regulatory authorities.

i. Disciplining Discretion under Uncertainty

Agency decision-making under conditions of radical uncertainty raises the spectre of unbridled discretion, with the prospect of limited accountability for the soundness of decisions and the risk of arbitrariness. Courts have had to face the background condition of radical uncertainty in the context of public authority decision-making invoking the precautionary principle in the light of existing scientific knowledge.[54] In such cases, EU courts have fashioned review modalities that do not cede authority to scientific or technocratic communities, but also do not juridify the regulator's decision-making procedure. In *Pfizer Animal Health*,[55] the Court of First Instance reviewed the withdrawal of authorisation of an animal feed additive, an antibiotic that favoured animal growth. The Commission (and the Council) had invoked the precautionary principle, citing the potential risk to human health if the additive led to antibiotic resistance in animals and humans. While a competent public authority is expected to consider the best available scientific data and international research in taking a decision, the Commission (and the Council) apparently disregarded the report of a Scientific Committee on Animal Nutrition (prepared at the Commission's request and suggesting the absence of new evidence about the harmful effect of the antibiotic).

The court recognised that the EU institutions had broad discretion to act even at a time when harmful effects were not apparent. However, in seeking to impose discipline on arbitrary decision-making under conditions of uncertainty,[56] the court did not limit itself to the procedural requirement that the public authority must *consider* high-quality, transparent and independent scientific advice prior to taking a decision. Recognising that it was not in a position to itself evaluate the substantive scientific merits, the court held that the competent authority could depart from the committee input, but must provide reasons for the decision that engage with the committee's advice and explain why the advice is being disregarded. Moreover, the public authority's 'statement of reasons must be of a scientific level at least commensurate with that of the [committee] opinion'.[57]

As a technique of judicial review, the foregoing approach is dialogic rather than hierarchical. It may be transposed as a mode of operationalising the duty to take utmost account of peer review opinions before taking a decision, which has been formalised in a number of EU market regulatory frameworks (see Chapter 3). The court does not cede authority to the specialist committee, recognising that the legal system has a different rationality and must protect different values. At the same time, its approach did not juridify the process of taking, interpreting and characterising the available evidence (including through a probabilistic framework), which would be inappropriate in assessing future risks that may not be well understood. Instead, the court – in an approach that Craig regarded as innovative[58] – required the competent authority to engage with the specialist

[54] Claims of anti-competitive harm may often be structured in a similar way, whereby the full harmful effects of business conduct are not fully observable at the time of taking a decision and in fact such conduct can often have short-term benefits for at least some market actors.

[55] Case T-13/99 *Pfizer Animal Health SA v Council of the EU* [2002] ECR II-03305.

[56] Ladeur (n 17).

[57] *Pfizer Animal Health SA* (n 55) [201].

[58] PP Craig, *EU Administrative Law* (Oxford, Oxford University Press, 2006) 417.

input at a commensurate level before departing from the advice. The technique is dialogic because it does not establish a clear hierarchy among the decision-makers. And instead of acting as the ultimate arbiter itself, the court dislodges further rounds of deliberation between the decision-maker and the specialist committee, which may both enhance the quality of decision-making and attenuate concerns about arbitrariness.

ii. EU Peer Review and National Judicial Oversight

Dialogic judicial review can be further enhanced when both the judicial and peer-review body have access to comparative evidence about similar implementation efforts of other authorities operating in a network. Accessing such peer evidence allows courts to perform more meaningful review of regulatory action compared to reliance on interpretation and the hierarchy of indeterminate norms. In *Koninklijke KPN and Others v Autoriteit Consument en Markt (ACM)*, a Dutch administrative tribunal had to perform legality review of a decision by the national telecoms regulator (OPTA)[59] to change the cost accounting basis for setting termination rates that telecommunications providers charge for delivering calls across their networks. OPTA's decision essentially followed an EU Commission Recommendation[60] (backed by a BEREC peer report)[61] effectively reducing the costs for calculating termination rates, with the intended effect of lowering final consumer mobile telephony charges. Dutch mobile telephony operators successfully argued before the national tribunal that OPTA's decision was inconsistent with Dutch national law and the principle of legality.[62]

The decisions of the Dutch tribunal, as well as the preliminary reference questions it ultimately submitted to the CJEU, focused on the question of the hierarchy of norms that framed the national authority's discretion. The national tribunal pointed out that the Commission's recommendation is non-binding, while following Dutch national law was mandatory for a Dutch regulator. While that much can be accepted, such an approach tends to simplify the discretion that is reposed in the NRA pursuant to the EU and national frameworks. It also ignores the usefulness of EU telecoms peer review in assisting the national tribunal's oversight function. On the one hand, it is true that the Dutch NRA was only under a duty to take utmost account of both the Commission's Recommendation and of BEREC's opinion under EU law, while it was bound by Dutch law. On the other hand, as the

[59] The sectoral Onafhankelijke Post en Telecommunicatie Autoriteit was subsequently merged into the Autoriteit Consument en Markt (ACM); see ch 1.

[60] Commission Recommendation (2009/396/EC) of 7 May 2009 on the Regulatory Treatment of Fixed and Mobile Termination Rates in the EU [2009] OJ L124, 20.May, 67–74.

[61] The powers of the Commission and BEREC within the oversight of national regulatory decision-making under the telecommunications package are described in ch 3.

[62] Dutch Trade and Industry Appeals Tribunal (College van Beroepvoor het bedrijfsleven), Judgment of 31 August 2011, s 4.8.3.7.

CJEU recognised, it is unlikely that the Dutch telecommunications law – promulgated under the EU telecoms framework – mandated only one and foreclosed any other cost accounting methodology for setting termination rates.[63]

In the preliminary reference proceeding before the CJEU, AG Mengozzi highlighted the uncertainty faced by NRAs in selecting the means to attain the broad telecoms framework objectives 'to promote competition in the provision of electronic communications networks and services, to contribute to the development of the internal market and to promote the interests of the citizens of the EU'.[64] The AG also pointed out that while EU law does not prevent a national tribunal from engaging in a searching review of the merits of regulatory decisions, the national tribunal should not require the NRA to demonstrate that any adopted measure (here the cost accounting method) will have the desired effects with *certainty*. And yet, the presence of uncertainty need not imply that the NRA's discretion is unconstrained or that the NRA is obliged to follow the peer consensus. Many Member States had in fact adopted the Commission's Recommendation,[65] and thus BEREC's opinion[66] in this case, rather than simply extolling the technocratic virtues of the recommended accounting method, could also provide useful comparative evidence about the observed effects of following the Commission's method on competitive conditions and retail prices in those other jurisdictions.[67]

Peer review can also assist the national tribunal in evaluating the NRA's observance of the principle of legality, a principle common to the Member States' legal systems, as well as other public law principles protecting the rule of law or fundamental rights. First, in assessing whether there was a change in market conditions that would justify OPTA's change in the accounting measure, the national tribunal can be assisted by contextual and comparative evidence. Comparative information about the experience of other authorities, including about the shortcomings of previously adopted regulatory measures, could be one of the factors that led to the change in the adopted measure. Second, apart from benefiting from peer review, courts can also spur specialised regulatory communities to incorporate rule of

[63] AG Mengozzi pointed out the relevant provisions of the Dutch Telecommunications Act were transposing specific articles of the EU telecoms legislative framework. See Case C-28/15 *Koninklijke KPN NV v Autoriteit Consument en Markt (ACM)* [2016] ECLI:EU:C:2016:692, Opinion of Advocate General Mengozzi (28 April 2016), paras 71–72. Both the Commission and other NRAs were apparently of the view that the law allowed more than one cost accounting methodology to be chosen in pursuing the framework objectives.

[64] *Koninklijke KPN NV v Autoriteit Consument en Markt* (n 63), Opinion of AG Mengozzi para [93].

[65] M Cantero-Gamito, 'The Private Law Dimension of the EU Regulatory Framework for Electronic Communications: Evidence of the Self-sufficiency of European Regulatory Private Law', DPhil thesis, EUI, 2015.

[66] BEREC Opinion in Phase II investigation pursuant to Article 7a of Directive 2002/21/EC as amended by Directive 2009/140/EC Case NL/2012/1284 – Call termination on individual public telephone networks provided at a fixed location in the Netherlands Case NL/2012/1285 – Voice call termination on individual mobile networks in the Netherlands, BoR(12)23. The opinion reports that an Expert Working Group was established to consider the case, though it does not report its composition.

[67] ibid 15–16. BEREC's opinion made only limited reference to comparative evidence in assessing the possible cross-border effects of OPTA's previous cost accounting methodology.

law and fundamental rights into their decision-making and peer review practices through the dialogic mechanism of conditional deference.[68] Such a mechanism is well known to EU lawyers: courts can conditionally defer to regulatory decisions so long as regulatory regimes demonstrate[69] that they develop and apply criteria ensuring that regulatory decision-making observes public law principles protecting the rule of law and fundamental rights.[70]

iii. Peer Review across Regulatory Silos

Judicial review proceedings also provide a forum for interacting peer-review frameworks from different specialised regulatory regimes. Again, the legislative documents establishing peer-review frameworks do not explicitly cover this question, though judicial review proceedings allow for systematic – rather than *ad hoc*[71] – consideration of different forms of peer input that are engaged in the same case. Where the same decision is reviewed under different regulatory frameworks, this can overcome some of the distortions of specialised regulation, including the risks for overt or soft capture, as well as the danger of confounding regulatory means with ends and ignoring unintended consequences.

For example, in two prominent competition cases, again involving pricing in the telecommunications sector, incumbent operators in two Member States, Deutsche-Telekom in Germany and Telefónica in Spain, were faced with conflicting injunctions from two different regulatory regimes. In both cases, the incumbent operators' pricing for broadband access was consistent with price regulation cost accounting rules imposed by their respective national *telecoms* sectoral regulators (pursuant to national laws transposing the EU telecoms framework package). While pricing consistently with national sectoral regulation, the incumbent operators were found by the Commission to violate Article 102 TFEU based on the theory that their pricing foreclosed downstream entry by competitors.[72]

[68] As shown by the GAL literature discussed in ch 3, transnational fora develop public law-like restraints when exercising public authority, though through dialogic review, traditional oversight institutions (such as courts) can encourage or enhance that process. *cf* G Teubner, 'Societal Constitutionalism: Alternatives to State-Centered Constitutional Theory?' in C Joerges et al (eds), *Transnational Governance and Constitutionalism* (Oxford, Hart Publishing, 2004).

[69] ECN guidance documents, for example, include rights-protection recommendations, albeit in a rudimentary form. See European Competition Network, *ECN Recommendation on Investigative Powers, Enforcement Measures and Sanctions in the context of Inspections and Requests for Information* (9 December 2013) [4], [39]; European Competition Network, *ECN Recommendation on the Power to Collect Digital Evidence, Including by Forensic Means* (9 December 2013) [6].

[70] This involves a transposition of the dialogic method from *Solange*, BVerfG, 29 May 1974, 37 Entscheidungen des Bundesverfassungsgerichts 271; BVerfG, 22 October1986, 73 Entscheidungen des Bundesverfassungsgerichts 339. See Y Svetiev, 'European Regulatory Private Law: Conflicts to Platforms' in KP Purnhagen and P Rott (eds), *Varieties of European Economic Law and Regulation* (Berlin, Springer Publishing, 2014) 168.

[71] Recall the discussion of the review of the Dutch ACM's sustainable chicken intervention in the Agricultural Markets Taskforce in ch 3.

[72] The Commission's decisions had been submitted to the Advisory Committee for review.

In reviewing the Commission's decisions in both cases,[73] the CJEU had to face the question whether pricing consistent with national sectoral regulation could nonetheless constitute a violation of EU competition law. It is worth recalling from our discussion in Chapter 3 that national telecom regulatory measures are subject to peer review (by the Commission and BEREC) and the Commission's competition decisions are subject to peer review (by the Advisory Committee).

One approach to resolving these cases, as in the OPTA example above, is to rely on traditional reasoning based on the interpretation and hierarchy of different legal obligations. Following such an approach by the CJEU, the Commission's antitrust violation finding prevails, given that Article 102 creates a Treaty obligation that overrides obligations under secondary legislation and regulatory decisions pursuant to national law. While providing a simple way to dispose of the conflict, such a 'dogmatic'[74] approach does not fully reveal the reasons for the conflicting approaches in light of the policy goals promoted by the two market regulatory regimes[75] or vis-a-vis comparative implementation experience. Again, just as in the previous example, neither EU or national telecommunications law nor EU competition law mandates a specific method for setting access prices by telecom incumbents. Both regimes allow discretion in choosing means through which to promote a number of different, and even mutually compatible, policy goals.

Hou has argued that, notwithstanding the similar legal issues presented to the court, the two cases were qualitatively different.[76] Interacting peer review across the two regulatory silos can shine a light on this difference in a way that aids the efficacy of judicial oversight. In *Telefónica*, the Spanish telecom regulator was said to have relied on outdated data in regulating the relevant rates, which was not updated to reflect market dynamics over a long period of time and allowed the Spanish telecoms incumbent to charge higher prices.[77] In the face of doubts about the appropriateness of its methodology, a court can inquire whether the Spanish NRA's approach could be justified by any legitimate policy rationale under the telecoms framework or under competition law. To the extent that such a rationale was not provided, the divergence appears to be attributable to the NRA's incompetence or capture.[78]

By contrast, the use of the higher cost basis for price-setting in *Deutsche-Telekom* was said to be justified by a different 'economic approach' to price regulation, whereby the German NRA aimed to stimulate dynamic infrastructure-based

[73] Case C-280/08 P *Deutsche Telekom AG v European Commission* [2010] ECR I-9555; Case C-295/12 P *Telefónica and Telefónica de España v European Commission* (CJEU Judgment of 10 July 2014) ECLI:EU:C:2014:2062.

[74] L Hou, 'Reshaping Market, Competition and Regulation in EU Utility Liberalization: A Perspective from Telecom' (2015) 52 *Common Market Law Review* 977, 982.

[75] *cf* C Joerges et al, 'A New Type of Conflicts Law as Constitutional Form in the Postnational Constellation' (2011) 2 *Transnational Legal Theory* 153.

[76] Hou (n 74) 1001.

[77] ibid 1001.

[78] D Geradin and R O'Donoghue, 'The Concurrent Application of Competition Law and Regulation: The Case of Margin Squeeze Abuses in the Telecommunications Sector' (2005) 1 *Journal of Competition Law and Economics* 355.

(rather than static or price) competition in the market.[79] Pursuing dynamic infrastructure-based competition as an objective is consistent with both the telecoms framework package and EU competition law. Peer review of comparative implementation experience would reveal the reasons for the German NRA's divergence from other authorities, but also whether and how other NRAs or NCAs have sought to accommodate dynamic forms of competition.[80] Finally, in a further extension of an experimentalist review architecture, the German regulator's approach could be conditionally allowed subject to ongoing *ex post* peer monitoring of the effects, including whether dynamic competition benefits through infrastructure upgrading resulted from the divergent measure.

B. Monitoring and Review of Implementation Efforts

Even the technique of mandating *ex post* monitoring as a way of coping with uncertainty, together with stimulating divergent implementation instruments, as well as testing their efficacy, is itself not wholly unknown in the practice of EU courts. It is already at least implicit in the early jurisprudence on the precautionary principle,[81] whereby the proportionate application of measures invoking this principle requires that regulatory frameworks must be open and revisable in light of new scientific evidence.[82] Similarly, the CJEU has held that regulatory instruments under conditions of uncertainty are proportionate where they include a sunset clause triggering review.[83] The CJEU has also suggested that monitoring can make a regulatory measure proportionate under conditions of uncertainty. In *Ordem dos Técnicos Oficiais de Contas (OTOC) v Autoridade da Concorrencia*,[84] the CJEU was faced with a Portuguese NCA decision against the national accounting professional association's (OTOC) measure mandating ongoing professional training of registered accountants and reserving a substantial part of such training to be provided by OTOC itself (rather than other training bodies). In evaluating OTOC's proffered objective for this measure, to 'guarantee the quality of the services offered by chartered accountants', the Court observed that – in the face of uncertainty – reserving a substantial part of

[79] Hou (n 74) 1002.

[80] ibid 1001. Hou suggests that Germany was the only Member State in which the market share of new broadband competitors shrank in the relevant period.

[81] On the limited practicality of probabilistic standards of review where the precautionary principle is invoked in the face of uncertainty, see J Zander, *The Application of the Precautionary Principle in Practice: Comparative Dimensions* (Cambridge, Cambridge University Press, 2010) 103–29.

[82] Case C-6/99 *Association Greenpeace France and Others v Ministère de l'Agriculture et de la Pêche and Others* [2000] ECR I-1651; see E Fisher, 'Precaution, Precaution Everywhere: Developing a "Common Understanding" of the Precautionary Principle in the European Community' (2002) 9 *Maastricht Journal of European and Comparative Law* 7.

[83] Case C-58/08 *Vodafone and Others v Secretary of State for Business, Enterprise and Regulatory Reform* ECLI:EU:C:2010:321: 'intervention is limited in time in a market that is subject to competition'.

[84] Case C-1/12 *Ordem dos Técnicos Oficiais de Contas v Autoridade da Concorrência* EU:C:2013:127, [2013] 4 CMLR 20.

the training to OTOC itself or using vague criteria to qualify training providers were not the only means to ensure quality of service:

> [T]he objective of guaranteeing the quality of the services offered … could be achieved by putting into place a *monitoring system* organised on the basis of clearly defined, transparent, non-discriminatory, *reviewable* criteria likely to ensure training bodies equal access to the market in question. (Emphasis added)[85]

The decision suggests that formalising an *ex post* monitoring mechanism is one way to cope with uncertainty about the selection of means (here, training providers) to deliver public policy objectives. Such monitoring can allow different training providers to subsist, while also imposing discipline on the discretion of the professional body through reporting and review of observed effects. Ultimately, such monitoring could even justify OTOC's otherwise *ex ante* unverifiable claim that only it could provide quality training for professional accountants.

Similarly, an experimentalist intuition is disclosed in the CJEU's decision on the implementation of the 'right to be forgotten', where the Court was considering whether the effective implementation of the right to de-referencing requires that the relevant links must be removed, without geographical limitation, from all the search engine domain names.[86] The Court recognised two uncertainty sources in pursuing the objective of protecting the right to de-referencing by undertakings: first, there is uncertainty about what constitutes an effective measure on the part of an undertaking to implement the right to be forgotten; and, second, there is also uncertainty about how protection of the right to be forgotten interacts with and may hamper the right to freedom of information.

To cope with those uncertainties, the Court invites both private operators and national competent authorities to experiment and monitor. With respect to the question of effective de-referencing measures, the Court observed that search engine operators must themselves identify 'sufficiently effective measures to ensure the effective protection of the data subject's fundamental rights', including having 'the effect of preventing or, at the very least, seriously discouraging internet users in the Member States from gaining access to the links in question using a search conducted on the basis of that data subject's name'.[87] On the question of balancing the rights of de-referencing and freedom of access to information, the CJEU observed that EU law does not require de-referencing on all versions of a search engine. Yet it also reminded national authorities that they can pursue divergent

[85] ibid para [99].

[86] Case C-507/17 *Google LLC v Commission nationale de l'informatique et des libertés (CNIL)* ECLI:EU:C:2019:772.

[87] Case C-507/17 *Google LLC v Commission nationale de l'informatique et des libertés (CNIL)*, Judgment of the Court of 24 September 2019, [70]. Such an obligation could only be effectively implemented by the undertaking periodically re-assessing the measures it has put in place in light of experience from specific de-referencing requests in a dynamic internet ecology, as well as comparing its own efforts to those of other undertakings. *cf Fisher v University of Texas*, 136 S Ct 2198 (2016) (outlining a dynamic obligation on universities to ensure that affirmative action admission programmes satisfy constitutional scrutiny).

solutions in applying a broader or narrower right to de-referencing, as they are free to apply national fundamental rights standards in balancing a data subject's right to protection of personal data with the right to freedom of information.[88]

All of the above examples are intended to provide contours of judicial review that support experimentalist problem-solving. Such review is dialogic, in the sense that it is neither indifferent to other frameworks of review of regulatory actors, nor does it seek to impose hierarchical supremacy (a 'final decider') in the face of uncertainty and the limits of hierarchy. Moreover, the examples illustrate how peer-review frameworks can aid the judicial review task by imposing accountability on agency decision-making, including identifying sources of uncertainty, the range of options available and comparative evidence about their use, efficacy or unintended consequences.[89] As such, a court's deference to regulatory discretion can be made conditional on justifications for divergence, a demonstration of how the rule of law or fundamental rights have been taken into account in decision-making, as well as the formalisation of *ex post* monitoring of implementation.

III. Private Antitrust Litigation and Experimentalist Governance

In this final part, we turn our attention to the role of civil courts in an experimentalist framework for competition law and market regulation. Stimulating private antitrust litigation has been identified for some time as an important objective of the EU Commission. Yet private antitrust litigation has not necessarily flourished in the Member States, even after the EU legislator went on to promulgate a directive providing a general framework for private antitrust litigation in national courts and tribunals.[90]

Private antitrust suits may be compatible with an experimentalist infrastructure for implementing competition law and regulation by generating enforcement innovation. Such innovation is important for experimentalism, given the scope conditions of uncertainty and the limits of hierarchical enforcement, suggesting that public authorities would not necessarily detect or be able to remedy all anti-competitive conduct. However, as we will see, the kind of private actions that the EU has sought to stimulate, namely civil suits for *damages*, may be problematic from an experimentalist perspective. Such suits may be helpful in the (increasingly limited) area of competition law where there is little enforcement uncertainty and

[88] *Google LLC* (n 86) [72].

[89] It is worth underscoring that such peer-review evidence can also bolster the political accountability mechanisms of regulators.

[90] Directive 2014/104/EU of the European Parliament and of the Council of 26 November 2014 on certain rules governing actions for damages under national law for infringements of the competition law provisions of the Member States and of the European Union [2014] OJ L349, 5 December (hereinafter 'the Damages Directive').

where experimentalism is possibly less relevant, though they could have spillover effects in disrupting experimentalist public enforcement.

A. Stimulating Private Damages Suits

Both the EU Commission[91] and the CJEU's[92] emphasis on the importance of private suits to enforce the competition law provisions in the Treaty is entirely consonant with the reliance – from a very early stage of EU integration – on private litigation to enforce EU law rights in the face of the EU Commission's limited enforcement capability. However, both the Commission's 2005 Green Paper and the responses to the Green Paper that framed the ensuing debate revealed considerable uncertainties about the mechanisms for stimulating private litigation at the national level for a number of different reasons.

In particular, for civil antitrust litigation to be a viable enforcement mechanism in national tribunals would require (re)calibrating national procedural law in the Member States, including rules governing: (i) the availability and format of representative litigation, such as through class actions; (ii) the rules for document discovery and obtaining evidence for private parties to be able to mount effective litigation in the absence of the investigatory powers of the state; (iii) the mechanisms through which litigation can be funded before a final decision on the merits; (iv) the rules about the award of legal costs, particularly for losing parties, as well as regulations on lawyers' fee recovery.[93] As such, the goal of promoting private antitrust litigation impinges on the rules of evidence and civil procedure which can be deeply embedded in local legal practice and may even be seen to embody fundamental normative commitments of the national systems of justice of the Member States.[94] The rules of evidence, civil procedure and the regulation of the legal profession can reflect broader national policy preferences about the use of litigation as an appropriate format for dispute resolution, including within regulatory fields beyond traditional private law.[95] To the extent that they are seen as part of national

[91] European Commission, *Green Paper: Damages Actions for Breach of the EC Antitrust Rules* (19 December 2005), https://eur-lex.europa.eu/legal-content/EN/TXT/PDF/?uri=CELEX:52005DC0672&from=EN. The objective is also noted in Recital 7 of Regulation 1/2003, though no substantive harmonisation provisions were enacted.

[92] Case C-453/99 *Courage Ltd v Bernard Crehan and Bernard Crehan v Courage Ltd and Others* [2001] ECR I-6297.

[93] EU Commission officials observed that 'research is required to establish the nature and extent of the potential obstacles to private enforcement of the competition rules' at the national level; see D Woods et al, 'Private Enforcement of Community Competition Law: Modernisation and the Road Ahead' (2004), http://ec.europa.eu/competition/speeches/text/2004_2_31_en.pdf. See also AP Komninos, *EC Private Antitrust Enforcement: Decentralised Application of EC Competition Law by National Courts* (Oxford, Hart Publishing, 2008) ch 3.

[94] *cf* A Olijnyk, *Justice and Efficiency in Mega-Litigation*, (Oxford, Hart Publishing, 2019).

[95] See HW Micklitz and A Stadler, 'The Development of Collective Legal Actions in Europe, Especially in German Civil Procedure' (2006) 17 *European Business Law Review* 1473.

legal traditions, such rules are even more resistant to reflection and change, even in cases where they may no longer be fit for purpose.[96] Unsurprisingly, both fealty to legal tradition by legal practitioners and fears of increased costly litigation by business drove Member State governments' opposition to the Commission's earlier harmonisation proposals.[97]

In light of uncertainty about locally appropriate mechanisms of civil litigation and the inability to impose a preferred common mechanism, one way to establish an experimentalist framework would be to define a common goal: stimulating private compensation claims for competition violations in national courts, while avoiding what were seen to be the 'excesses of the US litigation model',[98] including 'unmeritorious and even vexatious claims' and situations 'where defendants settle simply because litigation costs are too high'.[99] Pursuing the foregoing common objectives would require giving autonomy to the Member States to identify vehicles for private compensation suits (including collective claims) and tailoring the national rules of civil procedure and legal compensation. This is how I myself once framed the question about an experimentalist architecture for the evolution of private competition enforcement.[100]

However, quite apart from the reluctance about harmonising civil antitrust litigation rules by Member State governments, reservations about stimulating such litigation were also expressed by enforcement officials from the Commission[101] and NCAs.[102] Commission officials highlighted the need for 'coordination of public and private enforcement',[103] given the possible negative effects of civil litigation on the efficacy of the public enforcement system that had been built up at the EU and national levels, and strengthened through the Modernisation Regulation and the ECN. While having multiple private enforcers could ease the burden on public authorities, such litigation also has inevitable spillover effects on their

[96] Y Svetiev, 'The EU's Private Law in the Regulated Sectors: Competitive Market Handmaiden or Institutional Platform?' (2016) 22 *European Law Journal* 659; Gerstenberg (n 4); *cf* RD Kelemen, *Eurolegalism: The Transformation of Law and Regulation in the European Union* (Cambridge, MA, Harvard University Press, 2011).

[97] MA Sittenreich, 'The Rocky Path for Private Directors General: Procedure, Politics, and the Uncertain Future of EU Antitrust Damages Actions' (2009) 78 *Fordham Law Review* 2701, 2723.

[98] J Pheasant, 'Private Antitrust Damages in Europe: As the Policy Debate Rages, What are the Signs of Practical Progress?' (2007) 8 *Business Law International* 299. See also RVD Bergh, 'Private Enforcement of European Competition Law and the Persisting Collective Action Problem' (2013) 20 *Maastricht Journal of European and Comparative Law* 12.

[99] Neelie Kroes, 'Enhancing Actions for Damages for Breach of Competition Rules in Europe', speech at the Harvard Club, 22 September 2005, cited in Sittenreich (n 97) 2712.

[100] Y Svetiev, 'Networked Competition Governance in the EU: Delegation, Decentralization or Experimentalist Architecture?' in CF Sabel and J Zeitlin (eds), *Experimentalist Governance in the European Union: Towards a New Architecture* (Oxford, Oxford University Press, 2010).

[101] Sittenreich (n 97).

[102] Interview with a Bundeskartellamt official, Bonn, July 2009.

[103] ED Smijter and D O'Sullivan, 'The *Manfredi* Judgment of the ECJ and How it Relates to the Commission's Initiative on EC Antitrust Damages Actions', Competition Policy Newsletter, Autumn 2006, http://ec.europa.eu/competition/speeches/text/2006_3_23_en.pdf.

enforcement discretion and ability to shape competition policy. One such concern focuses on the effects of private litigation on the efficacy of public enforcement techniques, such as the use of leniency policies to detect cartels or commitment-type negotiated remedies. The availability of civil litigation may undermine such tools if it makes leniency applications or negotiated resolutions via commitments less attractive to target undertakings.

A second concern about stimulating private litigation arises from the enhanced role of national tribunals in shaping EU competition law based on the directly applicable EU provisions as well as the corresponding national rules. Such a development may also have spillover effects that are undesirable for public enforcement. For example, an enhanced role for national courts could produce a doctrinal drift in the interpretation and application of the competition rules, which could in turn affect public enforcement.[104] The US experience suggests that courts may narrow both rules of procedure and substantive antitrust doctrines as a way of discouraging and disposing of unmeritorious private claims, in turn hamstringing competition agencies' public enforcement efforts.[105]

As such, the 2014 Private Rights Directive may be characterised as a legislative intervention that aimed to optimise the efficacy of public enforcement by stimulating private suits in a way that does not 'unduly detract from the effective enforcement of competition law by a competition authority'.[106] A number of features of the Directive point towards this conclusion, including:

- the ready availability of private actions following on from public enforcement efforts;[107]
- the protection of evidence provided in leniency applications,[108] as well as limitations on liability for leniency applicants receiving immunity;[109]
- the regulation of access to the public agency's file for private parties.[110]

The question of the interaction of private antitrust litigation and public enforcement is also central in assessing the role of such litigation from an experimentalist perspective. In what follows, I wish to argue that the Directive's focus on stimulating private *damages* litigation for all kinds of competition violations may impair *experimentalist* public enforcement techniques.

[104] While competition agencies are typically not parties to antitrust civil damages litigation, Regulation 1/2003 guarantees NCAs the right to intervene in cases before national courts (art 15(3) and (4)) and gives the Commission the opportunity to provide its opinion at the court's request (art 15(1)).

[105] Svetiev, 'Antitrust Governance' (2007); see also DA Crane, 'A Neo-Chicago Perspective on Antitrust Institutions' (2012) 78 *Antitrust Law Journal* 43.

[106] Damages Directive, Recitals 21 and 32.

[107] ibid art 9.

[108] ibid, Recital 26.

[109] ibid, Recital 38.

[110] ibid, Recitals 21, 23 and 29; arts 6 and 7.

As both scholars[111] and the EU institutions[112] have pointed out, the function of civil antitrust litigation can be defined either from a traditional private law or a regulatory perspective. The private law perspective emphasises the corrective justice orientation of civil litigation to vindicate a private right to be compensated for harm from conduct that is wrongful from an interpersonal perspective. From the regulatory perspective, by contrast, civil litigation can aid the pursuit of public policy goals by deterring conduct that has been identified as socially harmful. Clearly, these two functions of civil damages suits can be in harmony where socially harmful conduct also constitutes an interpersonal wrong and inflicts private damage, and where harmed parties have both the information and the incentive to vindicate their rights. Civil litigation in such circumstances augments public enforcement against socially harmful conduct.[113] And if private compensation claims are costly and have uncertain prospects of success, private enforcers can be given further incentives to pursue such claims, as in the case of the US treble damages provisions for antitrust violations.

In the EU, the purpose of civil antitrust litigation has been limited to the compensating harm. However, irrespective of whether the purpose is to compensate private harm or to deter conduct contrary to the public interest, for civil suits to fulfil either purpose, it is necessary to be able to define what amounts to wrongful conduct, either from the point of view of interpersonal justice or that of the public interest. By contrast, as was elaborated in Chapter 2, Simon notes that experimentalist frameworks aim 'to bracket or sublimate issues of individual and retrospective fairness or blame' in hard cases.[114] This is precisely because hard cases engage conditions of uncertainty, whereby it is difficult or impossible to define *ex ante* what constitutes wrongful conduct. If we accept that in a growing share of contemporary competition problems, (i) it is difficult to identify any essential elements to anti-competitive conduct that can define a background set of rights against which harm can be determined retrospectively, and (ii) if anti-competitive conduct is principally delineated by virtue of its effects which are *ex ante* indeterminate, this leads to the conclusion that neither interpersonal justice nor deterrence provides an appropriate rationale for civil damages litigation to be embedded in an experimentalist governance architecture.

As already foreshadowed, one exception to the above conclusion may be 'easy' cases involving civil damages suits against hardcore clandestine cartels that involve price-fixing or market division purely to raise the participants' profitability and for

[111] See, eg, DA Crane, 'Optimizing Private Antitrust Enforcement' (2010) 63 *Vanderbilt Law Review* 675.

[112] European Commission, 'Commission Staff Working Paper Accompanying the White Paper on Damages Actions for Breach of the EC Antitrust Rules', 2 April 2008, https://eur-lex.europa.eu/LexUriServ/LexUriServ.do?uri=SEC:2008:0404:FIN:EN:PDF.

[113] Sittenreich (n 97) 2722.

[114] WH Simon, 'Toyota Jurisprudence: Legal Theory and Rolling Rule Regimes' in G de Burca and J Scott (eds), *Law and New Governance in the EU and the US* (Oxford, Hart Publishing, 2006) 38.

no other purpose.[115] It may be that the Damages Directive is principally oriented towards such actions, particularly as a follow-on to public enforcement, though the scope of the compensation rights is not limited in this way. Once we move beyond the area of such relatively clear violations defined *ex ante*, not only do the standard rationales for civil damages weaken, but the availability of private suits in the context of fuzzy rules and the need for complex assessments of effects can also only encourage opportunistic resort to litigation of the kind that both the EU and the Member States have sought to avoid.[116] The more that competition cases are in a zone of *ex ante* indeterminate effects, and the broader the scope of justifications and salient effects that competition enforcement takes into account (such as data protection or sustainability), the weaker the case for the availability of private damages suits: there is neither a background set of (interpersonal) rights to vindicate nor clearly identifiable (socially) wrongful conduct to deter.

B. Public Experimentalist Learning and the Compensation of Private Harm

To further probe the role of civil litigation within an experimentalist framework for competition law, it might be useful to consider the question of private compensation following on from public enforcement efforts under conditions of uncertainty. Dagan and Kreitner have argued that in contemporary regulation, many public agencies already supplement the role of civil courts in addressing interpersonal justice harms in addition to pursuing the public interest.[117] Moreover, as a normative matter, they argue that in many contexts prevalent in contemporary society, regulatory agencies may be a more appropriate forum for the vindication of compensatory rights than civil courts. Consistently with such views, in resolving cases through negotiated remedies, competition and market regulatory authorities have even sought commitments from defendants to compensate harm.[118]

In the light of uncertainty about the effects of business conduct on the public interest, experimentalist regulation attempts to identify competitive problems in their incipience through combining early diagnostic tools, the use of behaviour modification techniques and monitoring through participation of affected

[115] In addition, Crane has argued persuasively that neither compensation nor deterrence provides an adequate rationale for private damages suits even within a more traditional conception of antitrust enforcement. In his view, compensation fails because the typical harm sufferers are too diffuse and remote to compensate, while deterrence fails because of the time lag between a decision to engage in anti-competitive conduct and the ultimate consequences for the corporation and its officers from a liability finding. See Crane (n 111).

[116] Recall the earlier discussion suggesting that in an experimentalist framework, even infringements defined by object are a category that is open to revision in the light of new experience.

[117] H Dagan and R Kreitner, 'The Other Half of Regulatory Theory', 10 November 2018, https://ssrn.com/abstract=3031886.

[118] *cf* Parker (n 32).

parties to ensure error detection and adjustment of the remedy in the course of implementation. At the same time, following Dagan and Kreitner's intuition, an experimentalist public authority should be attuned to the fact that experimentalist enforcement pursuing the public interest may nonetheless result in harm to private parties, who may, as such, become victims of experimentalist learning. But to identify circumstances under which learning-oriented experimentation results in compensable private harm requires specification of a background set of rights (or entitlements) of private parties, which may be difficult to do if competition law is effects-oriented and if effects are *ex ante* indeterminate. Nonetheless, considering this question as part of the process of remedial design can help to understand whether an experimentalist approach to problem resolution appropriately seeks to either avoid or address harm to private parties.[119] Furthermore, defining a background set of compensation rights for affected third parties can also act as a penalty default to aid the efficacy of an experimentalist remedy.

Consider the question of the compensation of private harm when implementing a negotiated commitments remedy. First, at the time that a public authority is contemplating an experimentalist remedy, its investigation may already demonstrate that the defendant has committed a recognised competition violation, which has caused harm to private parties. As proposed earlier in this chapter, a judicial review standard which obliges the authority to explain the reasons for using a commitment decision would assist a civil court on the appropriateness of compensation of harm. In *Gasorba*, for example, the Commission accepted commitments to resolve concerns about the long-term supply agreements with non-compete obligations between Repsol and its service station tenants. The commitments were forward-looking, with Repsol agreeing not to enter into future long-term exclusivity agreements or to buy independent service stations, as well as to provide financial incentives for existing tenants to terminate their relationships.[120] The CJEU held that the Commission's commitment decision did not foreclose compensation claims by injured parties in civil proceedings, as it only provided an indication of possibly anti-competitive conduct and did not remedy any harm retroactively.[121] Moreover, if instead of treating the choice to proceed via commitments as an exercise of unreviewable prosecutorial discretion,[122] judicial review required an explanation for this choice, this would enhance the 'informational' value of the Article 9 decision for civil courts.[123] Not only would it assist the civil courts in deciding compensation claims following a commitments decision, but it would also ensure that such claims do not interfere with the experimentalist remedies by highlighting the sources of uncertainty.

[119] *cf* Damages Directive, Recital 5 (public enforcement decisions may give parties an incentive to provide compensation).
[120] *Gasorba SL* (n 35) [13]–[14].
[121] ibid [28]–[29].
[122] ibid, Opinion of AG Kokott at [40].
[123] S Makris and AR Faeses, 'Commitments and Network Governance in EU Antitrust: *Gasorba*' (2018) 55 *Common Market Law Review* 1959, 1970.

Similarly, the discussion of *Google Shopping* in Chapter 2 suggested that the Commission's principles-based remedy could be interpreted in experimentalist terms. As we pointed out, the Commission's decision identified a failure in Google's meta-regulatory obligations as a platform steward. Namely, Google's unilateral changes to the search platform design expropriated or devalued its collaborators' investments by reducing traffic for comparison-shopping websites, thereby causing them harm, quite apart from any harm to the public interest. In fact, the Commission itself suggested[124] that such harm could be compensable as a relational wrong to the comparison website operators, quite apart from the public interest remedy it had adopted.

Second, once an experimentalist remedy is adopted, monitoring of implementation through third-party input and adjustments to the remedy provide a sufficient mechanism to detect and avoid harm to third parties (even where such harm was not foreseen at the time of remedial design). In fact, complaints about the effectiveness of the remedy will typically be triggered by third parties suffering harm.[125] To the extent that remedial monitoring performs its diagnostic and error-correction functions, such third-party harm may be addressed in real time through remedial modifications, thereby alleviating the need for compensation.

However, it may also prove difficult or impossible to diagnose and avoid all third-party harm in the course of implementing an experimentalist remedy, including in cases where there is a substantial lag between remedial implementation and resulting harm. Moreover, third-party harm can result where the experimentalist remedy is achieving its desired effects, but is also producing unintended consequences. In such cases, there may be scope for an award of civil damages. Again, if such damages are claimed in a civil court, in order to limit interference with the experimentalist enforcement framework, the court would be assisted by an open disclosure of the reasons for the public authority's decision to adopt the commitment route, as suggested above. Alternatively, third-party compensation could also be incorporated into experimentalist remedial design by: (i) defining a background minimum set of rights of private parties (whether consumers, customers, suppliers or others); and (ii) obtaining a commitment from the undertaking to compensate such harm if it occurs. If there is asymmetry in knowledge between the authority and the defendant company about the likely effects of a negotiated remedy, defining a minimum set of rights of third-party compensation can act as a penalty default sustaining experimentalism. Such a penalty default can

[124] The Commission's press release points out that apart from the public remedy, Google may also be 'liable to face civil actions for damages that can be brought before the courts of the Member States by any person or business affected by its anti-competitive behaviour'. See European Commission, 'Antitrust: Commission Fines Google €2.42 Billion for Abusing Dominance as Search Engine by Giving Illegal Advantage to Own Comparison Shopping Service', 27 June 2017, https://ec.europa.eu/commission/presscorner/detail/en/IP_17_1784.

[125] FY Chee, 'Axel Springer Unit, Others Say Google Still Playing Unfairly, Want EU to Act', *Reuters*, 28 November 2019, https://www.reuters.com/article/us-eu-alphabet-antitrust/shopping-rivals-urge-eu-to-act-against-google-for-allegedly-favoring-own-service-idUSKBN1Y20W4.

disincentivise the defendant both from proposing implausible interventions and from dragging its feet in adjusting ineffective remedies.[126]

C. Stand-Alone Experimentalist Private Actions?

Finally, if we take seriously the constraints imposed by the scope conditions for experimentalism – uncertainty and the limits of hierarchy – it would be problematic to make all competition interventions contingent on action by public authorities. Specifically, there is no reason to believe that public competition authorities are solely capable of identifying all (including incipient and novel) forms of anti-competitive conduct, let alone addressing them in a timely fashion with limited enforcement resources. It follows that an experimentalist competition authority would welcome independent private causes of action, not only as a burden-sharing mechanism, but also as a source of different perspectives and innovation in the implementation of competition law.[127] However, based on the above discussion, there are at least three preconditions for stand-alone private actions to have an experimentalist character, including:

- the definition of a background set of rights of market participants that can trigger a private experimentalist remedy;
- the reconceptualisation of private antitrust remedies away from one-off damages awards towards participative problem-solving regimes;[128]
- the redefinition of the role of courts from one-off dispute resolvers towards that of 'catalysts'[129] that bring together actors and processes necessary for experimentalist problem-solving.

The experimentalist governance literature does disclose instances of cases brought before courts, in the face of the failure of public actors to effectively address persistent problems, which have resulted in the establishment of experimentalist regimes. For example, Sabel and Simon show how court proceedings have been used to destabilise and reform failing public organisations, such as schools, mental

[126] Hanoch Dagan has suggested the following example, which – although outside the scope of competition law – may usefully illustrate this point. Suppose that, in the face of uncertainty about the means of reducing gun violence, gun manufacturers propose an intervention of increasing gun ownership as a way of reducing gun-related deaths. If the state of current knowledge about the effects of widespread gun ownership is inconclusive, defining a background set of rights of compensation for harmed parties has the dual effect of addressing individual harm (by eliminating the need for *ex post* litigation with proof of causation), while also disincentivising opportunistic use of the experimentalist framework by proposing an implausible remedy.

[127] *cf* O Cherednychenko, 'Contract Governance in the EU: Conceptualising the Relationship between Investor Protection Regulation and Private Law' (2015) 21 *European Law Journal* 500.

[128] Crane (n 111).

[129] J Scott and S Sturm, 'Courts as Catalysts: Rethinking the Judicial Role in New Governance' (2007) 13 *Columbia Journal of European Law* 565.

health institutions, police departments and prisons.[130] In response to suits by the harmed users of such institutions,[131] the courts have noted the existence of persistent failures by the relevant institutions in the performance of their functions or the delivery of services. However, given the uncertainty about the effective means of institutional reform and the inability to reform an institution by either a simple injunctive decree or through damages awards, in such cases the courts fostered – by way of remedy – the creation of collaborative interdisciplinary governance regimes. Such regimes are based on broad stakeholder input into remedial design, monitoring of effects and recursive revision of reform mechanisms to respond to implementation failures. Note, however, that even if such suits were brought by private parties harmed by the failing institution, their main objective was ultimately not to obtain damages, but to achieve institutional reforms. As such, instead of relying on the palliative or (indirect) deterrence effects of damages or repeated litigation, the courts in such cases have overseen institutional reform through collaborative and iterated problem-solving.

It follows that stimulating private antitrust litigation of an experimentalist character involves legal and procedural reforms beyond incentivising damages claims. In *Réel/Alcan*,[132] given concerns about the foreclosure effects of Rio Tinto Alcan contractually tying the licensing of its smelting technology (in which it was said to have a substantial market share) with speciality crane equipment of Alcan's own subsidiary, the Commission accepted a remedy which may be seen as experimentalist. The commitment remedy was neither an outright ban on the tie nor an unqualified duty to deal imposed on Alcan,[133] but a 'non-discriminatory pre-qualification process for [equipment] suppliers' by way of an independent monitor 'with relevant industrial expertise' to ensure 'technically satisfactory exploitation of the technology'.[134] Since the remedy mimics private contracting mechanisms used to manage collaborative supply chain relationships through ensuring the trustworthiness and capability of downstream suppliers,[135] in principle it could also be implemented as part of a private dispute resolution process between the parties. The process of crafting such a remedy – in private as much as in public enforcement – requires retooling standard methods of judicial antitrust decision-making away from the determination of violation or liability and towards the diagnostic task

[130] CF Sabel and WH Simon, 'Destabilization Rights: How Public Law Litigation Succeeds' (2004) 117 *Harvard Law Review* 1015. See also KG Noonan et al, 'Legal Accountability in the Service-Based Welfare State: Lessons from Child Welfare Reform' (2009) 34 *Law and Social Inquiry* 523.

[131] While these were principally examples of public interest litigation, pursued by 'clients' of failing institutions or civil society organisations as claims for violations of constitutional rights, such cases could also be pursued through civil litigation citing ongoing harm.

[132] Commission Decision in Case AT.39230 *Rio Tinto Alcan*, 20 December 2012.

[133] See generally Svetiev (n 32) 492–93.

[134] *Alcan* (n 132) [113].

[135] RJ Gilson, CF Sabel and RE Scott, 'Contracting for Innovation: Vertical Disintegration and Interfirm Collaboration' (2009) 109 *Columbia Law Review* 431.

of problem-detection and problem-solving.[136] Problem-solving remedies have the added advantage of reducing incentives for opportunistic litigation in the hope of obtaining damages by an incompetent collaborator or disgruntled competitor. They may also be consensual and seen as favourable by both parties. While the traditional role of civil courts is focused on compensation, it may be that the Damages Directive's encouragement of consensual dispute resolution[137] could indirectly stimulate experimentalist private actions.

IV. Conclusion

Experimentalism may not sound very appealing when a competition or regulatory authority is facing judicial review, given that it may be seen to provide a carte blanche for discretionary problem-solving, which cannot be controlled either through rules or through a probabilistic framework for assessing anti-competitive effects. Yet, this chapter has sought to show that judicial review can support an experimentalist framework if review methodologies stimulate a frank acknowledgement of uncertainty and courts seek to incorporate peer-review mechanisms in creating dialogic disciplines on enforcement discretion. As such, form-based violations by object can be consistent with experimentalism if experience (rather than merely precedent) demonstrates certain conduct to have anti-competitive effects and if the definition of such violations is open to revision in the light of new contextual evidence. The judicial ambivalence about defining a probabilistic framework for reviewing anti-competitive effects may be seen as consistent with a concern about not hamstringing competition enforcement under conditions of radical uncertainty. While the courts' review framework may appear uneven or unsettled, this in itself may have the consequence of steering both the enforcer and the undertaking towards the commitments route, which allows for remedial flexibility, through experimentalist disciplines of monitoring and recursivity. Finally, oversight of regulators under conditions of uncertainty cannot be limited to courts applying legal norms to public actors, but can incorporate multiple accountability relationships,[138] so as to provide 'an interpretive and discursive schema' through which participants in different accountability relationships 'make sense of their own and each other's role[s]'.[139]

[136] See, eg, for a problem-solving judicial approach in the context of criminal enforcement, MC Dorf and CF Sabel 'Drug Treatment Courts and Emergent Experimentalist Government' (2000) 53 *Vanderbilt Law Review* 829; MC Dorf and JA Fagan, 'Problem-Solving Courts: From Innovation to Institutionalization' (2003) 40 *American Criminal Law Review* 1501.

[137] Damages Directive, ch VI.

[138] J Black, 'Constructing and Contesting Legitimacy and Accountability in Polycentric Regulatory Regimes' (2008) 2 *Regulation and Governance* 137, 152; see also Ladeur (n 17) 1464.

[139] ibid.

We have also aimed to provide a framework for understanding the role of private rights of action in experimentalist competition law as a market regulatory tool. Whatever the limits of antitrust civil damages in providing compensation and deterrence within a more traditional enforcement model, based on retrospective assessment of wrongful conduct, such limits are even more acute in an effects-based experimentalist framework under conditions of radical uncertainty. As such, stimulating private damages claims, as the focus of the EU Damages Directive, may only be salient for a subset of well-defined violations of competition law for conduct with unambiguously negative effects, such as clandestine hardcore cartels. However, much of the action in contemporary competition law focuses on conduct with *ex ante* indeterminate effects even with respect to consumer welfare narrowly defined, let alone if we take a broader conception of the effects salient in competition enforcement, such as data protection or sustainability. In such cases, private damages suits are conceptually problematic and may well distract from and discourage the creation of experimentalist frameworks.

Notwithstanding such scepticism, public enforcers may usefully reflect on the question of private harm in the context of designing experimentalist problem-solving remedies that pursue the public interest. Such reflection may suggest that third parties have already been harmed by the defendant's conduct prior to an experimentalist remedy being put in place or that parties may be harmed in the course of the implementation of such a remedy. In some circumstances, the latter type of harm may be avoided by remedial adjustment through real-time input, while in others, it may have to be accepted on the basis that in dynamic market interactions, there are inevitably both winners and losers. Further, experimentalist enforcers can also seek to pre-define a minimum set of rights of compensation of private parties (such as consumers, customers and suppliers) as part of a commitments-based remedy, triggered by defined milestones for the success or failure of the intervention. Such background rights of compensation can act as a penalty default that ferrets out implausible remedial proposals and enhances the defendant's dedication to the experimentalist framework. Finally, while private rights of action independent of public enforcement may be a source of enforcement innovation in competition law, such an outcome largely depends upon the institutional capability of civil courts – or other competent tribunals – to generate experimentalist problem-solving regimes as opposed to performing the more traditional function of awarding compensation.

5

Experimentalist Governance and International Antitrust

This final substantive chapter will explore the relevance of the experimentalist governance model for the evolution of global competition policy and cooperation. As it rose in prominence as a global competition regulator to rival the US, the EU also started both to encourage other jurisdictions to adopt competition instruments and to promote international cooperation in competition law and policy. Damro and Guay have argued that globalisation of economic activity via trade liberalisation created not only opportunities for European firms, but also challenges to the EU market from international anti-competitive conduct. As such, the EU became a prominent actor seeking to promote competition policies to 'support a vibrant and competitive environment that bolsters the ability of European firms to succeed in a global market place', as well as to 'nudge authorities in other countries' to develop similar policies.[1] Indeed, the past three decades have witnessed an exponential growth of jurisdictions adopting and enforcing competition laws even without a formal international instrument obliging them to do so, apparently based on the argument that competition law is a key institutional feature that is necessary for market forces to deliver broader economic and social benefits.[2]

At the same time as the international proliferation of antitrust laws, the emergence of experimentalist global governance regimes has been traced in various fields of market and social regulation.[3] The literature also suggests that through various pressures and mechanisms, the EU has played an important role in the formalisation of such transnational experimentalist regimes.[4] As we will see, the scope conditions of uncertainty and multi-polar distribution of power are also salient for transnational competition law and policy. The calibration of market competition goes to the fundamentals of economic organisation, including the relative role of

[1] C Damro and TR Guay, *European Competition Policy and Globalization* (London, Palgrave Macmillan, 2016) 4.

[2] D Rodrik, 'Institutions for High-Quality Growth: What They are and How to Acquire Them' (2000) 35 *Studies in Comparative International Development* 3, 4.

[3] See, eg, G de Búrca, RO Keohane and C Sabel, 'Global Experimentalist Governance' (2014) 44 *British Journal of Political Science* 477.

[4] J Zeitlin, *Extending Experimentalist Governance? The European Union and Transnational Regulation* (Oxford, Oxford University Press, 2015).

the state and the market in delivering economic and social policy outcomes.[5] As such, we can observe a resistance both to international rules and to hierarchical governance mechanisms, and reliance upon less formal as well as networked forms of cooperation and norm diffusion. In this chapter, we will examine in more detail the modalities of cooperation in global antitrust, including the development of best practice recommendations and the use of peer review in antitrust networks. However, we will also argue that – despite a superficial resemblance – the mere use of such cooperation mechanisms does not constitute experimentalist governance. Finally, we will explore the prospects for as well as limits impeding fully recursive experimentalist regimes at the global level. Notably, the size of a global network itself may be an obstacle to experimentalism, given that meaningful and manageable peer review and learning from difference takes place in clusters with mutually salient problems.

I. Globalising Competition Law and Policy

Throughout the twentieth century, efforts have been directed towards creating an international antitrust cooperation instrument through legally binding common rules, particularly as part and parcel of trade liberalisation, given the inextricable link between private and public restraints to market opening. International instruments to control anti-competitive business practices were proposed by the League of Nations in the 1920s, as part of the failed Havana Charter for the creation of the International Trade Organization (the pre-cursor to the World Trade Organisation (WTO)) in the 1940s,[6] as well as within the framework of the General Agreement on Tariffs and Trade (GATT) in the early 1990s.[7] All of these proposals failed and it was the EU that spearheaded efforts[8] to include competition law disciplines under the auspices of the WTO after its formation, by pushing to place antitrust on the agenda for the Doha Round of trade negotiations.[9] The EU's negotiating proposal was quite modest and incorporated experimentalist features. It envisaged very limited harmonisation (in the area of hardcore cartels),[10] while

[5] See EM Graham and JD Richardson, 'Issue Overview' in EM Graham and JD Richardson (eds), *Global Competition Policy* (Washington DC, Institute for International Economics, 1997) 3.

[6] S Weber Waller, 'The Internationalization of Antitrust Enforcement' (1997) 77 *Boston University Law Review* 343, 349–50.

[7] SL Snell, 'Controlling Restrictive Business Practices in Global Markets: Reflections on the Concepts of Sovereignty, Fairness, and Comity' (1997) 33 *Stanford Journal of International Law* 215, 229–31 (describing the proposal of a draft international antitrust code within GATT by a working group of scholars).

[8] European Commission, 'Report by the Group of Experts on Competition Policy in the New Trade Order: Strengthening International Cooperation and Rules' COM (95) 359 final; European Commission, *XXVIth Report on Competition Policy* (1996), paras 235–36.

[9] G Hufbauer and J Kim, 'International Competition Policy and the WTO' (2009) 54 *Antitrust Bulletin* 327, 328–29.

[10] This was the substantive area where consensus could be achieved most easily, given the widely held view about the pernicious effects of cartels.

extending the WTO's chiefly procedural principles, such as most-favoured nation, non-discrimination, national treatment, transparency and procedural fairness, to national competition policies. Moreover, the proposal also envisaged voluntary cooperation between jurisdictions through modalities such as peer review and technical capacity-building.[11]

Even such relatively modest proposals were met with resistance and ultimately dropped from the negotiations agenda. Commentators suggest that there was only lukewarm support from the US, as the other major antitrust player, for the EU proposal.[12] The US opposition was apparently based on a general aversion towards soft (non-binding) international commitments, combined with an unwillingness to be bound by international antitrust rules – inevitably based on compromise – given the well-established US domestic system. US antitrust was seen to be optimally targeted to capture anti-competitive conduct which results in efficiency losses,[13] and the US could credibly project its domestic regime extraterritorially based on the effects doctrine and the size and importance of its economy.

Developing countries, by contrast, were 'stoutly opposed' to any proposal for an antitrust instrument within the WTO.[14] Such opposition was based on uncertainty about the effects of adopting competition law disciplines on their policy autonomy, particularly in the pursuit of developmental goals. In fact, prominent commentators observed that 'it is not always the case that competition should be encouraged in [developing] countries'.[15] Moreover, given the limited experience of developing countries enforcing antitrust, there was uncertainty about the suitability of the instruments and categories of existing antitrust regimes, which 'require complex factual determinations of changed performance in specific markets as a result of designated actions'.[16] As such, developing nations faced uncertainty about the interaction of competition law with other development-oriented policies, leading to concerns about reducing the space to pursue 'industrial policies, investment screening techniques' or other policies promoting interfirm collaboration or national champions as a way of improving economic performance.[17]

Quite apart from the salience of the scope condition of uncertainty, polyarchy also presented a constraint, as neither of the dominant antitrust regimes – the US and the EU – was able to transpose its own rules into an international instrument.

[11] M Bode and O Budzinski, 'Competing Ways towards International Antitrust: The WTO versus the ICN' (2005) Marburg Economics Working Paper No 03-2005, https://ssrn.com/abstract=888682.

[12] Hufbauer and Kim (n 9) 330.

[13] EM Fox, 'Linked-In: Antitrust and the Virtues of a Virtual Network' (2009) 43 *International Lawyer* 151.

[14] Hufbauer and Kim (n 9).

[15] JJ Laffont, 'Competition, Information, and Development' in B Pleskovic and JE Stiglitz (eds), *Annual World Bank Conference on Development Economics* 1998 (Washington DC, World Bank, 1998).

[16] Hufbauer and Kim (n 9) 329–30.

[17] ibid 331. See generally, A Singh, 'Multilateral Competition Policy and Economic Development: A Developing Country Perspective on the European Community Proposals' (2004), https://unctad.org/en/Docs/ditcclp200310_en.pdf (arguing that competition law was inimical to development-oriented industrial policies and was to be introduced after the achievement of developmental goals).

Thus, in light of difficulties in achieving a formal instrument, the US initiated (with EU support) the establishment of an international competition network in 2001 as a dedicated forum for global antitrust cooperation.[18] The ICN was explicitly not intended to be a forum for binding rule-making or harmonisation of enforcement, billed instead as an informal forum for mutual learning and exchange about common problems among specialised competition regulators. In light of the salience of the scope conditions and the network's focus on mutual learning, we may well ask whether the ICN has provided the basis for the evolution of an experimentalist global antitrust regime.

II. An Informal Competition Network: A Stepping Stone to Experimentalism?

According to its Establishment Memorandum, the ICN was intended to provide a consensus-based informal venue for dialogue among 'leaders of antitrust agencies' aimed at the creation of a 'common competition culture' through maintaining regular contacts and sharing experiences about how problems of common interest are addressed in different jurisdictions.[19] Fox described the ICN as a 'voluntary forum' for 'sharing of views and experiences, for close cooperation, and for exploration of common issues', which would 'facilitate the sharing of information and experience, facilitate cooperation, and work towards consensus rules, principles, methodologies and procedures'. As such, the ICN was to encourage 'the dissemination of antitrust experience and best practices building on existing agency contacts and providing an opportunity to maintain "regular contacts" through meetings and conferences'.[20] Given that the ambition of creating an antitrust code for the world was explicitly disclaimed, such descriptions suggest that the ICN was envisaged as an information and exchange network, allowing regulators to meet, share experiences, discuss problems and 'brainstorm new approaches'.[21]

To the extent that such exchanges and mutual learning are purely informal, they do not constitute an experimentalist regime. As discussed in earlier chapters, experimentalist governance treats purely informal exchanges and learning as suspect from the perspective of both efficacy and accountability[22] to the extent

[18] CA James, 'Reconciling Divergent Enforcement Policies: Where Do We Go from Here?' in BE Hawk (ed), *International Antitrust Law and Policy* (New York, Juris Publishing, 2002) 5 (an initiative for a network 'all antitrust, all of the time').

[19] International Competition Network, 'Memorandum on the Establishment and Operation of the International Competition Network' (2001), https://www.internationalcompetitionnetwork.org/wp-content/uploads/2019/07/ICNMemo_on_Establishment.pdf (hereinafter 'ICN Establishment Memorandum').

[20] ibid; see Fox (n 13) 160–68.

[21] AM Slaughter, *A New World Order* (Princeton, Princeton University Press, 2005) 52.

[22] CF Sabel, 'Beyond Principal-Agent Governance: Experimentalist Organizations, Learning and Accountability' in ER Engelen and MSD Ho (eds), *De Staat van de Democratie: Democratie Voorbij de*

that the often unstated beliefs, assumptions or approaches that emerge in the context of closed epistemic communities are treated as tacit knowledge, which is not made explicit and so cannot be scrutinised by outside actors.[23] In such informal exchanges, officials from established regimes typically adopt the role of teachers, with new adopter officials doing the learning, even where their enforcement contexts and problems greatly differ.[24] Such an approach to learning and exchange can entrench the hegemony of established regimes, not least by silencing new adopters and limiting their innovation through tailoring competition rules to their specific policy needs and socio-economic conditions.

As Eleanor Fox has argued, developing countries may have 'a comparative advantage in designing competition systems that are well adapted to their nations and to the modern world' precisely because they are 'not constrained by path dependence' as 'their competition systems are sufficiently young and unformed'.[25] And yet, an emphasis on the creation of a 'common competition culture' through informal exchange and 'socialization'[26] may be seen as inimical to experimentalist innovation. Informal learning and acculturation reinforce the tendency towards homogeneity and isomorphism through soft coercion (such as technical assistance in return for adopting a certain set of norms), informal diffusion through imitation and peer pressures to comply with existing professional standards.[27] Isomorphism is the antithesis to the experimentalist approach to diffusion, which relies on disentrenching current practice via, local tailoring and innovation.

If we focus on its operations, even from its very first meeting, the ICN sought to move towards structuring the dialogue between enforcement officials, allowing for broad participation (at least in principle) and formalising the network's output. Thus, Monti described the standard mode of operation adopted by the ICN in its first decade as identifying 'issues for coordination, for which [the ICN] establishes a working group'. The working group would then carry out 'various surveys and consultations' with the member authorities and would then develop documents containing 'recommended practices in the given field', as well as

Staat (Amsterdam, Amsterdam University Press, 2004) (contrasting experimentalism where experts 'must frequently explain why their actions differ from those of peers' and 'justify themselves, again and again, in public' to the 'conventional presumption that [experts] are qualified to make complex decisions on the basis of their own informed judgment alone').

[23] For some evidence on the limitations of purely informal learning in the ICN, see Y Svetiev, 'The Limits of Informal International Law: Enforcement, Norm-generation, and Learning in the ICN' in J Pauwelyn, RA Wessel and J Wouters (eds) *Informal International Lawmaking* (Oxford, Oxford University Press, 2012); see also Y Svetiev, 'Partial Formalization of the Regulatory Network' (2010), https://ssrn.com/abstract=1564890.

[24] ibid 286–87.

[25] EM Fox, 'Competition Policy: The Comparative Advantage of Developing Countries' (2016) 79 *Law and Contemporary Problems* 69, 71–73. See also Y Svetiev, 'Competition Law and Development Policy: Subordination, Self-Sufficiency or Integration' in C Herrmann et al (eds), *European Yearbook of International Economic Law 2013* (Berlin, Springer-Verlag, 2013).

[26] Slaughter, *A New World Order* (2005) 198.

[27] PJ DiMaggio and WW Powell, 'The Iron Cage Revisited: Institutional Isomorphism and Collective Rationality in Organizational Fields' (1983) 48 *American Sociological Review* 147.

'workbooks or handbooks explaining how certain kinds of antitrust analysis ought to be carried out'.[28] This type of formalisation provides at least two advantages compared to purely unstructured exchanges: first, it allows for a broader set of experiences – beyond those of the established regimes – to be considered in the formulation of recommended practices by the network; and, secondly, it subjects the selection of recommended practices to open public deliberation, justification and contestation.[29] From that perspective, the selection of recommended practices within the ICN can – at least in principle – provide a first step in the recursive process of experimentalist rule-making based on implementation experience.

As Zaring has argued, regulation through best practice dissemination can be a form of 'localism or subsidiarity' in contrast to 'mandating a one-size-fits-all' regime.[30] Given that ICN recommended practices are not binding, they do not commit countries to any changes in their law or enforcement. As such, they can deliver the 'benefits of standardization without losing the useful innovation that comes from decentralized experimentation'.[31] But as Zaring has also pointed out, following best practices could end up being a very static and limited form of innovation if 'best practices work through copying'.[32] If regulators merely seek to 'keep up with the Joneses' and to copy the solutions developed by others rather than spurring local innovation and continuous improvement, best practice dissemination could instead result in 'sameness'.[33]

There are a number of features of the development and adoption of recommended practices in the ICN that tend towards the entrenchment of the existing consensus, as opposed to stimulating local divergence and experimentation, particularly by new adopters. One factor is the outsized role that mature jurisdiction agencies play both in agenda-setting and in contributing input for ICN deliberation.[34] Even by 2019, nearly two decades after the ICN was formed, the network's working groups were predominantly chaired by authorities

[28] G Monti, 'Unilateral Conduct: The Search for Global Standards' in A Ezrachi (ed), *International Research Handbook on Competition Law* (Cheltenham, Edward Elgar, 2012).

[29] The ICN also allows participation in its meetings by non-state actors such as the WTO, the OECD and UNCTAD, as well as private industry and consumer associations and non-governmental advisors, although there is no mechanism to ensure participation is either systematic or representative.

[30] D Zaring, 'Best Practices' (2006) 81 *New York University Law Review* 294, 297.

[31] HM Hollman and WE Kovacic, 'The International Competition Network: Its Past, Current and Future Role' (2011) 20 *Minnesota Journal of International Law* 274, 279.

[32] Zaring (n 30) 325–26.

[33] ibid 300.

[34] This problem was recognised by ICN steering committee officials. See, eg, John Fingleton, Chair-Elect, ICN Steering Group, 'Closing Speech to the Eighth ICN Conference' (Zurich, 5 June 2009), https://www.internationalcompetitionnetwork.org/wp-content/uploads/2020/01/SpeechChairFingletonclosing2009.pdf: 'we need to rise to the challenge … and work harder to ensure that the ICN continues to enable the fullest possible engagement of all its members, and that its work responds to the needs of newer agencies and those in smaller economies that are still finding their feet'. The role of mature jurisdictions in the ICN was described as an 'abuse of dominance' by at least one representative of a civil society actor that takes part in various global competition fora. Interview with a Consumer Unity and Trust Society official, Zurich, May 2009.

from industrialised countries or mature antitrust jurisdictions, as well as 'rule-promoting' jurisdictions from among emerging market economies.[35] While this may be understandable, given that agencies from such jurisdictions have more experience and resources to devote to the ICN tasks, it can also lead to the entrenchment of the current consensus, notwithstanding the open and broad-based deliberation made possible by the network.

The entrenchment effect is enhanced by the fact that the ICN working groups that structure the deliberations on recommended practices are organised principally around the competition law and policy categories already familiar in the mature regimes (such as cartels, unilateral conduct and mergers). In reflecting on the role and likely success of competition policies in developing countries, Rodriguez and Menon have identified reasons as to why such category entrenchment can be problematic for new antitrust adopters. As they point out, what to a trained competition lawyer may look like a cartel may in some contexts reflect pre-established local networks of production and distribution that are a source of local advantage.[36] Such production and distribution networks may even constitute the only way to efficiently organise production in light of other features of the local economy, such as weak contractual enforcement. On the one hand, these contextual factors may suggest pause about adopting rigid anti-cartel rules without reflecting upon the root cause of such production arrangements. On the other hand, policy-makers from such a jurisdiction may also benefit from considering to what extent cartel-like production networks impose costs on other actors, such as consumers. Deciding whether such production arrangements should be allowed to subsist or be outlawed may require root-cause analysis identifying local legal or institutional reforms beyond competition enforcement.

Another feature of ICN deliberations that may entrench the existing consensus is the method of collection of members' experience as a prelude to formulating recommended ICN practices, which is in principle open to input, though not necessarily systematic. Given that there is no obligation to report individual actions or decisions or remedies by member authorities (as in many of the EU frameworks discussed in Chapter 3), the ICN working groups typically proceed through survey questionnaires to member agencies, framed around familiar antitrust categories, as well as the analytical sub-categories for breaking down antitrust problems used in mature jurisdictions. A general review of such survey reports suggests that in most cases, around 30–40 agencies respond to such questionnaires

[35] U Aydin, 'Rule-Takers, Rule-Makers, or Rule-Promoters? Turkey and Mexico's Role as Rising Middle Powers in Global Economic Governance' *Regulation & Governance* (forthcoming) (distinguishing 'rule-promoting' from 'rule-making' antitrust jurisdictions).

[36] AE Rodriguez and A Menon, 'The Causes of Competition Agency Ineffectiveness in Developing Countries' (2016) 79 *Law and Contemporary Problems* 37, 61–63 (enforcement based on recognised competition law categories may undermine 'surviving institutional organizations' that overcome 'historical resource limits and institutional constraints' and are pre-competitive and economically advantageous).

including industrialised countries with mature regimes, rule-promoting antitrust jurisdictions and some developing recent adopters.

Relying on voluntary responses as a way of gathering the relevant background for the formulation of recommended practices is problematic for a number of reasons. Each authority must decide whether or not to file a response to a questionnaire presented by an ICN working group. Authorities from new adopter jurisdictions may not have any relevant experiences to share or may consider that their own experiences are unlikely to be of interest to the broader ICN membership. Such effects are particularly strong for a resource-constrained authority. While the answering of a questionnaire may seem like a fairly fine-grained contribution,[37]it requires a smaller relative investment of time and effort for a large well-staffed authority, including a separate section for international cooperation, versus a much smaller one that might be housed in a single office of a government department. Not only does a failure to respond by new adopters reduce the field of available experiences or contextual factors to consider in network deliberations, it also limits the learning potential of the survey exercise. An authority that responds to a survey is also going to be more invested in the entire benchmarking exercise and is therefore more likely to take an interest in the responses of others, as well as the conclusions reached by the working group, and compare these experiences and conclusions to its own domestic practices. For non-responding authorities, the exercise may remain remote and the final output is less likely to be viewed as salient. The process of reporting their jurisdiction's enforcement practices focuses actors' attention upon those practices (or their absence). It is precisely the reflection upon the authority's own practices and decisions that makes the otherwise abstract reports of other responding authorities salient, relevant and comprehensible.[38]

It is of course true that even if ICN recommended practices largely reflect the categories and approaches of mature jurisdictions, such practices are not binding on other jurisdictions. Moreover, most antitrust rules and analytical categories (such as market shares and barriers to entry) are fairly open-textured and require fact-intensive decision-making about the reasons and effects of business conduct. As such, the tailoring of recommended rules and practices can come about through their adoption and application in different jurisdictions. However, a number of factors may impede such a process of domestication and tailoring of consensus

[37] *cf* Y Benkler, *The Wealth of Networks: How Social Production Transforms Markets and Freedoms* (New Haven, Yale University Press, 2006) 100–01 (requires little investment of time and effort).

[38] For example, in a 2016 project of the Merger Working Group (led by the French NCA and the US Federal Trade Commission) to assess whether and how members' merger systems conform to the ICN's Recommended Practices for Merger Notification and Review Procedures, 80 jurisdictions responded to the survey. In addition to questions about conformity to ICN recommendations, 'members were also asked to report on which practices are most helpful, how the ICN influenced any reforms, and to identify new areas for prescriptive work'. See ICN, 'ICN Recommended Practices for Merger Notification and Review Procedures Member Self-Assessment Report on 2016 Survey Results' (April 2017), https://www.internationalcompetitionnetwork.org/wp-content/uploads/2019/04/MWG_NPRPssurveyreport2017.pdf.

antitrust rules and practices, as well as the ability of the broader ICN membership to learn from such domestication and tailoring.

First, market regulatory tools, such as antitrust, may remain largely dormant and unenforced in newly adopting jurisdictions, particularly where the domestic competition law is transplanted as a set of rules from a pre-existing template, which does not necessarily map onto the local 'demand' for law.[39] In fact, many jurisdictions with more limited resources and capacity to engage in individual search and comparison of international rules and practices tend to rely on a more passive process of transplant adoption of antitrust rules: following those of a mature jurisdiction because they reflected international consensus, or because a particular mature jurisdiction provided technical assistance funding offering its own law as a template,[40] or because it is a jurisdiction with which they share a legal system and tradition for historical reasons, such as prior colonial links.[41]

By contrast, jurisdictions that have undertaken more reflexive exercises of benchmarking of international experience, in an effort to identify or craft rules and practices that may more closely match their local needs and context, have typically had greater success in enlivening domestic competition enforcement and even becoming rule-promoters or rule-makers who develop innovative approaches. As South African officials have pointed out, the competition law rules in that jurisdiction were the result of an international benchmarking exercise, the results of which were subject to further deliberation within the National Economic Development and Labour Council (NEDLAC), a tripartite institution involving labour, business and government representatives responsible for economic policy. While the proposals were inspired by international experience and 'none of the ideas were unique' to South Africa, the discussion and review of the proposals within NEDLAC gave the law domestic 'legitimacy' and may be one of the reasons for its relatively quick uptake.[42]

Similarly, Wang and Krizic show that the enactment of the Chinese Anti-Monopoly Law did not involve a wholesale transplant of any particular template, but reflected a locally driven process of 'shopping around' to select suitable rules from various jurisdictions. As such, China sought to draw on 'inspiration from abroad' together with 'customization to domestic conditions'.[43] The rules

[39] D Berkowitz, K Pistor and JF Richard, 'Economic Development, Legality, and the Transplant Effect' (2003) 47 *European Economic Review* 165.

[40] Interview with Competition Commission of Pakistan official, Washington DC, March 2009 (noting that the EU provided funding).

[41] Interview with National Institute for the Defense of Competition and the Protection of Intellectual Property of Peru official, Zurich, June 2009 (observing that EU provisions or examples are followed, given that the Peruvian legal system is generally similar to that of Spain, Italy and Germany); interview with Fair Trading Commission of Barbados official, Zurich, June 2009 (making a similar point about Barbados' links with the UK legal system).

[42] Interview with South African competition official, Zurich, June 2009.

[43] L Wang and I Krizic, 'Beyond Legal Transplant: China's "Shopping around" Approach and Formation of Anti-monopoly Law' (2017) 40 *World Competition* 505.

chosen were not always those that reflected international consensus, but those that 'were regarded as the most appropriate to achieve [identified domestic] policy goals'. This process resulted in rule-borrowings from different jurisdictions, as well as some uniquely Chinese solutions.[44] Such a selection process, together with the decision to buck international consensus and – at least initially – assign the competition mandate to pre-existing regulatory bodies (rather than a new independent competition agency), may be among the factors for the relatively quick uptake of the Chinese law.[45] Moreover, stakeholders became engaged in specific Chinese enforcement initiatives from the very outset, bringing to the fore innovative arguments about the legitimate interests to consider in competition decision-making in that jurisdiction.[46]

Second, even if some jurisdictions or their agencies engage in innovation through tailoring antitrust rules or through the adaptation of recommended practices to their specific context, the ICN architecture does not necessarily provide the mechanisms through which to subject such divergent choices to scrutiny and review by other network members. Divergence from an ICN recommended practice may reflect local actors' misunderstanding of the recommended practice or its purpose. Such a divergence from consensus may also be due to the capture of the national legislator or agency by local interests, distorting competition law for protectionist or rent-seeking purposes.[47] Alternatively, a participating jurisdiction may find that a recommended practice provides a poor fit for its local enforcement context and may decide to reformulate and adapt it in a way that might also be useful to other agencies in the network.[48] In the absence of a systematic focus on reporting and reviewing implementation efforts, as in experimentalist architectures, ICN deliberations may neither distinguish between these reasons for divergence, nor use such divergent approaches in a recursive process of revising recommended practices. While the ICN recommended practices have been revised, such revision occurs occasionally and drawing again on voluntary survey responses.[49]

This brings us back to the earlier point that best practice benchmarking can be a governance tool for entrenchment of current consensus through copying, or a tool for subsidiarity through tailoring and innovation in the light of existing knowledge. To appreciate the difference between the two scenarios, we may recall the pragmatist disciplines used by firms in product design and production discussed in Chapter 2, which provide inspiration for the experimentalist

[44] ibid 521–24.

[45] Y Svetiev and L Wang, 'Competition Law Enforcement in China: Between Technocracy and Industrial Policy' (2016) 79 *Law and Contemporary Problems* 187.

[46] ibid. Svetiev and Wang suggest that already in early cases, different market stakeholders became engaged in the competition review process based on arguments about the effects of different types of investment, the protection of labour rights and experimenting with remedies, all of which diverged from the international technocratic antitrust consensus.

[47] Svetiev, 'Limits of Informal International Law' (2012).

[48] Fox (n 13) 172–73 (advocating for the principle of legitimate difference and the benefits of diversity versus conformity).

[49] See n 38 above.

governance framework. Notably, the pragmatist firm uses the benchmarking of best practices as part of a set of disciplines that disentrench or destabilise established organisational routines,[50] with the aim of generating continuous innovation and improvement in the design of products and production processes. Such disciplines are used to systematically provoke doubt about the firm's current practice, but also as a means of testing the performance and probity of information provided by collaborators (such as suppliers).[51]

In product design, benchmarking of best practice is 'an exacting survey of existing products and processes' together with an assessment of 'new and unproved techniques that might become available for use'.[52] In the firm context, this exercise obliges actors to reconsider current designs or processes and look for an answer in a novel set of possibilities, namely 'the set of best current or potential designs' that relate to the task at hand.[53] This is because it would rarely be possible – or desirable – for the firm to simply transplant or copy whatever it identifies as current 'best' practice. Furthermore, the process of product design all the way up to delivery of a product to market is ordinarily iterative: following the setting of initial design specifications, the design team may develop a simulation or prototype of the envisaged product, and benchmark its features and customer reactions as against currently available competitive products or other potential designs. A further round of benchmarking is used for the individual sub-systems of the product to implement the proposed design, whereby project teams benchmark 'the production processes central to their eventual products to ensure that the methods employed will meet or surpass the efficiency of their most capable competitor'.[54]

As discussed in Chapter 2, another discipline used to revise provisional initial plans that augments the disentrenching effect of benchmarking is error-detection and correction.[55] Error-detection focuses on interruptions in the process of production and aims to identify the root cause of such interruptions – by insistent questioning – so as to systematically divert attention from the most proximate cause of the breakdown and identify less apparent failures in a complex production system.[56] In this way, error-detection and correction can assist in displacing existing organisational routines since they 'reveal possibilities for improvement in unexpected (mis-)connections among the parts of complex endeavors; and the

[50] See generally S Helper, JP MacDuffie and CF Sabel, 'Pragmatic Collaborations: Advancing Knowledge While Controlling Opportunism' (2000) 9 *Industrial and Corporate Change* 443.

[51] WH Simon, 'Toyota Jurisprudence: Legal Theory and Rolling Rule Regimes' in G de Búrca and J Scott (eds), *Law and New Governance in the EU and US* (Oxford, Hart Publishing, 2006).

[52] CF Sabel and J Zeitlin, 'Neither Modularity nor Relational Contracting: Inter-firm Collaboration in the New Economy' (2004) 5 *Enterprise and Society* 388, 389.

[53] CF Sabel, 'A Real-Time Revolution in Routines' in C Heckscher and PS Adler (eds), *The Corporation as a Collaborative Community* (Oxford, Oxford University Press, 2006) 107.

[54] ibid.

[55] Helper, MacDuffie and Sabel (n 50).

[56] Recall Rodriguez and Menon's point earlier (Rodriguez and Menon, 'The Causes of Competition Agency Ineffectiveness' (2016)) that the root cause of cartels in some developing countries may be poor contract enforcement.

cumulative effect of these results is captured in improvements in the benchmark standards for various production processes.'[57]

Importantly, the firm must maintain a focus on the outcomes of its design and production processes because of the 'need to assure that the value created is captured within the organization'.[58] Such a focus on the firm's output ensures accountability in the selection and design process, since observed results ought to be attributed rapidly to earlier decisions or production practices. Most importantly, given customer and competitive pressures, problems with a particular product design or production decision are more likely to be detected relatively quickly. Once the product, or even a prototype, is developed, its performance will be tested both internally and in the market. Given the advantages of delivering new products to market quickly and the disastrous consequences of failure, the firm has every incentive to quickly identify reasons for failures or underperformance and correct them.

By contrast, legal rules and enforcement practices can be 'copied' into laws, enforcement manuals or guidance documents. Moreover, failures in the decision-making practices of a competition agency that is principally active in its own jurisdiction may go undetected for much longer. Within each individual jurisdiction, disruptions and errors in local implementation may be more obscure, particularly in the absence of the disciplines of monitoring effects of interventions through stakeholder input. The outcomes of local interventions may be influenced by multiple actors other than the agency and the regulated entity (courts, competitors and the executive), compounding problems of attribution in trying to explain implementation outcomes and identify areas for improvement. Even agencies themselves may not always be attentive to detection of errors or misconnections after finalising an intervention, let alone to the correction of enforcement errors. Where an implementation failure is identified, a local agency may have difficulty attributing such failure to some local enforcement constraint, as opposed to the inadequacy or poor fit of an ICN recommended rule or practice.

Precisely to ensure accountability and attribution, as preconditions for learning from difference, experimentalist governance requires the formalisation of obligations upon network members to report interventions and subject them to peer review by a central clearing house in a systematic rather than episodic way.

III. The ICN in its Second Decade: A Focus on Implementation

In an effort to improve the network mechanisms of cooperation and mutual learning, in its second decade the ICN sought to shift its focus beyond normative

[57] Sabel (n 53) 121.
[58] Benkler (n 37) 112.

guidance through elaborating recommended practices to address questions about actual implementation and agency effectiveness. As part of this shift in emphasis, the network undertook revisions of some of its earliest sets of recommended practices, such as those on merger notification.

As should be obvious, a focus on implementation does not produce experimentalist learning if it is merely focused on counting the number of jurisdictions that have formally adopted ICN recommended practices.[59] From the experimentalist point of view, the reasons for non-adoption, as well as experience with the actual implementation of adopted recommended practices, are much more important sources of learning. Network peer deliberations over implementation results can help to characterise local interventions – whether based on recommended practices or a divergence from them – as successes or failures. This is not least because, while the national enforcer may be most knowledgeable about the specific intervention in the local context, it also does not necessarily have the incentive or inclination to find fault with its own interventions.[60] In fact, it may often be impossible to characterise the success or otherwise of a local intervention without both considering input from affected stakeholders and comparing the local enforcement outcomes to outcomes of similar interventions elsewhere.

In a document entitled 'The ICN's Vision for its Second Decade' presented at the tenth annual ICN meeting, the ICN Steering Group[61] recalled the network's original objective of 'formulating proposals for procedural and substantive convergence through a results-oriented agenda and structure' and proposed to strengthen the ICN's mission 'to advocate the adoption of superior standards and procedures in competition enforcement and policy around the world', emphasising a dynamic objective of continuous improvement in recommended standards and procedures. The document went on to explain that 'convergence' in the ICN context is defined as the 'voluntary adoption of widely-accepted norms of competition policy, substantive standards, procedures and levels of institutional capability' based on a three-stage process:

> The first is decentralised implementation, as different jurisdictions experiment with diverse processes and substantive standards for solving specific problems. The second stage involves sharing these experiences and building consensus through the identification of best practices or techniques. In the third stage, individual jurisdictions opt in to the consensus norms.[62]

[59] *cf* Fox (n 13) 169–71.

[60] S van Uytsel, 'The International Competition Network, Its Leniency Best Practice and Legitimacy: An Argument for Introducing a Review System' in M Fenwick et al (eds), *Networked Governance, Transnational Business and the Law* (Berlin, Springer-Verlag, 2014).

[61] The ICN Steering Group at the time was composed of representatives of the competition authorities of Australia, Brazil, Canada, the EU, France, Germany, Italy, Japan, Mexico, the Netherlands, Russia, South Africa, South Korea, Turkey, the UK and the US (both the Department of Justice and the FTC) and by the co-chairs of the ICN working groups. See https://www.internationalcompetitionnetwork.org/wp-content/uploads/2018/07/ICN2dDecade2011.pdf.

[62] ibid 5.

According to the vision document, in areas 'where differences are relatively narrow … the ICN provides a forum for members and [non-governmental advisers] to develop consensus Recommended Practices', which are intended to be 'dynamic, revised periodically to reflect the continuous experimentation in the pursuit of better practices at the domestic level'. By contrast, 'where differences are greater due to different domestic economic histories, development and priorities (such as the analysis of unilateral conduct), the ICN facilitates "informed divergence": identifying the nature and sources of apparent divergence and understanding and respecting any underlying divergent rationale'.

Thus formulated, the ICN's approach appears to be based on a view of a core of consensus, whereby on most competition law topics and issues, the differences would be relatively small to allow consensus best practices to be widely adopted. By contrast, on a narrower set of issues (unilateral conduct is provided as an example), seemingly persistent divergence has to be understood and tolerated, as it is seen to be rooted in differences in history, levels of development or policy priorities, and thus potentially unbridgeable through mutual learning.

However, from the experimentalist perspective, both of the above claims of the ICN vision document can be contested. In all areas of competition regulation, it is probably possible to identify both some common ground and some reasons for divergence, and it is the combination of these factors that allows jurisdictions to learn from each other, even as a means to better understand their own system and its fundamental concerns. First, even with seemingly technical questions that appear to involve pure coordination, such as merger notification rules, different rules and thresholds for notification, have an impact on the substantive reach of a jurisdiction's competition regime and the types of mergers it can target.[63] Similarly, with respect to leniency (another 'consensus' area identified in the vision statement), van Uytsel observes that there is considerable uncertainty about the efficacy of different leniency approaches in detecting cartels at the international level, and, as we saw in Chapter 1, leniency programmes can also have implications for national rules of evidence, commitments to fundamental rights and rule of law protections of due process.[64] Moreover, while the vision documents suggest that even consensus rules and practices should be dynamic and subject to revision, it does not identify where the impetus for continuous improvement comes from if most jurisdictions plug into the consensus rules and practices, nor does it identify the process and criteria through which superior practices would be identified and selected.

Second, the mere fact that some competition rules, such as those on unilateral conduct, may be more contested – due to historical, philosophical or developmental legacies of different jurisdictions – does not mean that such differences

[63] Fox (n 13) 169.
[64] Van Uytsel (n 60).

are irreducible or that jurisdictions cannot learn from each other. Thus, while the different US and EU approaches to unilateral firm conduct are said to have a different history and underlying philosophy, this also has not meant that the two systems cannot learn from each other.[65] For example, in cases involving global market players, such as Microsoft and Google, where these two jurisdictions have frequently followed divergent approaches to enforcement, mutual engagement and peer review can clarify whether the divergence is best explained by: (i) a different interpretation of the available evidence about the likely competitive significance of the same conduct; (ii) a difference in the effects of the same conduct in the two jurisdictions because of a different competitive structure of the market or different consumer behaviour; (iii) a difference in the kinds of effects considered relevant in each jurisdiction or the timeframe in assessing the likely effects; or even (iv) a conclusion by the agency of one jurisdiction that the remedial approach pursued by the other was ultimately ineffective in pursuing similar objectives.[66]

On the questions of ICN processes and governance mechanisms, the vision document did propose reforms to promote 'diversity, inclusiveness and transparency' in the operation of the network. The reforms were relatively modest and related to the chairing and deliberations of the Steering Group and the Working Groups. Such reforms may contribute towards greater inclusiveness and voice for developing countries and new adopters, but importantly they did not include reforms that would have moved the ICN closer to an experimentalist governance network, such as through a requirement of systematic reporting and peer review of interventions by the member agencies. At the same time, ICN documents have recognised that there is some degree of overlap between the ICN's activities and those of other international competition fora, which raises the prospect that an experimentalist regime may be assembled by linking a set of different institutional components hosted in different fora, as we outlined in the EU context in Chapter 3. Thus, while it does not host peer reviews itself, the ICN has suggested that its 'Recommended Practices remain a key benchmark in … the peer reviews conducted within OECD and UNCTAD'.[67]

[65] EM Fox, 'Monopolization and Dominance in the United States and the European Community: Efficiency Opportunity and Fairness' (1986) 61 *Notre Dame Law Review* 981, 982, 1020; WE Kovacic, 'Achieving Better Practices in the Design of Competition Policy Institutions' (2005) 50 *Antitrust Bulletin* 511.

[66] Y Svetiev, 'Scaling Experimentalism: From Convergence to Informed Divergence in Transnational Competition Policy' in J Zeitlin (ed) *Extending Experimentalist Governance: The EU and Transnational Regulation* (Oxford, Oxford University Press, 2015) 177; see also C Damro and T Guay, 'Transatlantic Merger Relations: The Pursuit of Cooperation and Convergence' (2012) 34 *Journal of European Integration* 643.

[67] ICN, *Merger Working Group: ICN Recommended Practices for Merger Notification and Review Procedures Member Self-Assessment, Report on 2016 Survey Results* (April 2017), https://www.internationalcompetitionnetwork.org/wp-content/uploads/2019/04/MWG_NPRPssurveyreport2017.pdf, 1.

IV. Transnational Peer Review in Competition Law and Policy

The OECD's Competition Committee has produced in-depth country reports on competition law and policy since 1998 and has conducted peer reviews of national competition policy enforcement since the early 2000s, and its review exercises are not limited to OECD members.[68] In addition, the United Nations Conference on Trade and Development (UNCTAD) hosts an Intergovernmental Group of Experts (IGE) in competition law and policy, which was formed precisely to focus on the competition enforcement needs and experiences of developing countries.[69] Given such an objective, the UNCTAD Secretariat also decided to formalise its own peer-review mechanism precisely to make peer-review exercises more relevant to the problems faced by developing countries, as well as to draw on the experience of other developing countries in conducting reviews.[70] Importantly, UNCTAD's Secretariat follows up on the formal peer-review exercise with specific initiatives to disseminate the results of the peer review, as well as to assess the capacity-building needs of the reviewed agency and develop a technical assistance programme to address the peer-review recommendations. The first UNCTAD peer reviews of Kenya and Jamaica were conducted in 2005 and 10 years later, UNCTAD also conducted both a review of implementation (principally examining the degree to which peer-review recommendations have been implemented in the reviewed jurisdictions),[71] as well as an external evaluation of its peer-review mechanism.[72]

The extent to which peer review within UNCTAD may complete an experimentalist regime depends, as discussed in Chapter 3, on whether such peer reviews have an experimentalist character to stimulate the tailoring of competition law by interacting transnational best practice guidance with local stakeholder engagement, or whether they are conducted in a top-down manner so as to approximate countries' competition rules and practices to existing templates (as in the soft convergence or technocratic peer-review models). A full and comprehensive account of the peer-review frameworks in competition law at the OECD and UNCTAD are beyond the scope of this book. However, for present purposes, review of UNCTAD peer-review reports combined with observation of the public deliberation sessions that

[68] OECD, *Country Reviews of Competition Policy Frameworks*, https://www.oecd.org/daf/competition/countryreviewsofcompetitionpolicyframeworks.htm.

[69] P Brusick and L Cernat, 'Competition Law and Policy' in S Kasahara and C Gore (eds), *Beyond Conventional Wisdom in Development Policy: An Intellectual History of UNCTAD 1964–2004* (New York, United Nations, 2005) 183.

[70] Interview with a former UNCTAD Secretariat official, Lucerne, March 2014.

[71] MM de Fays, 'UNCTAD Peer Review Mechanism for Competition Law: 10 Years of Existence' (UNCTAD, 23 June 2015), https://unctad.org/en/PublicationsLibrary/ditcclp2015d4_en.pdf.

[72] LV Melikyan, 'External Evaluation of UNCTAD Peer Reviews on Competition Policy' (UNCTAD, 23 June 2015), https://unctad.org/en/PublicationsLibrary/ditcclp2014d5_en.pdf.

complete the peer review process did not appear to disclose an experimentalist orientation of the peer-review exercise.[73]

Focusing on the review reports, two such reports that provided the basis for the UNCTAD IGE peer review in 2018 of Botswana[74] and Argentina,[75] were written by a current and former competition official (from Tanzania and Spain respectively) with assistance from the UNCTAD Secretariat. The reports typically set out the general legal and administrative framework for competition enforcement in the reviewed jurisdictions and assess (sometimes implicitly) the rules and practices on the reviewed jurisdiction vis-a-vis pre-existing templates for competition law and enforcement. The reports typically note problems that have been identified in competition enforcement in the reviewed jurisdiction, though without always moving beyond a proximate to a root-cause analysis of such enforcement problems. The reports also list specific enforcement interventions and cases decided in the reviewed jurisdiction, though the principal focus is on the *legal* outcomes of those cases, such as whether the competition prosecution was successful in identifying violations, the kind of remedy that was imposed or whether the decision survived judicial review or appeal. Importantly, there appears to be less emphasis in the reports on *ex post* evidence about the actual effects of specific enforcement exercises on the operation of local markets, including any unintended consequences of such interventions. Both because of their episodic nature and because they aim to provide a fairly comprehensive snapshot of the legal and enforcement landscape in the reviewed jurisdiction, country reports may tend to obscure details which could have the diagnostic function of revealing locally specific problems, let alone helpful divergences from consensus practices that disclose promising tailoring, innovation or room for improvement.

A similar impression of an overall focus on convergence emerges from the open sessions during the annual UNCTAD IGE meeting, which provide the occasion for deliberation based on the country peer-review report. In particular, in such sessions, officials from the reviewed jurisdictions are questioned by a review panel (usually made up of enforcement officials and academics) on issues arising from the country report. Officials from the reviewed jurisdiction can, in turn, also pose questions to the reviewing panel and – given that the sessions are open – representatives of other jurisdictions or NGOs present at the IGE meeting can join the discussion. The proceeding as a whole, including both the questions that are posed and the answers, can appear quite ritualised. The idea that all officials present are part of a community of interest leads to the perception that participants need to pay general obeisance to a set of consensus norms.[76] In such sessions,

[73] This section is based on the author's participation in and observation of the peer-review sessions of the UNCTAD IGE annual meetings between 2016 and 2019.

[74] UNCTAD, *Voluntary Peer Review of Competition Law and Policy: Botswana* (20 July 2018), https://unctad.org/en/PublicationsLibrary/ditcclp2018d1_en.pdf.

[75] UNCTAD, *Voluntary Peer Review of Competition Law and Policy: Argentina* (19 July 2017), https://unctad.org/en/PublicationsLibrary/ditcclp2017d1_en.pdf.

[76] E Goffman, *The Presentation of Self in Everyday Life* (New York, Anchor Books, 1959) 9: 'maintenance of this surface of agreement, this veneer of consensus … facilitated by … statements which assert values to which everyone present feels obliged to give lip service'.

the officials from the reviewed jurisdiction typically acknowledge 'deficiencies' with their own system, so that the learning in peer review is perceived as one-directional and convergence-oriented. As indicated, UNCTAD does follow up the peer-review exercises with dissemination initiatives within the reviewed jurisdiction and technical assistance programmes. However, the assessment report of the efficacy of the peer-review programme appears to be principally focused on the degree of implementation of the recommendations rather than on the degree of tailoring or the effects of implementation.[77]

Interestingly, by contrast to the country-focused peer reviews, the thematic roundtables presented at the annual meetings of the UNCTAD IGE follow a format that more closely approximates an experimentalist form of peer review. This is because of their focus on specific enforcement problems, the consideration of comparative experience and input from market stakeholders.

The thematic roundtable presentations at the UNCTAD IGE are problem-driven, typically responding to requests by agencies that have commonly identified specific enforcement challenges. For example, at its sixteenth annual session, the UNCTAD IGE participants requested UNCTAD to prepare a briefing on the 'challenges faced by developing countries in competition and regulation in the maritime transport sector' in order to facilitate a thematic roundtable at the following IGE meeting. The request was motivated by a number of identified problems and concerns in this sector, including the fact that maritime transport is significant for trade and development (with over 80 per cent of merchandise trade by volume carried by sea), and the fact that the industry – already concentrated – witnessed even greater consolidation during 2016. Such consolidation was seen to lead both to potential efficiencies and to concerns about competitive distortions. The UNCTAD Secretariat was tasked with preparing a background report focusing on both the effects of such recent developments 'with regard to competition and concentration in the sector' and the specific challenges and enforcement options for developing countries. The focus was on three questions:

a) How is increasing market concentration and global alliances in liner shipping affecting competition in the sector, including effects on shippers, seaports and shipping companies, particularly in developing countries?
b) In view of the international nature of shipping services, what kind of challenges and options do national competition authorities have when dealing with competition issues in the liner shipping industry?
c) What kind of policy measures could help ensure that the improvements achieved in terms of efficiency and connectivity are passed on to the clients of liner shipping carriers in the form of enhanced reliability of services and reduced freight charges?[78]

[77] De Fays (n 71).

[78] UNCTAD Intergovernmental Group of Experts on Competition Law and Policy, Seventeenth Session, Geneva, 11–13 July 2018, Agenda, https://unctad.org/en/pages/MeetingDetails.aspx?meetingid=1675; Challenges faced by developing countries in competition and regulation in the maritime transport sector, Note by the UNCTAD Secretariat.

The background report prepared by the UNCTAD Secretariat set out a number of observable trends in the maritime shipping sector, as well as competition concerns that arise from those trends (drawing on sectoral reports and the relevant academic literature), as well as describing regulatory frameworks and enforcement options based on the experiences of jurisdictions that have undertaken enforcement or regulatory activity in this sector. At the seventeenth session of the UNCTAD IGE in 2018, the roundtable discussion included presentations drawing on UNCTAD's background paper, together with presentations by representatives from three competition authorities (Brazil, Hong Kong and the EU Commission) reporting on their activities and competition enforcement approaches in the maritime transport sector. The problem-oriented format of deliberations allowed the identification of similarities and differences in the problems faced and the interventions by the three jurisdictions. Moreover, the agencies, drawing on specific enforcement examples in the sector, highlighted both the uncertainties they faced in developing an enforcement strategy and drew out possible reasons for divergences in their respective enforcement approaches.

The substantive discussion based on peer exchange and comparison of concrete examples was enhanced by the presence on the panel of two representatives of industry stakeholders commenting on the approaches of the different authorities.[79] Furthermore, the ensuing interactive debate commenced with a number of additional formal interventions from jurisdictions (Japan, Algeria, Romania and South Africa) describing their own recent regulatory and enforcement activity in this sector, including remedies pursued and implementation challenges faced, as well as the interaction of competition enforcement with sectoral regulation of maritime transport. All of the participant officials in the roundtable and interactive debate emphasised the uncertainty about the competitive performance of the sector and the effects of the various regulatory approaches in the face of ongoing sectoral dynamics of change. In the face of such uncertainties, the roundtable agency and stakeholder participants highlighted the importance of ongoing monitoring of the sector and the effects of enforcement measures that have been adopted, though it is worth noting that the maritime sector was not scheduled for discussion at the following UNCTAD IGE meeting.

In terms of focus, content and participation, the thematic roundtable on competition enforcement in the maritime sector described above, although not styled as a 'peer review', resembles much more closely the experimentalist format of peer review described in Chapter 3. The review of enforcement practice in the roundtable was problem-oriented and based on a specific emergent challenge, and involved deliberation upon specific measures adopted by different agencies. Such a format allows for the comparison of the design and effects of the different interventions, including how agencies with actual experience in dealing with the

[79] However, it is worth noting that the market stakeholders present at the roundtable were *industry* representatives of the users and suppliers of maritime transport (the Global Shippers Forum and the World Shipping Council), but without representatives of more diffuse interests.

identified problem assessed the likely sources of harm locally (highlighting important differences in both the economic and regulatory context), the way in which they dealt with uncertainty and enforcement limitations, as well as preliminary assessments of the effects of their interventions. The need for ongoing monitoring of implementation efforts vis-a-vis industry developments was also identified in the roundtable interactive debate.

V. Experimentalism and Shared Enforcement Context

The above discussion suggests the importance of a degree of shared context for the workability of an experimentalist regulatory framework, where shared context is understood as a set of mutually-salient implementation problems. As such, it suggests that the size of a network such as the ICN may limit its ability to formalise experimentalist disciplines of systematic reporting and review. At its founding, the ICN was envisaged as a broad-based antitrust focused network without restrictive membership criteria. Under the Establishment Memorandum, the only criterion for a member of the ICN is to be 'national or multinational competition agenc[y] entrusted with the enforcement of antitrust laws' and, as a result, the ICN has grown over two decades to over 140 member authorities. Imposing an obligation of reporting and peer review of competition interventions by all members in such a broad-based network presents a significant challenge even just for collecting and managing information, let alone for engaging in meaningful and systematic comparison and peer review of such interventions.

Again, a comparison to the use of benchmarking in the context of product and process design by the firm may be instructive. Benchmarking of best practices used by other firms is problem-oriented, in that it is triggered when the firm confronts a specific problem of designing a product or improving a product feature or the production process. For it to be an effective disentrenching strategy that directs attention away from current local practice, benchmarking must examine a set of actual and potential solutions that are sufficiently 'like' the problem at hand. This set is initially open, but ultimately bounded so that the task of comparison is manageable rather than a 'fool's errand'.[80] When the alternatives to be considered are too numerous, the search process may take too long, add many confounding variables, making meaningful comparisons between different alternatives difficult or impossible, which may tend to reinforce the *status quo*.

However, at the same time, the UNCTAD roundtable example given above illustrates that a global broad-based regulatory network can provide a venue for experimentalist learning. A broad-based global regulatory network can contribute towards the emergence of experimentalist governance by acting as a network of networks, which facilitates both the creation of clusters of shared enforcement

[80] Sabel (n 53) 124.

context and the dialogue between such clusters. In this setting, a cluster of shared enforcement context is not necessarily constituted by a group of jurisdictions that are sufficiently similar so that they can easily converge on a common set of competition norms and practices.[81] Instead, the clusters of shared context may be thought of as groups of jurisdictions that face enforcement problems that are mutually salient, so that the agencies participating in such clusters can engage in meaningful and systematic peer review of both the design and effects of specific interventions.[82] Where the problems are mutually salient, participant authorities can tailor divergent implementation efforts in the face of uncertainty, while also being attentive to the problems of regulatory arbitrage that may undermine divergent regulatory solutions.

Moreover, as a former Brazilian competition official has observed, joining different competition networks – particularly for agencies from new adopters and smaller antitrust jurisdictions – can be beneficial both from the perspective of reduction in enforcement costs and from the perspective of learning:

> Developing nations need to join different networks … to explore their own interests more centrally … More generally, by joining a network a member may reduce their enforcement costs by building upon the experiences of what other jurisdictions have accomplished. And this is especially important for developing economies which usually have limited budgets.[83]

Perhaps unsurprisingly, we can observe examples of such clusters of shared enforcement context being formed, which can contribute towards assembling a global experimentalist regime. For example, Gal has highlighted the growth of regional competition law agreements and cooperation fora.[84] For a number of obvious reasons, the problems faced by competition agencies of jurisdiction in the same region are more likely to be mutually salient. Jurisdictions in a regional forum are more likely to have trading links due to trade agreements, as well as firms that operate across borders, which may formulate cross-border anti-competitive and

[81] *cf* American Bar Association, *The Internationalization of Competition Law Rules: Coordination and Convergence* (1999) 36–37 (arguing that 'clusters of nations are tending to adopt one or another of' three different models: the US model in the Americas, the EU model in Europe and the Japanese model in Asia).

[82] The importance of mutually salient problems for competition agency networks is recognised by enforcement officials: 'to get these kinds of [competition] forums to work, you need to have … *very concrete projects* to work over. If you just come and have a meeting once in [a] while and … there is nothing to work over in between, they don't happen'. Interview with a South African official, Zurich, June 2009.

[83] Transcript of the panel discussion on International Best Practices with Mariana Tavares de Araujo, partner of Levy & Salomão Advagados, Rio de Janeiro, 22 May 2014 in Beijing at Antitrust in Asia: China co-sponsored by the ABA Section of Antitrust Law and the Expert Advisory Committee of the Anti-monopoly Commission of the State Council (cited in L Wang, 'Domestic Regulatory Reform and Transgovernmental Networks: Brazil and China in the Global Competition Regime' *Regulation and Governance* (forthcoming)).

[84] See, eg, MS Gal, 'Regional Competition Law Agreements: An Important Step for Antitrust Enforcement' (2010) 60 *University of Toronto Law Journal* 239.

market allocation strategies. Moreover, the EU itself has encouraged the creation of regional competition fora, particularly in the context of negotiating trade agreements with third countries. In fact, the EU sometimes participates in such regional networks itself, leading to exercises of formal reporting and review of implementation resembling those we observed in the ECN.[85] Finally, competition agencies from different jurisdictions have also formed thematic cooperation clusters that focus on specific and mutually salient enforcement problems.[86]

As we observed in the UNCTAD setting above, transnational networks can both help to identify members who face mutually salient problems and contribute to the peer review of enforcement efforts. In fact, one important concern with respect to enforcement clusters (whether regional or thematic) is that they may lack sufficient competence or that they may too easily converge on a particular solution or approach, which then becomes too difficult to dislodge due to a combination of groupthink and an absence of relevant comparators.[87] Such a concern can be attenuated both by authorities participating in multiple networks and by the existence of a global 'network of networks'[88] that can facilitate the brokering of relevant information and experience across clusters.

VI. Conclusion

The failure of the EU's initiative for the creation of an international antitrust instrument under the WTO umbrella was to a large extent attributable to uncertainties about the desirability of competition, as well as the role of competition policy in the promotion of developmental objectives by jurisdictions without much experience of competition enforcement. As such, there was both resistance by developing nations to any one-size-fits-all antitrust rules and a resulting inability by the mature regimes such as the US and the EU to impose their model at the global level. However, at the same time, the creation of a global regulatory network, such as the ICN, has not – based on the account presented here – provided an experimentalist framework for international antitrust cooperation, not least because of the ICN's

[85] Svetiev, 'Scaling Experimentalism' (2015) 192 (in the context of the Cotonou Agreement between the EU and the African, Caribbean and Pacific states, the EU-Cariforum Agreement and the Andean Community).

[86] ibid; C Damro and T Guay, 'Transatlantic Merger Relations: The Pursuit of Cooperation and Convergence' (2012) 34 *Journal of European Integration* 643.

[87] A Schrank and J Whitford, 'The Anatomy of Network Failure' (2011) 29 *Sociological Theory* 151, 162 (describing an 'involuted' network, a network failure whereby 'partners have for one reason or another become overly dependent on each other and therefore fail to absorb information from outside the network – information they need to maintain their competencies in a world of intense innovation and competition').

[88] See L Viellechner, 'The Network of Networks: Karl-Heinz Ladeur's Theory of Law and Globalization' (2009) 10 *German Law Journal* 515.

focus on normative convergence and its consequent inability to give a voice to the specific problems and enforcement constraints faced by new adopters.[89] Moreover, even if a network such as the ICN were to formalise (or incorporate) reporting and peer review of implementation, this may not be sufficient for it to become experimentalist. For transnational antitrust cooperation to evolve in an experimentalist fashion, exercises of reporting and mutual peer review can be made both manageable and meaningful within clusters of members with mutually salient problems. In assembling a transnational experimentalist regime, a global network such as the ICN (or UNCTAD) can act as a network of networks, which provides a venue for the creation of such clusters and facilitates the dialogue between them.

[89] In fact, many of the concerns and problems raised in the preceding pages are also reflected in feedback provided to the ICN Steering Group by its membership. See ICN, *ICN Vision for its Second Decade, Annex 1* (May 2011), https://www.internationalcompetitionnetwork.org/wp-content/uploads/2018/07/ICN2dDecade2011.pdf, 15ff (suggesting the creation of fora 'tailored specifically to groups of agencies with common interests, such as smaller or younger agencies or agencies in developing or small economies' within the ICN and suggesting that the ICN should 'conduct work on evaluating/assessing the impact of competition enforcement efforts on consumer welfare').

Conclusion

Since the original efforts to chart the emergence of experimentalist governance as an architecture in EU policy-making and market regulation,[1] authors working in different policy fields and from different disciplinary backgrounds have sought to understand to what extent experimentalism provides a robust model for regulatory problem-solving in the EU, which is also consistent with the fundamental normative commitments of the EU and national legal and constitutional orders. Beyond scholarly reflection, as we observed in Chapter 2, the experimentalist governance literature is also having an impact on policy and decision-makers looking for alternatives to relentless centralisation, fragmentation or differentiated integration as models for the evolution of the EU project.

At the same time, the scholarly reflection on experimentalist governance may arguably be constrained by the methods and objects of study within specific disciplinary traditions.[2] On the one hand, schematising broadly, writers within the political science and European studies disciplinary traditions have been focused on the question of whether governance arrangements observed in different fields of EU law and policy are indeed experimentalist or new governance, or some variant of hierarchy.[3] A further question of interest within this scholarly tradition relates to the causative factors that account for the emergence of experimentalism in specific policy fields.[4] Consistent with this disciplinary methodological orientation, scholars have focused on identifying markers to distinguish experimentalist from other forms of governance, as well as generalisable findings about variables that cause actors to choose experimentalist mechanisms. Authors working in this tradition may be sceptical of 'just so' accounts, particularly because – as we observed – different observed governance architectures can be consistent with multiple theoretical accounts, whether hierarchical, informal or experimentalist, to name but a few.[5] At the same time, because experimentalist frameworks

[1] CF Sabel and J Zeitlin, 'Learning from Difference: The New Architecture of Experimentalist Governance in the EU' (2008) 14 *European Law Journal* 271; and the original contributions in CF Sabel and J Zeitlin (eds), *Experimentalist Governance in the European Union: Towards a New Architecture* (Oxford, Oxford University Press, 2010).

[2] *cf* L Vicente and HW Micklitz, 'Interdisciplinary Research: Are We Asking the Right Questions in Legal Research?' (2015) *EUI Department of Law Working Paper No 4.*

[3] TA Börzel, 'Experimentalist Governance in the EU: The Emperor's New Clothes?' (2012) 6 *Regulation and Governance* 378. *cf* LE Lynn, 'The Persistence of Hierarchy' in M Bevir (ed), *The SAGE Handbook of Governance* (London, SAGE, 2011).

[4] See, eg, B Rangoni, 'Architecture and Policy-Making: Comparing Experimentalist and Hierarchical Governance in EU Energy Regulation' (2019) 26 *Journal of European Public Policy* 63.

[5] Börzel, 'Experimentalist Governance' (2012).

can incorporate elements of hierarchical governance[6] (such as the penalty default, rule-based enforcement or judicial review) or because governance practice may be transformed (from top-down to experimentalist regimes and vice versa) using the same regulatory architecture,[7] these factors may make it difficult to nail down descriptive and causative accounts of experimentalist governance.

While a social science orientation may largely eschew normative questions, the legal scholarship is keenly concerned with normative aspects of experimentalism, as well as new governance models more generally.[8] Thus, legal scholars have focused on questions of the consistency of experimentalist governance – including the open acknowledgement of uncertainty and the limits of hierarchy, the grant of discretion to pursue differentiated solutions – with fundamental normative commitments, such as the rule of law,[9] democratic control of public authorities[10] and the protection of fundamental rights.[11] Legal scholars have also focused on the role of independent courts as guardians of such commitments through legal rules that maintain institutional balance and provide legal certainty.[12] From this perspective, experimentalist forms of regulation cause concern for a number of reasons, including: (i) the expansion of regulatory discretion largely unconstrained by binding rules; (ii) the need for learning and adjustment through differentiated regulatory solutions leading to unequal legal treatment; (iii) the collaborative design of interventions possibly without democratic input and control; and (iv) the risk that the outcome-orientation of regulatory action may undermine fundamental rights.

This book has sought to elaborate a general framework for competition law as an experimentalist tool of market regulation in the EU (and beyond) through focusing on emergent practice. Such a competition law is effects-oriented, though it eschews indeterminate debates about the proper goals of competition policy. Instead, it accepts the (not necessarily controversial) view that markets are always work-in-progress constructions[13] with competitive rivalry as one instrument through which to align market conduct with the public interest. Experimentalist

[6] See eg, TA Börzel and T Risse, 'Governance without a State: Can it Work?' (2010) 4 *Regulation and Governance* 113.

[7] JE Fossum, 'Reflections on Experimentalist Governance' (2012) 6 *Regulation and Governance* 394; Rangoni (n 4).

[8] G de Búrca and J Scott, (eds), *Law and New Governance in the EU and the US* (Oxford, Hart Publishing, 2006). See M Kumm, 'Constitutionalism and Experimentalist Governance' (2012) 6 *Regulation and Governance* 401.

[9] M Wilkinson, 'Three Conceptions of Law: Towards a Jurisprudence of Democratic Experimentalism' (2010) 2 *Wisconsin Law Review* 673.

[10] *cf* M Dawson, 'Transforming into What? New Governance in the EU and the Managerial Sensibility in Modern Law' (2010) 2 *Wisconsin Law Review* 107.

[11] But see G de Búrca, 'Human Rights Experimentalism' (2017) 111 *American Journal of International Law* 277.

[12] C Ford, 'New Governance in the Teeth of Human Frailty: Lessons from Financial Regulation' (2010) 2 *Wisconsin Law Review* 441.

[13] *cf* J Black, 'Reconceiving Financial Markets: From the Economic to the Social' (2013) 13 *Journal of Corporate Law Studies* 401. See also RC Hockett and R Kreitner, 'Just Prices' (2017) 27 *Cornell Journal of Law & Public Policy* 771.

competition law is transversal in both scope and objectives, and so it can act as a diagnostic tool to identify weaknesses in competitive, network and regulatory disciplines on business conduct from either a relational or a public interest point of view. In making this argument, I have followed an approach to the study of experimentalist governance that attempts to hybridise the two methodological orientations schematised above.

I. From Spontaneous Workarounds to Deliberate Experimentalism

At least two reasons might explain the scholarly focus on the extent and causes of a (spontaneous) emergence of experimentalist governance as a distinct mode of regulation. The first is the notion that experimentalist solutions are built bottom-up, not least because there is no privileged top-down vantage point that can guide problem-solving under conditions of uncertainty, particularly given the need for tailoring interventions to local context and the limits of coercive enforcement. The second reason arguably relates to the fact that the literature on experimentalist governance draws inspiration from the pragmatist disciplines of firm governance and interfirm collaboration that firms have developed to cope with uncertainty, generating an infrastructure for continuous improvement and for generating trust between collaborators. And yet, it may be conceptually difficult to speak of a fully spontaneous emergence of experimentalist governance in regulation or even in policy-making more broadly. The incentives of private firms to capture joint value[14] and the greater flexibility they have for structuring collaborations across interfirm boundaries through contract[15] make it easier for private (firm) orderings to iteratively and spontaneously formalise pragmatist solutions compared to regulators.

Interviews with competition and market regulatory officials confirm this point. Regulatory officials may be reluctant about pursuing differentiated solutions that openly acknowledge uncertainty and proceed iteratively, precisely out of concern that such solutions would be seen as inconsistent with the public law framework within which they operate.[16] Moreover, regulators (and their overseers) may view the objectives of public competition or regulatory authorities, their

[14] Y Benkler, *The Wealth of Networks: How Social Production Transforms Markets and Freedoms* (New Haven, Yale University Press, 2006).

[15] RJ Gilson et al, 'Contracting for Innovation: Vertical Disintegration and Interim Collaboration' (2009) 109 *Columbia Law Review* 431.

[16] *cf* NR Parrillo, 'Federal Agency Guidance and the Power to Bind: An Empirical Study of Agencies and Industries' (2019) 36 *Yale Journal on Regulation* 165, 168 (notwithstanding their intended flexibility, agencies use guidance documents rigidly due to internal organisational routines and perceived rule of law concerns).

target undertakings and other affected market stakeholders as being irreducibly in conflict. Such a view underscores regulatory and enforcement officials' understanding of their role as watchdogs rather than co-equal participants in collaborative governance to shape business strategy, as outlined in Chapters 1 and 2.[17]

In light of the above, the principal object of the book should not be seen as testing the hypothesised emergence of experimentalist governance in EU competition law as a tool of market regulation. Instead, the goal has been both more limited and more ambitious. On the one hand, I have sought to show how a number of (perhaps surprising) developments in both the substantive evolution and the enforcement instruments of competition law may be understood as consistent with the elaboration of an experimentalist governance framework for regulating markets.[18] Many of the procedural and substantive innovations presented in the preceding chapters may be seen as responses to the scope conditions of uncertainty and the limits of hierarchical enforcement. At the same time, however, when actors recognise and seek to respond to these scope conditions, they need not ineluctably be led to experimentalist solutions. Responding to uncertainty about choosing instruments to achieve policy objectives, legislators, regulators and even courts may seek to improve access to knowledge and technocratic expertise through *ex ante* mechanisms of consultation and input so as to improve the quality of decision-making. Similarly, responding to the limits of hierarchical enforcement may lead to the proliferation of rules or tools for surveillance, compliance-monitoring and deterrence to control public authorities and to enhance their ability to identify and sanction violations.[19] However, as should be evident from the preceding chapters, such changes in the enforcement architecture and practice would not necessarily lead to experimentalist solutions, which elide the distinction between *ex ante* rule- or decision-making and *ex post* implementation, as well as sidestepping both retrospective violation findings and compliance verification.

Nonetheless, what we have observed throughout this book is that public authorities and private actors faced with the constraints of uncertainty and hierarchical enforcement have developed mechanisms and solutions that can be rationalised by experimentalist governance. However, the book has also sought to show that a robust move towards experimentalism in competition law would require refinement of the mechanisms discussed, as well as promoting interactions between those mechanisms. In turn, such refinement requires more active recognition by relevant regulatory actors (as well as legislators and courts that define and supervise their mandate) and market stakeholders that they are engaging in experimentalism and that experimentalist governance provides a framework for

[17] MJ Piore and A Schrank, *Root Cause Regulation: Protecting Work and Workers in the Twenty-First Century* (Cambridge, MA, Harvard University Press, 2018).

[18] I Tavory and S Timmermans, *Abductive Analysis: Theorizing Qualitative Research* (Chicago, University of Chicago Press, 2014); C Ansell, 'Pragmatist Interpretivism' in M Bevir and RAW Rhodes (eds), *Routledge Handbook of Interpretive Political Science* (Abingdon, Routledge, 2016).

[19] *cf* M Power, *The Audit Society: Rituals of Verification* (Oxford, Oxford University Press, 1997).

regulating markets that is normatively attractive: both because it can effectively pursue the public interest mandate and because it is consistent with fundamental normative commitments. Within such an experimentalist framework, the promotion of competition through competition law can be seen to play a dual role. The first role is the broadly recognised function of competitive rivalry as (only one) discipline on market actors, which limits the exercise of power so as to improve market outcomes. The second role for experimentalist competition law is to ensure that a multiplicity of market institutions are generated and maintained both as sources of learning and as an antidote to lock-in through path dependence.[20]

By showing how the experimentalist account rationalises developments in EU competition law and market regulation, the more ambitious goal of this book is to provide a framework, as well as an invitation for competition and market regulators, other public actors and market participants, to engage with two normative questions that cannot be avoided if experimentalism is to take hold. These include the questions of whether an experimentalist governance framework for market regulation is normatively desirable and whether it is feasible. Much of the focus of the preceding chapters has been on demonstrating the feasibility of experimentalist governance in light of the governance innovations that have been introduced into competition law and sectoral market regulation over the last few decades. Moreover, by outlining the alternative mechanisms to hold regulators accountable and how such mechanisms of peer accountability can interact with standard tools of regulatory oversight, I have aimed to show – along with others – that experimentalist governance is not unbridled technocratic discretion and does not trample normative commitments to the rule of law, democratic governance and rights protection. And to further underscore the point that experimentalist competition law as a market regulatory tool need not be seen as a revolutionary project, I have sought to show how existing institutions either already play an experimentalist function or can be easily repurposed to do so through tweaking their orientation (particularly with respect to modes of justification in the face of uncertainty) rather than through wholesale abandonment or replacement. In that spirit, the book has also sought to chart concrete pathways towards a more fully fledged experimentalist elaboration of competition law.

At the same time, this book invites further engagement with the normative questions about the desirability and feasibility of an experimentalist competition law in the regulation of markets in the EU and beyond. With respect to the first normative question about the desirability of experimentalist governance, such a debate is already immanent in the literature in recognition of the limits of pre-existing competition law templates in dealing with contemporary problems. At least three interrelated developments may be seen to underlie such debates and to reinforce the desirability of a broader more explicit adoption of experimentalist

[20] R Bronk and W Jacoby, 'Uncertainty and the Dangers of Monocultures in Regulation, Analysis, and Practice' (2016) MPIfG Discussion Paper 16/6, www.mpifg.de/pu/mpifg_dp/dp16-6.pdf; *cf* H Dagan and M Heller, *The Choice Theory of Contracts* (Cambridge, Cambridge University Press, 2017).

governance in competition law and market regulation. These include the emergence of the information technology-mediated and data-driven economy, the recognition of the value of maintaining diverse market and regulatory institutions, and developments in disciplines, including economics, which have informed the content of competition law and market regulation.

A. The Information-Based Economy

In many examples discussed in this book, antitrust enforcers and market regulators have had to cope with the competitive implications of information technologies in shaping production and distribution models. Enforcement to address these problems has sharpened the focus on novel forms of production and distribution that were both meant to cope with – and in turn also contribute to – more volatile market environments.[21] Developments in information technology have transformed competitive rivalry from being based on efficient processing of raw materials towards the processing of information.[22] Such transformation in production and distribution has somewhat discordant implications for the role of competition as a disciplining tool on market actors. On the one hand, competitive rivalry as between market actors has increasingly been based on innovation through the delivery of new and better-quality products and services rather than price.[23] On the other hand, production processes increasingly rely on networked collaboration, undermining the stability of markets, including the significance of the distinction between horizontal and vertical relationships in production and distribution. Platform-based networked production is deeply collaborative and involves the sharing of intimate information across firm boundaries, creating the scope for new forms of predation and opportunistic conduct vis-a-vis other producers, as well as new forms of harm vis-a-vis users.

These developments have at least two implications for the use of competition law and regulation to discipline market actors. One implication, discussed earlier, relates to the focus on dynamic forms of competition, including the need to assess the social benefits of innovation, leading to heightened uncertainty in enforcement efforts. As Ford has argued, the relationship between market regulation and innovation is a troubled one, not least because innovation cannot be regarded as an unqualified good and may often be directed at circumventing regulation.[24] As a

[21] Y Svetiev, 'Antitrust Governance: The New Wave of Antitrust' (2007) 38 *Loyola University Chicago Law Journal* 593; PJ Weiser, 'The Future of Internet Regulation' (2009) *University of California Davis Law Review* 529; S Helper et al, 'Pragmatic Collaborations: Advancing Knowledge While Controlling Opportunism' (2000) 9 *Industrial and Corporate Change* 443.

[22] CF Sabel, 'A Real-Time Revolution in Routines' in C Heckscher and PS Adler (eds), *The Corporation as a Collaborative Community* (Oxford, Oxford University Press, 2006).

[23] See, eg, A Ezrachi and ME Stucke, 'The Curious Case of Competition and Quality' (2015) 3 *Journal of Antitrust Enforcement* 227.

[24] C Ford, *Innovation and the State: Finance, Regulation, and Justice* (Cambridge, Cambridge University Press, 2017).

former competition official has observed, 'online sales and "platformisation" have opened multiple new distribution dimensions that may require a fresh look on the application of competition rules'.[25] While such developments bring potential benefits to consumers, for the enforcer it may be difficult *ex ante* to distinguish between business models that are aimed at protecting investments that benefit consumers and those aimed at shielding market players from competition.[26]

One approach to dealing with the difficulty of gauging the social benefits of innovation is for enforcers or regulators to stay their hand,[27] so as not to stunt innovation, until negative effects become apparent.[28] However, the combination of network effects, algorithmic decision-making and machine learning[29] may mean that *ex ante* unforeseen negative effects may already be systemic by the time they are observed, while both the dangers of lock-in and the difficulty of reversing it may be heightened. As we have seen, in the absence of a comprehensive *ex ante* regulatory framework, competition law provides a nimble diagnostic tool for innovating market regulation by identifying incipient harm, prototyping solutions and providing a mechanism for ongoing learning through stakeholder participation in monitoring the effects and adjusting such prototypes.[30]

A second, and related, implication concerns the categories of competition enforcement. Consistent with the respect for legal certainty and predictability, the analysis of novel forms of competitive harm has – in the EU, as elsewhere – been inflected through pre-existing categories of antitrust analysis about the exercise of market power and its entrenchment. But as Radin[31] has argued in a different context, *ad hoc* incorporation of novel developments into pre-existing doctrinal (or analytical) categories can result in a 'deformation' of the law and a consequent poor fit between legal categories and the underlying normative commitments that animated them.[32] Avoiding such deformation of antitrust and market regulation requires reconceptualising both the kind of power that competition law seeks to

[25] C Fonteijn, 'Keynote Address' (IBA Communications and Competition Law Conference, Amsterdam, 6 June 2016), https://www.acm.nl/nl/publicaties/publicatie/15872/Speech-Fonteijn-bij-the-IBA-Conference-Amsterdam.

[26] ibid.

[27] ibid: 'this is not the moment … to rush to label more types of vertical arrangements as hard core, or to crush budding business models'.

[28] *cf* ibid: 'we value a problem-oriented approach. When no problem is found: no regulation is necessary'.

[29] See, eg, ME Stucke and AP Grunes, *Big Data and Competition Policy* (Oxford, Oxford University Press, 2016).

[30] As such, experimentalism can bridge *ex ante* regulation (which may often be inexistent) and *ex post* enforcement under conditions of uncertainty. *cf* Ezrachi and Stucke (n 23) 257.

[31] MJ Radin, 'The Deformation of Contract in the Information Society' (2017) 37 *Oxford Journal of Legal Studies* 505.

[32] Kar and Radin liken the resulting deformation of contract law to the 'medieval use of "epicycles" to try to square geocentric theories of planetary motion with recalcitrant observations of a nongeocentric universe'. RB Kar and MJ Radin, 'Pseudo-contract and Shared Meaning Analysis' (2019) 132 *Harvard Law Review* 1135.

control and the potential harms that competition enforcement seeks to avoid. In networked collaborative production settings, antitrust enforcement is not always targeted at the more familiar market failure resulting from exercise of static market power.[33] Instead, it may need to focus on network failures,[34] such as righting a temporary imbalance in power between collaborating parties 'involved in long-term, reciprocal exchange'.[35] The seemingly inextricable link between relational and public harm may even require rethinking the old adage that competition law protects competition rather than competitors.[36]

Similarly, the harm to final users (such as the harm from unrestrained data collection, retention and re-use) is an extension of networked modes of production and the incorporation of final users into the value-creation process. As a former head of the Dutch NCA has observed:

> While competition and privacy interests may coincide, they may at times also conflict. For example, online platforms may have an incentive to reserve consumer data for their own use. Competitors may face an insurmountable barrier if certain data is really crucial to their business but is not available. On the other hand, forcing online platforms to share data with others may be against consumer interest from a privacy perspective. How do we balance competition and privacy interests in this context? This is a dynamic problem and it requires dynamic thinking.[37]

Experimentalist governance may offer both a 'conceptual tool kit' to make sense of regulatory or enforcement efforts[38] in a dynamic networked environment and the institutional formats through which they can be implemented in a deliberate and systematic rather than *ad hoc* manner.[39] The combination of rich sources of data with computational power, artificial intelligence and machine learning tools speed up the market effects of business innovations. To regulate such tools through continuous problem-solving, avoiding lock-ins and systemic unintended consequences, requires agile real-time *regulatory* platforms that adopt the error-detection and correction logic of experimentalist market regulation. The networked and polycentric modes of modern production, service delivery and distribution make it quite unpredictable where diagnostic (problem-detection) information might come from, which is an argument against the silo or corporatist regulatory models and in favour of transversal forms of market regulation, such as experimentalist competition law.

[33] Svetiev, 'Antitrust Governance' (2007).
[34] *cf* A Schrank and J Whitford, 'The Anatomy of Network Failure' (2011) 29 *Sociological Theory* 151, 169.
[35] ibid.
[36] EM Fox, 'We Protect Competition, You Protect Competitors' (2003) 26 *World Competition* 149.
[37] Fonteijn (n 25).
[38] WW Powell, 'Neither Market nor Hierarchy: Network Forms of Organization' (1990) 12 *Research in Organizational Behavior* 295.
[39] Schrank and Whitford (n 34) 153, 169.

B. Diversity of Economic Institutions

The harmonisation framework for building – what we have called a 'shallow'[40] version of – the EU internal market by reducing costs of cross-border transactions has also increasingly come under pressure. As we have seen, criticism has been variously expressed in both public and scholarly debate, and one key concern of such criticism is about the homogenising effect on economic, market and regulatory institutions exerted by EU competition and internal market law that seeks to promote cross-border transactions through flattening local modes of production and public (or private) regulation.[41]

We may assume for the present purposes that EU law – being functional to the internal market – has such a flattening effect on business practices, though this is of course an empirical question, which may yield different answers in different sectors and Member States.[42] Assuming that in the evolving political climate, allowing greater scope for local diversity in economic and regulatory institutions is seen as desirable, there seem to be alternative pathways to achieve it.

One pathway, envisaged in some of the scholarship on the market-functional orientation of EU law, is to aim for a stricter delimitation of competences as between EU and national law in a way that leaves a clear demarcation of measures (both regulatory measures and business practices) that are not subject to scrutiny under the disciplines of EU law.[43] Such an approach can be justified if the maintenance of diversity in economic and regulatory institutions can be valued in itself as a way of preserving different ways of economic life.[44] As discussed earlier, it can also been justified on an argument based on the varieties of capitalism – the idea that business practices are embedded in – and therefore complementary to – regulatory frameworks as well as formal and informal economic institutions.[45]

But two types of objections can be levelled at the strategy for maintaining economic and regulatory diversity through strict competence delimitation. One is that such a solution may leave considerable scope for either disguised or overt protectionism by limiting scrutiny of local business or regulatory practice vis-a-vis

[40] Y Svetiev, 'The EU's Private Law in the Regulated Sectors: Competitive Market Handmaiden or Institutional Platform' (2016) 22 *European Law Journal* 659.

[41] *cf* GT Davies, 'Internal Market Adjudication and the Quality of Life in Europe' (2015) 21 *Columbia Journal of European Law* 289.

[42] It may also be that EU law leads to the hybridisation of local business practices or regulatory rules rather than flattening or substituting them. See Svetiev (n 40).

[43] GT Davies, 'Democracy and Legitimacy in the Shadow of Purposive Competence' (2015) 21 *European Law Journal* 2; *cf* G Monti and J Mulder, 'Escaping the Clutches of EU Competition Law: Pathways to Assess Private Sustainability Initiatives' (2017) 42 *European Law Review* 635.

[44] See Davies, 'Internal Market Adjudication' (2015). *cf* Dagan and Heller, *The Choice Theory of Contracts* (2017).

[45] See, eg, P Zumbansen, 'Varieties of Capitalism and the Learning Firm: Corporate Governance and Labour in the Context of Contemporary Developments in European and German Company Law' (2007) 8 *European Business Organization Law Review* 467.

the disciplines of EU law (which are not only market-making but also substantively public interest-oriented). A second and related objection is that such an approach may limit the learning potential for local actors to adjust local business practices and regulations in the face of broader drivers of transformation – such as changes in tastes and identities or technology and modes of production – precisely through dialogic interaction with EU law disciplines and institutions.

By contrast, the experimentalist pathway to maintaining diversity in local practice does not rely on the sharp division of competences between the EU and the Member State levels. The 'Jack-in-the-Box' character of EU internal market law is advantageous precisely because it provides a trigger for deliberative dialogue in various fields of market regulation.[46] Where a new technology disrupts local modes of production or local regulations, EU law might constrain measures that merely seek to protect prior ways of doing things, but it also triggers a process of local re-evaluation of the goals or values that local business or regulatory practices were advancing in the face of new market possibilities. Such a dialogic process can transform local practice or regulation, so as to continue to advance the same goals and values in the face of technological development, perhaps benefiting from the comparative experience of other actors coping with the same problem. This has two further benefits. At the EU level, thus transformed, local business practice or regulation can be a source of continued diversity in market institutions. At the local level, the process leads to a re-assessment of both the salience of the goals of existing trading or regulatory practices and the continued efficacy of such practices in the face of technological change.

C. Developments in Economics and Policy-Making

As we have seen in earlier chapters, the experimentalist approach to market regulation may also rationalise and incorporate developments in regulatory theory. At first blush, it is also consistent with developments in economic policy-making away from mere reliance on *ex ante* modelling based on assumptions of rational behaviour towards experimental design, which have been driven by a set of interrelated factors. In the economics profession, sustained input by economists working within the behavioural tradition has made inroads in shaking up confidence in *ex ante* modelling of markets based on the assumption of rational behaviour.[47] One consequence has been a methodological shift towards understanding behaviour in

[46] T Wilhelmsson, 'Jack-in-the-Box Theory of European Community Law' in L Kramer (ed), *Law and Diffuse Interests in the European Legal Order: Liber Amicorum Nobert Reich* (Baden-Baden, Nomos Verlag, 1997).

[47] eg, ME Stucke, 'Behavioral Economists at the Gate: Antitrust in the Twenty-First Century' (2006) 38 *Loyola University of Chicago Law Journal* 513.

specific (heterogeneous) contexts and, as a corollary, a context-specific experimental approach to learning about the effects of policy interventions.[48] Many regulators and competition authorities report efforts to understand and incorporate behavioural economics insights about human behaviour into the design of regulatory or enforcement instruments[49] and in evaluating specific decisions or interventions.[50] Apart from reliance on *ex ante* behavioural insights, market regulatory authorities have themselves engaged in policy experimentation,[51] including in settings involving novel technologies where the underlying environment is highly unstable and there is a need for learning and iteration.

The above developments suggest a possible background reason for cautious endorsements for experimentalism as the basis for the elaboration of competition law by enforcement officials discussed in Chapter 1. However, in concluding the book, it is worth highlighting the different forms of incorporating experimental insights and designs into market regulation, and the extent to which they are consistent with the experimentalist governance model of competition law presented in this book.

In a contribution on the use of experimentalist techniques in environmental regulation and the promotion of sustainability, Ansell and Bartenberger have sought to distinguish 'varieties of experimentalism', each of which may entail different values, purposes and stances towards knowledge.[52] They underscore the point – already made by Dorf and Sabel,[53] and Sabel and Zeitlin[54] – that philosophical pragmatism provides a framework that rationalises 'adaptive, reflexive and problem-oriented' governance based on experimentation. This is for at least three reasons, including: the pragmatists' 'emphasis on inquiry and creativity'; the pragmatist view of 'means and ends as interdependent and shaped experimentally through action'; and the pragmatist understanding of 'meaning as indeterminate until "fixed" in relation to a particular situation or purpose'.[55]

[48] See generally JH Kagel and AE Roth (eds), *The Handbook of Experimental Economics Volume 2* (Princeton, Princeton University Press, 2015); N Bardsley et al, *Experimental Economics: Rethinking the Rules* (Princeton, Princeton University Press, 2010).

[49] J Hinloopen and HT Normann, 'Experimental Economics and the Practice of Competition Policy' in J Hinloopen and HT Normann (eds), *Experiments and Competition Policy* (Cambridge, Cambridge University Press, 2009).

[50] WE Kovacic, 'Evaluating Antitrust Experiments: Using *Ex Post* Assessments of Government Enforcement Decisions to Inform Competition Policy' (2000) 9 *George Mason Law Review* 843.

[51] AE Roth, 'Experiments in Market Design' in JH Kagel and AE Roth (eds), *The Handbook of Experimental Economics* (2016).

[52] CK Ansell and M Bartenberger, 'Varieties of Experimentalism' (2016) 130 *Ecological Economics* 64, 64.

[53] MC Dorf and CF Sabel, 'A Constitution of Democratic Experimentalism' (1998) 98 *Columbia Law Review* 267.

[54] CF Sabel and J Zeitlin, 'Experimentalism in the EU: Common Ground and Persistent Differences' (2012) 6 *Regulation and Governance* 410.

[55] Ansell and Bartenberger (n 52) 65.

Despite such commonality, Ansell and Bartenberger identify and distinguish three 'logics' of experimentation within the regulatory craft, including:

- controlled experimentation, aiming to 'discern causal effects' by controlling different factors that could influence outcomes of interest;
- Darwinian experimentation, aiming to increase the systemic capability for innovation through enhancing variation ('letting a thousand flowers bloom') and even buffering experiments within protective niches (presumably to attenuate regulatory arbitrage);
- generative experimentation, aiming to prototype solutions to specific problems followed by iterative adaption to refine the prototype and, we might add, possibly scale it up or diffuse it.

As these authors point out, in all of the above scenarios, experimentation is used as a technique to cope with uncertainty. However, they argue that both the form of experimentation and the type of learning that results differ. Controlled experimentation proceeds in a deductive fashion, principally aimed at making inferences about cause and effect,[56] with the hope that such inferences may be generalisable in policy formulation.[57] Darwinian experimentation proceeds inductively, stimulating variation in policy development through parallel experimentation,[58] whereby solutions may be generalised by generating a best-practice portfolio.[59] Finally, they argue that generative – like Darwinian – experimentation does not rely on controlled experiments to identify causality, since generative experimental solutions evolve through iteration and adaptation to findings and changed circumstances, and, as such, can be responsive to contextual factors.

Experimentalist governance as used within this book relies on both persistent variety and iterative learning within individual solutions (or remedies) implemented. As such, experimentalist governance does not, at least principally, rely on the tool of controlled experiments. As Sabel and Zeitlin explain, experimentalist mechanisms 'provoke doubt about [actors'] own assumptions and produce on-going readjustment through comparison'.[60] Referencing Dewey,[61] Bender suggests that 'experimentalism refers not to experiments but rather to experience'.[62]

[56] ibid 66

[57] *cf* N Bardsley, 'Sociality and External Validity in Experimental Economics' (2010) 9 *Mind and Society* 119.

[58] Ansell and Bartenberger (n 52) 67

[59] See, eg, DP Ellerman, 'Parallel Experimentation and the Problem of Variation' (2004) 16 *Knowledge, Technology & Policy* 77.

[60] CF Sabel and J Zeitlin, 'Experimentalist Governance' in D Levi-Faur (ed), *The Oxford Handbook of Governance* (Oxford, Oxford University Press, 2012) 170.

[61] J Dewey, *Logic: The Theory of Inquiry* (New York, Henry Holt and Company, 1938).

[62] B Bender 'Experimentalist Governance in the European Competition Network' in J Bailleux and A Vauchez (eds), *Exploring the Transnational Circulation of Policy Paradigms: Law Firms, Legal Networks and the Production of Expertise in the Field of Competition Policies* (Fiesole, EUI Robert Schuman Centre, 2014) 10.

To appreciate this point, it is important to underscore the constraining effects of the scope conditions of radical uncertainty and the limits of hierarchical coercive enforcement. Their combined effect would suggest that there is no agent with a privileged vantage point and superior rationality that would be able to design or coordinate controlled experiments, either by *ex ante* hypothesising possible (chiefly exogenous) causative factors to control for or by identifying the optimal degree of diversity. While experiments that study human behavioural patterns or ones that test policy options may inform or even morph into experimentalist governance,[63] such controlled or field experiments are not the principal tools of this form of experimentalism. As such, the conception of experimentalist governance adopted throughout this book suggests caution about ideas of controlled, orchestrated or coordinated experimentation through optimal diversity. The bottom-up and participative nature of experimentalist governance and its emphasis on contestability of designs by the participants themselves elides the distinction between designers and subjects of an experiment, in the same way that it elides the distinction between rule-making and rule-enforcement.

It is true that within the network of interconnected (regulatory and market) actors, we speak of central (or 'higher-level') actors (such as the Commission, national competition or regulatory authorities, industry associations or even courts), which can both authorise and supervise experimentalist mechanisms.[64] However, in order to be able to authorise regulatory innovation, experimentalist governance does not require such higher-level actors to have (or pretend to have) either superior knowledge or enforcement capacity. On the contrary, experimentalist authorising actors are aware of and openly acknowledge the constraints of uncertainty and the limits of coercion, including the limitations of pre-existing decision-making and regulatory templates.[65] Moreover higher-level actors also appreciate the importance of maintaining diversity and are attuned to the risk that local enforcement efforts may be undermined by interdependence and regulatory arbitrage. They may even wield penalty default powers. But their principal role is as a central clearing house of implementation information.

II. Experimentalist Governance: Prospects, Limits and Constraints

In the remaining pages, we turn our attention to possible challenges to sustaining experimentalist competition law as a tool of market regulation that may be

[63] JP Voß and A Simons, 'A Novel Understanding of Experimentation in Governance: Co-producing Innovations between "Lab" and "Field"' (2018) 51 *Policy Sciences* 213; KW Abbott and D Snidal, 'Experimentalist Governance 2.0: Taking "Experiments" (More) Seriously', working paper.

[64] EL Rubin, *Beyond Camelot: Rethinking Politics and Law for the Modern State* (Princeton, Princeton University Press, 2007).

[65] G Stoker, 'Translating Experiments into Policy' (2010) 628 *Annals of the American Academy of Political and Social Science* 47, 56 (experimenters should be 'self-aware and critical').

more salient in the light of developments beyond the apparently technocratic fields of competition law and market regulation. Such developments include an emergent and growing scepticism about the role of markets, international economic integration and technocratic regulation, leading us to question whether such an environment is more propitious or more hostile to experimentalist governance.[66] In discussing the challenges to experimentalist governance, the aim here is to underscore the point made repeatedly that the market regulatory experimentalism as outlined in the preceding pages is neither a project of (covert) harmonisation nor one that privileges market-based solutions to public policy problems. Furthermore, to the extent that experimentalism can be seen as the means for hybridising policy objectives of different participants in multi-level governance,[67] I will explore the extent to which a minimum threshold of policy compatibility is required in the face of immanent scepticism about both the EU and open competitive markets.

A. Identifying and Disseminating Success

Experimentalist governance relies on higher-level actors authorising locally tailored solutions to achieve commonly agreed-upon goals. A key aim of the architecture is learning from difference, including learning about superior means for pursuing policy objectives under conditions of uncertainty. Moreover, such learning through implementation may identify 'best' implementation practices, which could be generalised across other lower-level units. Two possible objections can be made to this conception of experimentalist governance: one about the obstacles to the selection process and the other about its self-limiting nature.

The first objection relates to the problem of identifying successful solutions and isolating the specific features of such solutions that could be adopted elsewhere. As discussed above, an experimentalist architecture does not principally rely on controlled or coordinated experimentation to make general findings about the causes of successful intervention. Implementation efforts are shaped mainly through a bottom-up participative process embedded in a local context. While it is true that experimentalism relies on 'root-cause' analysis that diverts attention from proximate causes of problems, such analysis is contextual. It seeks to identify the complex interconnections between different factors in light of an identified failure, recognising that 'every problem potentially implicates any of the parts of the system'.[68] However, the nature of interconnections in one system may be quite different from another. As Simon explains, the phrase 'root cause analysis' can

[66] G Stoker, 'Can the Governance Paradigm Survive the Rise of Populism?' (2019) 47 *Policy and Politics* 3.

[67] Svetiev (n 40).

[68] Simon (n 51) 50.

be 'misleading to the extent that it implies that we are interested in a historical or scientific account of how the error happened. The search is, not so much for a retrospective description, as for opportunities for improvement'. Since experimentalism does not generate general laws of causation, but identifies room for local improvement, it need not necessarily generate templates for successful implementation across different local contexts.

For this reason, I have argued that the generation and generalisation of best enforcement or regulatory practices is neither a necessary nor a sufficient condition for an experimentalist architecture.[69] Ansell and Bartenberger observe that experimentalist governance combines the logic of Darwinian and generative experimentation. Tools such as error-detection and correction, and root-cause analysis generate improvements within local implementation efforts. To the extent that such improvements are incremental and specific to the local circumstances, even what amounts to success in pursing regulatory objectives may be difficult to gauge in the immediate term. Further, even a successful solution in one setting need not be easily transposable to a different setting in any event.[70] The more a particular problem has polycentric effects, the more difficult it may be to identify successful practices that can be easily generalised.

Take by way of an example a Dutch regulatory decision to allow a merger between the Dutch telecoms incumbent KPN and the principal installer of fibre technology Reggefiber. The policy objective was to stimulate the roll-out of a fibre network in the Netherlands while maintaining market openness, and the venture was originally approved subject to a commitment that 'consisted in implementing a functional and operational separation between the joint venture and parent company KPN, in combination with an obligation to provide non-discriminatory open access based on reasonable prices in a particular fibre infrastructure'.[71] The success of this intervention in achieving the specified objectives has been contested. As the former head of the Dutch ACM has pointed out, the negotiated remedies in that case were subject to monitoring and review by the authority in the light of outcomes and market developments.[72] Leaving aside questions about its success or otherwise the generalisability of the Dutch solution to other settings may be constrained by differences in market structure, relevant local actors (such as municipalities and social housing providers) and differences in terrain, other local regulations, population size or density.[73] Similarly, in Botta and Svetlichnii's examples, the use of competition law to discipline excessive

[69] Y Svetiev, 'Scaling Experimentalism: From Convergence to Informed Divergence in Transnational Competition Policy' in J Zeitlin (ed), *Experimentalist Governance? The European Union and Transnational Regulation* (Oxford, Oxford University Press, 2015).

[70] *cf* T Madon et al, 'Implementation Science' (2007) 318 *Science* 1728.

[71] PW de Bijl, 'Broadband Policy in the Light of the Dutch Experience with Telecommunications Liberalization' (2011) 1 *Journal of Information Policy* 77, 90.

[72] Fonteijn (n 25).

[73] BM Sadowski et al, 'Providing Incentives for Private Investment in Municipal Broadband Networks: Evidence from the Netherlands' (2009) 33 *Telecommunications Policy* 582; H Rood, 'Very High Speed

pricing may be seen as appropriate in some jurisdictions where small market size or demographic decline make new entry quite unlikely, even if it may be out of place in other settings.[74]

As Simon explains, experimentalist regimes 'require standardization to facilitate comparability'.[75] However, such standardisation is not necessarily oriented towards generalising specific practices, which would be self-limiting in any case as it would extinguish diversity. Instead, the objective is to standardise regulatory knowledge and to make the goals pursued and instruments selected by local actors explicit and subject to contestation by regulatory peers and local stakeholders. Best-practice benchmarking in an experimentalist regime also provides the spur for identifying metrics of successful implementation to aid comparison of the effects of different enforcement approaches. Peer review makes the decisions of authorities from different jurisdictions mutually observable and comprehensible. As a result, quite apart from regulatory peers, national actors also benefit from such comparisons, including local stakeholders and oversight actors (such as legislatures, executives and courts), as was discussed in Chapter 4.

B. Putting Experimentalism to the Test: Beyond the Tacit Knowledge of Experts

As has been pointed out, the book also aims to stimulate debate on the question of whether experimentalist elaboration of competition law is normatively desirable and feasible. It should be recalled that a key premise for the claimed superiority of experimentalism is that under the scope conditions of radical uncertainty and the limits of coercive enforcement, it would not be possible to elaborate and enforce detailed rules for competition law and market regulation that simultaneously ensure the attainment of public policy objectives and regulatory accountability.

At the same time, some authors have argued that 'simple rules' are appropriate to cope with 'a complex world'.[76] They argue that simple rules 'save time and effort' by focusing attention and simplifying the processing of information.[77] Moreover, simple rules are said to work because they enable sound choices when information is scarce and time is short, while allowing synchronisation of the activities for members of a community.[78] Such synchronisation may also reduce

Broadband Deployment in Europe: The Netherlands and Bulgaria Compared' (2010) TPRC 2010, https://ssrn.com/abstract=1989172.

[74] A Svetlicinii and M Botta, 'Article 102 TFEU as a Tool for Market Regulation: "Excessive Enforcement" against "Excessive Prices" in the New EU Member States and Candidate Countries' (2012) 8 *European Competition Journal* 473.

[75] WH Simon, 'Solving Problems versus Claiming Rights: The Pragmatist Challenge to Legal Liberalism' (2004) 46 *William & Mary Law Review* 127, 190.

[76] See, eg, DN Sull and KM Eisenhardt, *Simple Rules: How to Thrive in a Complex World* (New York, Houghton Mifflin Harcourt, 2015).

[77] ibid 5.

[78] ibid 6.

the administration costs of interpretation, monitoring and enforcement.[79] At the same time, simple rules are said to 'confer flexibility to pursue new opportunities, while maintaining some consistency'.[80] Sull and Eisenhardt rely on case studies of complex systems with multiple interdependent parts that change frequently and unpredictably, to conclude that simple rules are a weapon against otherwise overwhelming complexity.[81]

And yet, a careful examination of the supporting case studies suggests that Sull and Eisenhardt's argument and conception of simple rules may in fact be consistent with the experimentalist approach. Their key claim is that the complexity and dynamism of the underlying context cannot be adequately met with regulatory or legal complexity, which results from an attempt to elaborate a comprehensive set of rules that cover different situations and contingencies.[82] The simple rules that are said to work effectively to deal with complex problems in the settings studied by Sul and Eisenhardt have a number of key features. First, they are not immutable and 'can evolve in light of new evidence, shifting objectives, and changed conditions'.[83] Second, they are 'tailored to the situations of the particular people who will use them' and to well-defined activities or decisions as opposed to 'one-size-fits-all rules' that apply across the board.[84] Since such rules are tailored to specific decision-making contexts, yet are flexible, their reformulation would have to be done by actual practitioners in real time[85] rather than through more cumbersome rule-making processes far removed from those who have to implement them.[86] As such, these are not the generally applicable rules – or indeterminate standards – of command and control regulation. The formulation and continuous revision of such rules can be done by practitioners through the disciplines of error-detection and correction and root-cause analysis.[87] At the same time, however, as will be underscored below, experimentalism does not ask us to blindly trust the judgement of expert practitioners, but subjects them to deliberative disciplines of peer review and dialogic justification.[88]

Consider Ho's study of experimentalist peer review in a Washington State health department. It involved a randomised controlled trial with half of the food

[79] *cf* RA Epstein, *Simple Rules for a Complex World* (Cambridge, MA, Harvard University Press, 1997).

[80] Sull and Eisenhardt (n 76) 6.

[81] ibid 7–8.

[82] ibid 13: 'the parts of a complex system can interact with one another in many different ways, which quickly overwhelms our ability to envision all possible outcomes'.

[83] ibid 15.

[84] ibid 22.

[85] Sull and Eisenhardt (ibid 5) point to the rules medical doctors use to provide urgent care.

[86] *cf* Parrillo, 'Federal Agency Guidance' (2019) 168 (regulatory guidance as a less costly and time-consuming form or rule-making).

[87] ibid. Parrillo's discussion of the growing use of regulatory guidance documents suggests that such guidance can provide the soft revisable rules of experimentalist governance.

[88] This appears to be one key difference between the experimentalist model and the root-cause regulation model outlined by Piore and Schrank (n 17).

safety inspectors assigned to a treatment group incorporating experimentalist peer review over a four-month period. The aim was to study whether experimentalist peer review would lead to more effective and consistent implementation of food safety standards compared to purely discretionary decision-making based on tacit expert knowledge.[89] It was motivated by concerns that in a large number of cases, individual inspectors disagreed as to whether a specific observed situation involved a food safety violation or not. Peer review was used to identify challenging problems and to develop guidance documents for inspection. The experimentalist intervention resulted in an increase in detection of food safety problems and a reduced variation in assessment of identical cases across inspectors. Moreover, interview evidence suggested that incorporating peer review had a number of collateral organisational benefits, even if it was also more costly in terms of time and human resources.[90]

Similarly, Sabel has pointed to quasi-experimental evidence about the effects of introducing an experimentalist framework for special education delivery in Finland. The framework relied on diagnostic testing to identify problem cases, considerable discretion for frontline special education teachers, consultation with a broad range of experts in developing individual education plans, and peer review of the effects of plans and strategies for improvement by a multi-disciplinary Student Welfare Group at the school level.[91] To assess the effects of this framework, Sabel points out that while each quintile of Finnish students outperforms peers from other countries in the Programme for International Student Assessment testing, the bottom quintile of students outperform by the most.[92] Further, he points to a quasi-experimental historical comparison study by Moberg and Savolainen comparing the performance of a similarly situated group of students with learning problems before and after the introduction of the customised special education regime in Finland, which showed both an improvement in outcomes under the new framework and a reduction in variation in student performance.[93]

Finally, Sabel contrasts evidence from Finland with the experience of Denmark as a similarly situated Nordic country, which also granted frontline special education professionals considerable discretion, but without experimentalist monitoring and peer review as in Finland. In particular, the Danish approach relied on purely informal means of stimulating organic cultural change by encouraging emulation of thoughtful, engaged and experienced teachers.[94] Reliance on informal emulation of successful teachers apparently leads to a haphazard development of special

[89] DE Ho, 'Does Peer Review Work: An Experiment of Experimentalism' (2017) 69 *Stanford Law Review* 1.

[90] ibid 70–73.

[91] CF Sabel, 'Rethinking the Street-Level Bureaucrat: Tacit and Deliberate Ways Organizations Can Learn' in P Osterman (ed), *Economy in Society: Essays in Honor of Michael J Piore* (Cambridge, MA, MIT Press, 2013) 128–30.

[92] ibid 125.

[93] ibid 133.

[94] ibid 136.

education strategies and could account for poorer student outcomes in Denmark. Moreover, as in Ho's study, the Finnish schools' peer-review framework not only improved service delivery outcomes, but also provided a mechanism of accountability on public officials, which can either substitute or augment other oversight mechanisms (as we observed in Chapters 3 and 4). By contrast, diffusing tacit knowledge informally through the emulation of experienced teachers in order to enhance expertise and common culture, as the main disciplines on decision-makers' discretion, makes the exercise of expert discretion largely inscrutable to outside observers.

There are a few take-away points from the above discussion. First, Sull and Eisenhardt's key argument is that normative (including legal) complexity is not an effective problem-solving response in a complex and dynamic underlying environment. This conclusion finds support in the work of legal scholars, including those who favour[95] and who are sceptical[96] of public regulation. Such scholars have suggested that legal complexity increases the costs of rule-making, compliance and enforcement,[97] while potentially stifling innovative responses to novel situations by both regulators and regulated entities.[98] Moreover, legal complexity also inadequately constrains the discretion of public officials, not least because such complexity makes it necessary for regulators to choose which rules to enforce or prioritise or how to balance inconsistent commands.[99]

At the same time, as discussed in Chapter 4, experimentalist governance does not wholly disclaim reliance on rules where such rules can help practitioners deal with complexity, but are also revisable in the light of new experience. Such a conclusion may suggest that the governance alternatives to command and control regulation are protean: you can always find experimentalism if you look hard enough. However, the examples outlined above suggest that it is possible to distinguish the experimentalist framework from other regulatory models, including purely rule-constrained discretion and informal mechanisms, such as emulation, socialisation, professionalism or culture. While the above examples do not conclusively establish the superiority of experimentalist governance in competition or market regulation in the face of uncertainty and the limits of hierarchy, they suggest methods to both distinguish and evaluate alternative governance frameworks.

[95] PH Schuck, *Why Government Fails So Often: And How it Can Do Better* (Princeton, Princeton University Press, 2014).

[96] Epstein (n 79).

[97] ibid 30–31.

[98] Sull and Eisenhardt (n 76) 18.

[99] Parrillo (n 16) 177 points out that legal complexity leaves regulated entities at the mercy of regulators, thus enhancing regulatory discretion. See also Piore and Schrank (n 17).

C. Technocracy, Democracy and Experimentalism?

Finally, we turn to the question about the prospects for the broader uptake and consolidation of experimentalist competition law as a tool of market regulation in light of the political winds that have buffeted the EU, its Member States and the world since the early 2010s. As discussed in the Introduction, both in the run-up and particularly in the aftermath of the global financial and the European sovereign debt crises, prominent voices in public and scholarly debate suggested that the competitive market orientation of EU legal integration undermines the sustainability of the European project.[100] While such criticism was fuelled by the response to the sovereign debt crisis and the imposition of austerity and harsh structural adjustment on net debtor nations,[101] as discussed in the Introduction, it has also been cast more broadly to suggest that EU competition law (as internal market law) imposes a straitjacket on national regulation,[102] the diversity of economic life in Europe[103] and the social market economy model as a European aspiration.[104] Furthermore, in an extension of the democratic deficit argument, European integration through building and regulating the internal market is seen as further enhancing the delegation of power to non-majoritarian technocratic institutions.[105]

Scholarly criticism has been coupled with a growing politicisation of EU integration and governance, driven also by political actors who publicly oppose EU integration, leading to the electoral success of 'populist' and Eurosceptic parties across different Member States, as well as the successful referendum for the UK's exit from the Union.[106] In fact, from a longer-term perspective, some have observed a rupture in the permissive consensus for an elite-driven EU integration process.[107] While Eurosceptic political leaders have mainly focused on the

[100] D Chalmers et al, 'The Retransformation of Europe' in D Chalmers et al (eds), *The End of the Eurocrats' Dream: Adjusting to European Diversity* (Cambridge, Cambridge University, 2016) 21 (describing the market integration model as 'empirically over and normatively unsustainable').

[101] See, eg, M Everson and C Joerges, 'Facticity as Validity: The Misplaced Revolutionary Praxis of European Law' in E Christodoulidis et al (eds), *Research Handbook on Critical Legal Theory* (Cheltenham, Edward Elgar, 2019) 425 (criticising the CJEU-sanctioned view that eurozone governance is a technocratic exercise that cannot be subject to democratic legitimacy or rule of law constraints). They point out that 'technical expertise cannot be neatly separated from … normative assessments and policy choices', which applies to competition law and market regulation more broadly.

[102] Monti and Mulder (n 43).

[103] Davies (n 41).

[104] FW Scharpf, 'The Asymmetry of European Integration, or Why the EU Cannot Be a "Social Market Economy"' (2010) 8 *Socio-Economic Review* 211.

[105] *cf* P Mair, *Ruling the Void: The Hollowing of Western Democracy* (London, Verso, 2009) (arguing that the EU was 'constructed by national political leaders as a protected sphere in which policy-making can evade the constraints imposed by representative democracy').

[106] P de Wilde et al, 'Introduction: the Differentiated Politicisation of European Governance' (2016) 39 *West European Politics* 3.

[107] L Hooghe and G Marks, 'A Postfunctionalist Theory of European Integration: From Permissive Consensus to Constraining Dissensus' (2009) 39 *British Journal of Political Science* 1.

charged themes of austerity or migration, EU market regulation has not been spared, including by Eurosceptics on the left.[108] And where Eurosceptic parties have gained power in the Member States, observers have noted both institutional and substantive changes in competition enforcement and market regulation. For example, Bernatt, in a detailed study of Poland and Hungary,[109] suggests that these Member States have implemented changes in NCA personnel and appointments procedures so as to be able to appoint officials who may be 'receptive to signals from the government', thus undermining the authorities' independence. He also suggests that interventions in judicial appointments may have an impact on the impartiality and expertise of courts reviewing competition and regulatory decisions. Finally, he points to specific decisions[110] of the NCAs, as well as changes to substantive[111] or procedural[112] law in those jurisdictions that diverge from common EU-level practices. As he argues, these changes may lead to enforcing competition law in a protectionist manner, as well as favouring state-owned enterprises, national companies or politically connected firms or sectors.[113]

Such developments have led authors to question whether EU economic law can cope with policies, rules and enforcement approaches that manifest 'national economic particularlism' to the extent that they may even re-establish national market organisation and regulation.[114] Is 'national economic particularism' just a form of economic nationalism or 'patriotism' and a cover for protectionism that cannot be made consistent with EU law disciplines, including those of competition law and market regulation? And in light of the argument presented in this book, can an experimentalist framework discipline or even accommodate such

[108] See, eg, J Guinan and TM Hanna, 'Forbidden Fruit: The Neglected Political Economy of Lexit' (2017) 24 *IPPR Progressive Review* 14 (arguing that the EU is a neoliberal project and that EU competition law, state aid and sectoral regulation hamper progressive economic policies at the national level, including some of those proposed by the UK Labour Party in the post-referendum 2017 election); however, see also F Mor et al, 'EU Constraints on Economic/Industrial Policy' (House of Commons Library, September 2017).

[109] M Bernatt, 'Illiberal Populism: Competition Law at Risk?', January 2019, https://ssrn.com/abstract=3321719.

[110] ibid (with reference to the Polish NCA decision to speedily approve the PGE/EDF merger subject to conditions, UOKiK decision of 4 October 2017, DKK-156/2017).

[111] ibid (with reference to the enactment in Hungary of art 93/A of the Competition Act dealing with anti-competitive agreements in the agricultural sector).

[112] ibid (with reference to the enactment in Hungary of art 24/A of the Competition Act, whereby the government can authorise a merger deemed of strategic importance for the national interest without any involvement of the NCA).

[113] Scholars have noted that following the financial and economic crises, all Member State governments have intervened more intensively in the operation of markets in ways that challenge EU competition or state aid disciplines. See, eg, AM Weaver, 'Convergence though the Crisis: State Aid Modernization & West European Varieties of Capitalism' (2015) 21 *Columbia Journal of European Law* 587.

[114] See, eg, M Varju and M Papp, 'The Crisis, National Economic Particularism and EU Law: What Can We Learn from the Hungarian Case?' (2016) 53 *Common Market Law Review* 1647. See also M Varju (ed), *Between Compliance and Particularism: Member State Interests and European Union Law* (Cham, Springer, 2019).

particularities in market regulation? Or are such instances of national particularism fundamentally incompatible with and, as such, likely to undermine the evolution of an experimentalist framework?

We should recall that within experimentalist governance architectures, autonomy is granted to lower-level regulatory actors (including national agencies or firms) to select locally appropriate means to pursue commonly defined framework goals. The *quid pro quo* for such autonomy is the obligation to report specific interventions and subject their design and effects to peer review. It follows that experimentalism, in contrast to rigid harmonisation or convergence models, seeks to accommodate national particularities, especially when they are understood as local conditions to which enforcement must be tailored to pursue common framework goals. However, accommodating national particularities may appear more challenging where national measures respond to local policy or political objectives and, more specifically, objectives that appear prima facie incompatible with the common framework goals.

As I have argued elsewhere, EU competition law[115] and sectoral regulation[116] (as with EU law more generally) can provide experimentalist institutional platforms for the hybridisation of different policy goals within multi-level governance. One template arises out of the book-pricing dispute, where in the face of a competition law challenge by the Commission, Germany's private accord between publishers and retailers for book resale price maintenance was defended as a practice that supported that country's book reading and literary culture.[117] In the light of strong German commitment to the accord, the Commission doubted its ability to mandate its preferred solution of prohibiting it.[118] As such, the Commission sought to accommodate this national business practice through procedural disciplines,[119] including the requirement to translate it into public legislation and minimise the effects on the internal market. While such governance disciplines allow for some national deliberation on the role of the book-pricing accord and its effects and costs for local consumers, an experimentalist framework requires even stronger deliberative disciplines. The mere fact that this was a pre-existing business practice does not in itself justify the claim of cultural peculiarity – the

[115] Y Svetiev, 'European Regulatory Private Law: From Conflicts to Platforms' in K Purnhagen and P Rott (eds), *Varieties of European Economic Law and Regulation* (Cham, Springer International, 2014).

[116] Svetiev (n 40).

[117] *cf* CU Schmid, 'Diagonal Competence Conflicts between European Competition Law and National Regulation: A Conflict of Laws Reconstruction of the Dispute on Book Price Fixing' (2000) 8 *European Review of Private Law* 155.

[118] Backhaus and Hansen report doubts within the Commission about an enforcement action based on the obligation 'to respect cultural differences' between the Member States under art 151 of the Treaty of Amsterdam. JG Backhaus and R Hansen, 'Resale Price Maintenance for Books in Germany and the European Union: A Legal and Economic Analysis' in A Marciano and JM Josselin (eds), *From Economic to Legal Competition: New Perspectives on Law and Institutions in Europe* (Cheltenham, Edward Elgar, 2003) 88.

[119] J Mulder, '(Re)Conceptualising a Social Market Economy for the EU Internal Market' (2019) 15 *Utrecht Law Review* 16.

link between this business practice and local culture cannot be left tacit. In other words, an experimentalist framework requires the culture-generating mechanism to be made explicit, such as, for example, the cross-subsidisation effect, whereby profits of bestselling books provided a cushion for a diverse range of publications and the survival of a vibrant retail network.

The experimentalist discipline of peer review could reveal, as Tagiuri has shown,[120] that there was nothing particularly German about this book pricing practice, but that it was a functional contractual restraint transplanted in different forms in many jurisdictions beyond Germany. It could also reveal that the same practice had been abandoned elsewhere due to the costs it imposed on final consumers, unintended consequences or because of a change in book-purchasing habits or novel modalities for book distribution.[121] None of these is a sufficient reason to abandon the practice in Germany, though the imposition of a legislative sunset clause may be combined with the experimentalist obligation of peer review (including through input by domestic stakeholders) of the effects of the practice in the light of changing distribution technology or reader habits and identities.

The above provides an illustration about how arguments based on national particularities, including cultural and way of life claims, can be brought within the fold of EU economic law and can even be promoted through experimentalist mechanisms. But such an outcome requires the justificatory frameworks in EU competition (and internal market) law to remain elastic.[122] Such elasticity allows experimentalist competition law to both accommodate and impose deliberative discipline on the pursuit of policy goals that may traditionally be seen to be outside of the scope of competition law, such as environmental sustainability or even redistribution.[123] For instance, the exploitative (excessive pricing) abuse findings disclosed by Botta and Svetlichnii pursued by NCAs in some new Member States directed at price gouging in relatively small markets with little likelihood of entry may be understood in redistributive terms.[124] Similarly, Member States' regulatory controls on prices for essential utilities, such as energy (discussed in the Introduction) could have a redistributive focus in the face of rising energy prices in liberalised markets.[125] The CJEU has held that Member States can maintain

[120] G Tagiuri, 'The Cultural Implications of Market Regulation: Does EU Law Destroy the Texture of National Life', DPhil thesis, Bocconi University, 2018.

[121] See Backhaus and Hansen, 'Resale Price Maintenance' (2003).

[122] Case C-230/16 *Coty Germany GmbH v Parfümerie Akzente GmbH* ECLI:EU:C:2017:941. See Y Svetiev and G Tagiuri, 'The Opportunities and Dislocations of Technological Change: EU Law as a Coping Mechanism?' (2018) 24 *Columbia Journal of European Law* 612. As was discussed in ch 2, while the Commission has sought to narrow the justificatory framework, the EU Courts have maintained its elasticity. See also M Bernatt and M Mleczko, 'Public Interest and a Place for Non-competition Considerations in Polish Competition Law' (2017) Concurrences No 1-2018, https://ssrn.com/abstract=3056521.

[123] C Shapiro, 'Antitrust in a Time of Populism' (2018) 61 *International Journal of Industrial Organization* 714, 717 (arguing against bringing redistribution into antitrust analysis).

[124] Svetlicinii and Botta, 'Article 102' (2012).

[125] S Pront-van Bommel, 'A Reasonable Price for Electricity' (2016) 39 *Journal of Consumer Policy* 141.

such price regulations, despite the market liberalisation objectives of the EU energy regulatory framework, if they demonstrate that the competitive mechanism is not working effectively in the relevant markets, as well as appropriately motivate the regulated tariffs and include a sunset clause so as to recursively revisit such tariffs.[126]

In discussing the varieties of experimentalism, Ansell and Bartenberger argue that experimentalist governance principally aims to stimulate 'political learning', namely 'learning that leads stakeholders to alter their preferences, goals, frames and commitments'.[127] Political learning is understood as being 'relative to one's own set of perspectives, attitudes, interests and concerns'. As such, they point out that not all parties involved in experimentalist implementation need to learn the same thing, allowing facts and values to 'productively co-exist',[128] as we observed in the discussion of the Dutch sustainability cases in Chapter 2.

At the same time, some of the characteristics of illiberal populist governments discussed by Bernatt, including their claim to unambiguously represent the popular will of the (local) majority, a confrontational approach towards those with different views and resistance to international or regional regulatory frameworks, appear to be inimical to experimentalist learning through dialogue. While bucking the technocratic consensus is not inconsistent with experimentalist governance, denial of the interdependencies, uncertainties and complexities that beset the regulated environment,[129] an insistence on specific regulatory solutions and an unpreparedness to monitor and disclose the effects of such solutions as the basis for their (re-)evaluation would all short-circuit the deliberative dialogic processes that undergird experimentalist learning. In a sense, such approaches to regulation deny the existence of the scope conditions for experimentalism.

It is beyond the scope of this book to predict how such political developments will unfold, apart from highlighting the constraints they may create for the experimentalist elaboration of competition law and market regulation in the EU. Yet it may be worth making two further observations. First, at least in some of the instances recounted by Bernatt, such as the formulation of the agricultural cartel exceptions in Hungary, we can detect potential for the hybridisation of a local political objective and the EU competition framework. As Bernatt points out, the final version of Article 93A of the Hungarian Competition Act, exempting

[126] Case C-265/08 *Federutility v Autorità per l'Energia Elettrica e il Gas* [2010] ECR I-03377, ECLI:EU:C:2009:640; Case C-36/14 *European Commission v Republic of Poland* ECLI:EU:C:2015:570.

[127] Ansell and Bartenberger (n 52) 70, contrast political to epistemic learning, suggesting that the latter 'expands or refines our scientific knowledge of the world'. *cf* T Freyburg et al, 'Democratic Governance and Transgovernmental Networks' (2017), https://www.peio.me/wp-content/uploads/2016/12/PEIO10_paper_46.pdf.

[128] Ansell and Bartenberger (n 52) 71. An openness to both epistemic and political learning may attenuate Bernatt's concern about populist governments' appointment of non-experts to staff NCAs and regulatory authorities. As a Czech competition official pointed out, such authorities even two decades after the passage of their competition law had no competition economics experts and staff had to learn on the job and from their EU colleagues.

[129] Sull and Eisenhardt (n 76) 19.

agricultural cartels, provides that 'infringement of the prohibition of anticompetitive agreements with respect to agricultural products shall not be established if the anticompetitive agreement is open to all market participants and does not lead to undue revenue for the participants'. Such a formulation may balance traditional competition law goals with redistributive concerns as between farmers and consumers. Deciding whether producers are receiving 'undue revenue' cannot be done through either interpretive or technocratic methods; it requires monitoring of the effects of the exemption provision in specific agricultural markets. Thus, by including a specific reference to the effects of the exemption on trader revenues, the revised law creates a potential trigger for its experimentalist elaboration.

Second, as we have discussed already, one technique for unblocking collaborative experimentalist solutions is the penalty default, which imposes an unambiguously undesirable scenario on, among others, a recalcitrant lower-level unit. As pointed out in Chapter 1, some provisions of Regulation 1/2003 may be understood as penalty defaults, such as the Commission's power to relieve an NCA from deciding a specific case, particularly given the relatively easy threshold of establishing an effect on intra-EU trade. While the Commission has not made much use of such provisions, it did reject the request – pursuant to Article 9(2)(a) of the EU Merger Regulation – by the Polish NCA to assess the merger between pay-TV providers Discovery and Scripps.[130]

Reflecting more broadly on the connection between antitrust and democracy, in light of emergent populist antitrust proposals in the US context, Shapiro has argued that competition law is not an appropriate tool through which to address concerns about the threat of market concentration to democracy.[131] In his view, this is a task better left to more targeted interventions, such as limits on corporate financial contributions to politicians. And yet in some market contexts, the objectives of competition law may be aligned to the protection of democratic institutions, for example, in the case of the media.[132] Bernatt points to a poignant example, whereby the Hungarian government approved a transfer of 400 media outlets to the Central European Press and Media Foundation founded only months before the transaction, which in turn gave the Foundation ownership of approximately 80 per cent of all Hungarian media.[133]

[130] As Bernatt (n 109) points out, the Commission subjected the merger to conditions designed to safeguard the functioning of TVN-24, 'a leading information TV station … often critical of the current government'.

[131] Shapiro (n 123) 716. While a general competition rule against market concentration may be over-inclusive, as Tagiuri ('The Cultural Implications' (2018)) has shown, measures oriented at protecting viable small businesses in specific markets may be justified on relational and cultural bases, or in order to ensure continuity of supply to remote or vulnerable communities, as well as for reasons of urban planning or environmental sustainability.

[132] J Drexl, 'Economic Efficiency versus Democracy: On the Potential Role of Competition Policy in Regulating Digital Markets in Times of Post-truth Politics' in D Gerard and I Lianos (eds), *Reconciling Efficiency and Equity: A Global Challenge for Competition Policy* (Cambridge, Cambridge University Press, 2019).

[133] Bernatt (n 109).

Quite apart from the question of concentration, competition law as a transversal tool can act as an early diagnostic mechanism for business model transformations in the media industry, which could undermine the media's role in supporting democratic institutions. For instance, early complaints by traditional suppliers of news content, such as newspapers, about use of their content by online platforms were a source of diagnostic information about changes in business models for news distribution triggering competitive dynamics that degrade quality journalism.[134] Similarly, consumer protection concerns in online commercial transactions, including the effects of misleading or fraudulent product reviews, provide further diagnostic information about how in an online environment users may be vulnerable to unverifiable misleading content.[135] Given that many online platforms use the same algorithms for both commercial and other content,[136] such pieces of diagnostic information were available long before the phenomenon of 'fake news' was seen as a threat to democratic participation and deliberation. As discussed earlier, market regulatory authorities can use complaints from competitors, customers or final users to identify market or network failures, conduct that infringes non-market values, as well as to identify regulatory failures[137] (such as the inexistence or inadequacy of a targeted regulatory regime).

D. Recursivity versus Stability

As Stoker[138] argues, invoking Urbinati,[139] to meet populist challenges:

> Governance procedures … need to be promoted as open to revision; backed by a recognition that they can develop faults – networks can become too closed and markets can become too controlled by a narrow set of interests. To be open to revision is a better answer to claims of dissatisfaction with political processes than a dubious claim of having achieved smartness. Networks and markets as forms of governing need to be defended not as stable parts of the governing system but as constantly open to revision through sunset clauses, periodic reviews and stringent accountability.

Quite apart from being open to revision through contestation from below, an experimentalist framework subjects local policy-making to the discipline of peer review of both the design and effects of local interventions. *Ex ante* peer review

[134] S Hubbard, 'Why Fake News is an Antitrust Problem', *Forbes*, 10 January 2017, www.forbes.com/sites/washingtonbytes/2017/01/10/why-fake-news-is-an-antitrust-problem/#1a3e446330f1 (a former antitrust enforcer points out that a focus on the problem of 'fake news' reveals how changes in technology of content production and consumption alter the competitive conditions in news publishing).

[135] Drexl (n 132).

[136] ibid.

[137] Drexl's (ibid) discussion about the German BKA's consideration of the complaint by German press publishers against Google is an example of competition enforcement producing diagnostic information about the unintended consequences of the ancillary copyright for press publishers provision enacted in Germany, which apparently harmed media plurality.

[138] Stoker (n 66) 14.

[139] N Urbinati, *Democracy Disfigured: Opinion, Truth and the People* (Cambridge, MA, Harvard University Press, 2014).

makes local decision-makers aware of alternative mechanisms for pursuing even locally defined (or inflected) goals, while peer monitoring of the effects of implementation measures evaluates their effects and unintended consequences.

However, according to Stoker, one key challenge that populism presents to new governance is its rejection of diversity,[140] not least because it draws strength from anxieties about social change driven by globalisation, free movement and even technological change. As such, it has a 'nostalgic commitment to an older order of less diverse and more settled communities',[141] including the idea of a return to a simpler and more predictable existence. By contrast, the claim that experimentalist governance is a normatively desirable regulatory architecture is based precisely on the fact that instability and dynamism inevitably constrain traditional market regulation. As such, experimentalist law is based on defeasible rules, which are constantly subject to revision in light of joint problem-solving and monitoring.

Drawing on systems theory, Calliess and Renner[142] have argued that one of the functions of law is to stabilise normative expectations[143] and that governance regimes can blend into legal regimes only to the extent that they can assume such a stabilisation function. To the extent that experimentalism takes persistent instability for granted,[144] this means that public authorities cannot rely on hard rules, habitual practices or templates to regulate markets; they must themselves innovate to keep pace with an unstable environment by collaborating with regulated entities through corrigible prototypes, based on continuous monitoring and rolling, ever-evolving standards. In experimentalist regulation, normative expectations are stabilised at best temporarily and are always subject to revision. Nostalgia aside, stability in the underlying environment and in normative expectations may be seen as valuable from various perspectives, ranging from the relational to the personal or even psychological.[145] Persistent environmental instability may undermine the capability of law to stabilise normative expectations, particularly if we take seriously experimentalist scepticism about closed and self-referential communicative systems and insistence on constant dialogic interactions without a final decider. However, the question of whether imposing stability is a worthy or realistic goal for contemporary market regulation[146] and one that is compatible with an experimentalist governance framework remains a question for another day.

[140] Stoker (n 66) 9.

[141] ibid.

[142] *cf* GP Calliess and M Renner, 'Between Law and Social Norms: The Evolution of Global Governance' (2009) 22 *Ratio Juris* 260.

[143] In particular, they argue that 'law is defined as a system of communications which are marked by the binary code legal/illegal' (ibid 266).

[144] *cf* W Scheuerman, 'Democratic Experimentalism or Capitalist Synchronisation? Critical Reflections on Directly-Deliberative Polyarchy' (2004) 17 *Canadian Journal of Law and Jurisdiction* 101 (experimentalism as a 'normatively problematic synchronization of the legal system with contemporary high-speed capitalism').

[145] *cf* J Gleick, *Faster: The Acceleration of Just about Anything* (New York, Vintage, 1999).

[146] Y Benkler, 'A Political Economy of Oligarchy: Winner-Take-All Ideology, Superstar Norms, and the Rise of the 1%', September 2017, www.benkler.org/Political%20economy%20of%20oligarchy%2001.pdf: 'you cannot legislate away [a] fundamental technological shift'; *cf* AE Tay, 'Smash Permanent Rules: China as a Model for the Future' (1973) 7 *Sydney Law Review* 400.

INDEX

www.ingramcontent.com/pod-product-compliance
Lightning Source LLC
Chambersburg PA
CBHW071257180926
51613CB00001B/57

* 9 7 8 1 5 0 9 9 1 0 6 7 0 *